Archite ... of Betrayal

How Parliament Tried to Thwart Brexit, from Chequers to the Meaningful Vote

By Jack Buckby

1st Edition
Copyright © 2019

www.jackbuckby.co.uk

ISBN: 9781799296607

For Sylvia

Table of Contents

Introduction..1

Chapter One
Where We Are and How We Got Here......................3

Chapter Two
July 2018...19

Chapter Three
August 2018..42

Chapter Four
September 2018..86

Chapter Five
October 2018..122

Chapter Six
November 2018..159

Chapter Seven
December 2018...216

Chapter Eight
January 2019..259

Chapter Nine
February 2019...309

Chapter Ten
March 2019..348

Chapter Eleven
Brexit Delayed, the People Betrayed....................371

Introduction

This book chronicles the Brexit negotiation process, focusing on the progress of Prime Minister Theresa May's Brexit withdrawal deal, known as the 'Chequers Deal'. I log the progress of this proposed agreement from its inception, to the ultimate Meaningful Vote on the deal in the House of Commons.

The Meaningful Vote is the name given to Section 13 of the UK's European Union (Withdrawal) Act. It is a vote that decides whether Parliament gives consent to the deal put forward by Theresa May and the European Union.

I have written this book in the form of a diary. It reports on and analyses the day-to-day business of politicians involved in the Brexit negotiations, the constant attempts at sabotage, the Prime Minister's indecisiveness, and the utter disdain that elected representatives have shown to the people of Britain.

I intend this to be a reference book – a time capsule into one of the most turbulent times in British politics. Find a month and date in the book, and you'll know what happened in the Brexit negotiation that day, who the key players were, and how the media reacted. It is a way of ensuring that we never forget the way in which our political leaders handled this situation.

Call it negligence, call it malicious, or call it a betrayal – the Brexit negotiation process took too many years, and divided British society. It brought chaos to Parliament and plunged the UK into a constitutional crisis, in a way we've never seen before.

This book isn't an easy read. It is long, it can be confusing, and the story is chaotic. But it is important. What the politicians did to this country won't be forgotten any time soon, but *how* they did it *will*. The British voters will forget exactly how the snobs and charlatans in Westminster – the architects of this appalling betrayal – went about frustrating the Brexit negotiation process.

For almost three years, our parliamentarians have done nothing but attack, deride and smear the British people, all the while pretending to be decent elected representatives with the wellbeing of their constituents in mind. It's the greatest con of modern times, and it works because the decisions being made in Westminster are so complex and long-winded that regular voters tune out. Spend enough years banging on about the same old complicated topics and loopholes, and people are bound to tune out.

A tired population won't be motivated to head to the polls and beat the system, and so the cycle continues. This must end, and hopefully, this book plays a part in that. This is a historical document; a time capsule into the daily misdeeds that were performed without a moment's contemplation. Without it, these acts will fade into the archives of the BBC News homepage and accessed only by those with great interests in history.

Chapter One
Where We Are and How We Got Here

23rd June 2016

I'll always remember the day of the Brexit vote. I walked to the polling station with my dog Dennis, knowing that for the first time ever my vote might actually mean something. For a long time before then I'd been regularly spoiling my ballot paper, refusing to lend my support to any particular party. But on this occasion, I felt for the first time that my vote could really change things.

I put my cross on the ballot, checking ten times that it was clearly and unmistakably in the box for 'Leave'. The rest of the day was fairly normal. I worked, I wrote, I went for another walk with Dennis. I think I even stopped off at the pub for a bit.

That night, I invited two friends to come over for drinks. They were both Remainers who were confident that the referendum didn't pose any threat to Britain's continued membership of the European Union. And you know what? I agreed with them.

I didn't for a moment think that it might actually happen. After months of scaremongering and lies from the politicians, I figured the British people were sufficiently terrified about the prospects of leaving the EU, and that they would vote accordingly. I cracked the odd joke and made the occasional sly dig to my Remainer friends, but I knew inside that our cause seemed hopeless.

Throughout the evening, my opinion didn't change. We watched the rolling coverage of the referendum on the television, sipped wine, had a laugh, and that was that. They soon left, confident that the results we'd seen thus far were showing a victory for Remain.

I locked up the house and called a Republican friend of mine in Washington DC. He and I continued to watch the rolling news together, lamenting what seemed to be an inevitable loss. We discussed the prospects of a future under the European Union, the potential of Turkey gaining access to free movement, and the likelihood that we wouldn't have another opportunity to leave during our lifetime.

On our screens, Nigel Farage appeared. The press waited eagerly for the man who'd campaigned for Brexit all his adult life to admit defeat. Surrounded by microphones, his colleagues looking tired and defeated, Farage admitted defeat:

> *"The Eurosceptic genie is out of the bottle and it will now not be put back, but perhaps even more remarkably, the biggest change in this referendum is not what's happened in the United Kingdom, it's what's happened across the rest of the European Union. We now see in Denmark, the Netherlands and even in Italy, up to around 50% of those populations want to leave the European Union. I hope and pray that my sense of this tonight, and my sense of this – and no, I'm not conceding – is that the government's registration scheme, getting 2 million voters on, a 14-hour extension, is maybe what tips the balance. I hope I'm wrong."*

He said he wasn't conceding, but he was. And when Nigel Farage says he thinks we've lost, we've lost.

Chapter One: Where We Are and How We Got Here

Most of you will already be aware of the government's schemes to ensure that that majority of people would vote Remain. Farage had mentioned the plot to register as many people as possible with an extension deadline. This referred to the decision by the government to extend the deadline by 14 hours; an extension that conveniently aided the application of more young voters. In fact, the proportion of applicants coming from the younger age groups was high, with over 77%[1] of the hundreds of thousands registering late being under the age of 45. Go figure. Young people like me were late to the game and so the government gave us another chance to register, knowing very well we'd more likely to vote Remain.

The government had plenty of dirty tactics like that up their sleeves. In April, they sent a leaflet to every single home in the country which explained 'Why the government believes that voting to remain in the EU is the best decision for the UK'. Just think about that; every single home in the United Kingdom was sent a leaflet crammed full of falsehoods and flat out lies, suggesting we'll lose our jobs, the economy would suffer, and Britain simply wouldn't thrive outside of this political union. It cost the government, or should I say *the taxpayer*, almost £10 million.

I remember the day I received it. It was a Monday morning, 11th April 2016. I felt like I was a citizen of a fascist or communist regime. There I was, at home having a cup of tea, and through my letterbox I'm receiving communication from my government telling me not to vote against their interests or there will be dire consequences.

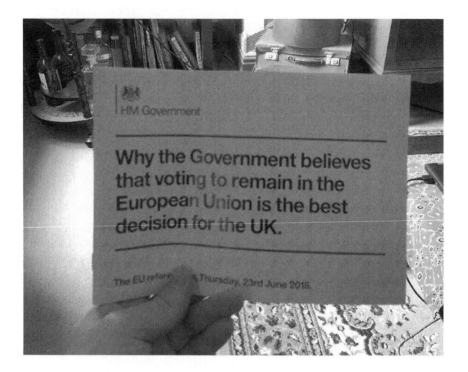

It's something I'll never forget, even if I don't have the leaflet to hand any more. My friends and I took some small joy in burning it that night.

But despite their best efforts, despite Project Fear warning us that we'd all lose our jobs, the sky would fall in and we'd starve to death, the British people didn't back down. The naysayers were wrong.

It was the moment when Sunderland's results came in that everything changed. My friend and I suddenly stopped talking doom and gloom and sat in silence, watching intensely as the news reporters announced that Sunderland had voted to leave the European Union by a much bigger margin than expected. This city in the North East of England – a corner of the country seemingly forgotten by Labour politicians and Westminster toffs – had been expected to vote to leave the EU by around six points. By the time all votes had been counted, Leave had won by a massive 22 points. And it changed everything. The markets instantly reacted, the press went into meltdown, the attendees at the count cheered and danced in excitement, and the whole country began believing we could do it.

I remember wondering why I was surprised. I genuinely shed tears of joy, and I questioned how I'd ever fallen for the lies by the press. How could I have believed that Sunderland, a forgotten city, would have voted to leave by such a small margin? Some were still sceptical about a win. Farage said it was 'fantastic' but that he thought 'Remain might just nick it', but I knew. They were so wrong about Sunderland, and they were wrong about many other places. Even Newcastle's Remain victory was tighter than expected.

From here on in, region after region announced Leave vote after Leave vote. It seems like a blur looking back. I remember smoking a cigarette as I saw the sun slowly coming up outside when Jenny Watson appeared on our screens. She's the former chair of the Electoral Commission; a typical metropolitan feminist type who spent a lifetime campaigning for left-wing causes and working a three-hour week for a £100,000 salary. So, when she stood up on the stage in Manchester and announced to the country at about half four in the morning that the UK had voted to Leave the European Union, the look of sheer horror on her face was understandable.

We did it. We won.

A Brief History of the European Union

For readers outside the United Kingdom or those who have never really paid attention, it's important to know a little about the history of the European Union to understand exactly what we won.

In 1950 the French Foreign Minister Robert Schuman wrote the Schuman Declaration, a plan that preluded the 1952 Treaty of Paris setting up the European Coal and Steel community in Belgium, Italy, France, Luxembourg, the Netherlands and the Federal Republic of Germany.

Then, in 1957, these six countries signed the Treaty of Rome creating the European Economic Community and the European Atomic Energy Community. The new treaty created a common market that allowed goods to move freely across this region of Europe. By this time, the EEC had become the most important European community. It had assembled a council of ministers and a Parliamentary Assembly of members drawn from the National Member State Parliament.

In 1961, Britain, Ireland and Denmark all applied to join the EEC. It was championed by Harold Macmillan, former British conservative Prime Minister. However, French president Charles de Gaulle wasn't too pleased and saw this as a threat to his goal of amplifying France's voice in the world.

Two years later, Britain's membership of the EEC was vetoed by de Gaulle citing Britain's lack of commitment to integration with Europe. The goal of the European project was clear from the beginning; integration and federalism have always been the aim.

Fast forward to 1968, and all import tariffs were removed between member states - and in 1973 Denmark and Ireland finally joined the European Community. Britain then held a referendum in 1975 which successfully entered our country into the community as well, after renegotiating entry terms.

In the late 1980s, Portugal and Spain also joined the EC and the famous blue and gold flag was unveiled. This was followed by the implementation of the Single European Act, which modified the Treaty of Rome and completed the formation of a European Union, abolishing veto powers of member states and increasing the legislative powers of the European Parliament.

In 1993 the Maastricht Treaty was accepted by the Danes but only after a second referendum vote. So yes, the European Union does indeed have a history of holding multiple referenda until they get the result they want.

In France, a referendum won support for the treaty with just a 0.4 per cent majority. Two years later France, Germany, Portugal, Spain, Greece, Sweden and Finland began removing their own national border control.

The Amsterdam treaty is signed four years later, removing more national vetoes and it takes only another two years until the public first sees evidence of fraud and mismanagement in the Union. In 1999, all 20 commissioners resigned as a result of fraud and nepotism and a new President is appointed.

The Euro currency was adopted by 11 countries in this same year and by more in 2002. Thankfully, the UK kept the Pound Sterling. The former French president Valéry Giscard d'Estaing spent 2002 and 2003 drafting the first EU constitution, which set out the goals of simplifying and replacing EU treaties and expanding the power of the Union.

By 2004, the EU begins its enlargement. European elections were held that June and on the 29th of October, EU leaders signed the new constitution. The plans were plunged into chaos in 2005, however, when the French and Dutch voters reject government plans to ratify this Constitution, meaning that it would not come into effect.

The United Kingdom was promised a referendum on the ratification of the Constitution under Gordon Brown's government. Ireland was promised the same, but the referendum never came. Instead, the bureaucrats of the European Union drew up the Lisbon Treaty. This contained many of the same measures of the Constitution and amended previous treaties as opposed to replacing them. A cunning plan, which allowed the Union to grab even more power without any mandate from the European people.

And here we are today – half in, and half out, still dealing with the corruption within this vicious, poisonous, and festering pit of corruption, hatred, and vengeance. This is a project with grudges to bear, and goals to achieve, and they hate that we saw through them. Their corruption, their love affair with power, and their boundless, immeasurable striving for a uniform world can be seen in this exceptionally short history above.

I hope, also, that this book will serve as further proof that this institution never intended to allow our government to honour the result of our referendum.

What the People Voted Against

While I was shocked to win the referendum, I wasn't shocked that it was the working-class people of Britain who swung the vote. This was an unexpected Peasant's Revolt – a revolution at the ballot box that working-class people had been waiting to do. They might have been afraid to drift from their traditional parties, but they certainly weren't afraid to tell the politicians where to stick it.

Working class people were, and are, angry. For too many years working class communities have been brushed aside and considered collateral damage while the politicians move forward with their mass immigration project. I have no intention to be a sensationalist when I say that the transformation of working-class communities was completely intentional. Tony Blair's speechwriter Andrew Neather said as much when he said New Labour opened the floodgates to "rub the right's nose in diversity"[2].

That same man, today, you can find writing about his love for fine wines, climate-controlled wine walls, and spiral cellars[3]. He's a true connoisseur of London luxury, and it stinks.

This is what the British people voted against. There is a political elite in this country that doesn't understand what it's like to be a regular person. They have no idea what it's like to go to work every morning and raise a family while having to count every penny. It wasn't really about the European Union all along – it was about reminding the politicians who are in charge. And we did that alright.

We were angry about matters of sovereignty, mass immigration, and the economy. Huge parts of the United Kingdom have not only been left virtually unrecognisable as a result of mass immigration, but local economies have been decimated and largely ignored by a political elite who seem to care more about big business and big cities.

Voting to leave the European Union won't solve these problems, and I think most people who voted to leave do know that. Britain is still in dire need of politicians who want to act on major domestic issues, and until that happens, nothing will change – Brexit or not.

Once we leave the European Union, Britain will still face an immigration crisis from outside the EU. Local authorities will still have to deal with segregated communities, gang violence, and grooming gangs. We will still have radical hate preachers on our own soil, we'll still export terrorists to the rest of the world, and we'll still have a gaping, vacuous hole where our national pride used to be. A lot of work needs to be done, and the British people hoped that a vote to leave the European Union might just be, at least, the *start* of solving those problems.

We voted against the system but trusted the politicians would be true to their word. David Cameron told us that the government would implement that decision we made. The literature posted through our letterboxes said it too. We were told this was a "once in a generation decision", and "the government will implement what you decide"[4]. This has proven to be one of the biggest, if not *the* biggest, lies in British political history.

Just days after we made our decision, the result was already being challenged.

The Immediate Calls for a Second Referendum

Within a week of the Brexit vote on 23rd June 2016, we were bombarded with demands for a second referendum. Every major media outlet was discussing the possibility, printing op-eds that espoused the benefits of immediately putting the question back to the public to double check. We were treated like imbeciles who had made a simple mistake, but we knew exactly what we were doing.

Labour MP David Lammy wrote for The Guardian on the 26th June – just three days after the vote[5]:

> *"We need a second referendum. The consequences of Brexit are too grave".*

Let's break this down: if calling for a second referendum is really about democracy, then those who propose it should argue simply that the voters have the right to change their mind. Instead, Lammy and others give their game away when they cite "economic disaster" and the "destruction of the union with Scotland". They might scoff when we call them losers and claim they simply can't accept the result because it didn't go their way – but isn't that exactly what is happening?

When Lammy says "the consequences of Brexit are too grave" he's explaining why Brexit cannot happen, and therefore, why he believes a second referendum must take place. This is about reversing the decision and making the 'right' choice. It has absolutely nothing to do with democracy.

It was around this same time that millions of people began signing an online petition that demanded new rules to be implemented. The petition suggests a second referendum must have a majority of 60% or more, and turnout of more than 75%[6]. The rules were being rewritten days *after* the vote had successfully taken place.

These tactics are tried and tested when it comes to European referenda, which is why this happened. The Dutch accepted the Maastricht Treaty in 1993, but only after a second referendum vote. In France, Maastricht was approved by a majority of 51% to 49%, with a turnout of 69.7%. So Europe and pro-EU leaders are willing to accept small margins when the outcome is in favour of the union, but not a majority of 52% to 48%, with a turnout of 72.21%, if the outcome doesn't favour the union. The hypocrisy is clear.

"Hard" and "Soft" Brexit

By the end of June and the beginning of July, the terms "Hard" and "Soft" Brexit became part of the national lexicon. The terms just seemed to come from nowhere, but they were being defined by academics and regularly printed in the national press. In July 2017, the Public Policy Institute for Wales defined the terms[7].

Soft Brexit was defined as remaining in the European Economic Area, and Hard Brexit was defined as exiting the EU on World Trade Organisation Rules.

A study from King's College London asked: "What sort of Brexit do the British people want?"[8].

In early July, the BBC explained in great detail the new divide between Hard and Soft Brexit[9].

These terms would soon become tools in a campaign to deceive the public. The issue was no longer the fact that Leave had won the referendum, but what voters really *meant* by "Leave". Creating a divide between Leave voters meant politicians could muddy the Brexit waters, create confusion, and divide the unified. If they make Leave bicker amongst themselves, it's easier to slip Remain through the net.

Cameron Steps Down and Brexit Begins

The day after the Brexit vote, Prime Minister David Cameron resigned. Speaking outside No 10, Cameron said: "the will of the British people is an instruction that must be delivered". He, it seemed, wasn't the man to deliver it.

Cameron first promised a referendum on the Lisbon Treaty back before the 2010 general election and pledged again in 2014 to offer a referendum on EU membership. He made this offer for one reason – the United Kingdom Independence Party had just won the 2014 European elections, returning more Members of European Parliament than any other party in the UK. Cameron wanted to ward off that threat and put an end to the matter of independence once and for all. It didn't go his way, and he was forced to step down and make way for a Prime Minister who could deliver what the British people voted for.

A Tory leadership election ensued. Home Secretary Theresa May put her name forward, along with Andrea Leadsom, Michael Gove, Stephen Crabb, and Liam Fox. Boris Johnson was expected to throw his hat in the ring, as one of the most prominent Tory Leave campaigners, but was "stabbed in the back' by Michael Gove who decided to run last minute.

Tory leadership elections are defined by the party constitution. Tory MPs vote on a list of candidates until that list is whittled down to two. Those two candidates are then presented to Tory members who decide who will be the party's leader, and in this instance, the Prime Minister. The 2016 Tory leadership election didn't end up requiring the consent of members, however.

In the first round, Theresa May obtained 50.2% of the vote. Andrea Leadsom came second with 20.1%. Liam Fox was eliminated on that ballot, and Stephen Crabb withdrew his candidacy later in the day. In the second round of voting, Michael Gove was eliminated. May got 60.5% of the vote, Leadsom 25.5%, and Gove 14% - a 0.6% reduction from the first ballot.

However, before Tory members were given the opportunity to choose between popular Leave campaigner Andrea Leadsom and Remainer Theresa May, Leadsom withdrew from the race following press controversy. Leadsom had told The Times[10] that being a mum meant she had a "very real stake" in Britain's future – implying, of course, that Theresa May did not.

May became the leader of the Conservative Party on the 11th of July 2016 and made one very clear promise: "Brexit means Brexit, and we will make a success of it"[11].

This became a slogan Mrs May repeated over and over again, in an attempt to reassure the public that despite campaigning for Remain, she was the woman to deliver the Brexit people voted for.

On the 29th March 2017, the United Kingdom invoked Article 50 of the Treaty of the European Union. Article 50 is the legal mechanism by which a member state leaves the European Union. The invocation, or triggering, of Article 50 meant that the UK had officially notified the EU of its impending withdrawal. It meant that the UK would cease to be a member of the European Union on the 30th March 2019 at 00:00 Brussels time. In the UK, that's the 29th of March at 11pm.

In June 2017, Theresa May held a snap general election in the hope that she could increase her Parliamentary majority and pass Brexit legislation more easily. The election was a complete and utter disaster, with the Conservative Party losing 13 seats and being forced to agree to a "Confidence and Supply" agreement with the Democratic Unionist Party (DUP).

The DUP are a pro-unionist political party in Northern Ireland who won 10 seats, and therefore enough votes in Parliament to provide the Tories with the majority they needed to form a (reasonably) stable government. This dynamic would prove to be a pivotal part of the Brexit negotiation process, with Irish matters becoming even more important. Step one foot wrong over the delicate matter of Ireland, and the DUP could withdraw their support and deprive May of her majority.

Following the formation of May's new government and the announcement of her Chequers Plan for leaving the European Union, came the most shocking display of disdain for the voting British public. Politicians on both sides of the House did everything in their power to delay, frustrate, or even cancel Brexit.

Chapter One: Where We Are and How We Got Here

The biggest democratic exercise in the UK's history was on course to be betrayed by hundreds of MPs who thought they knew better than us.

References

[1] BBC News, "EU referendum: 430,000 apply to register during extension deadline.", BBC News, 10th June 2016
https://www.bbc.co.uk/news/uk-politics-eu-referendum-36496047

[2] The Telegraph, "Labour wanted mass immigration to make UK more multicultural, says former adviser.", Tom Whitehead, 23rd Oct 2009.
https://www.telegraph.co.uk/news/uknews/law-and-order/6418456/Labour-wanted-mass-immigration-to-make-UK-more-multicultural-says-former-adviser.html

[3] Homes & Property, "The ultimate climate-controlled wine walls and spiral cellars.", Andrew Neather, 18th March 2015.
https://www.homesandproperty.co.uk/luxury/property/the-ultimate-climatecontrolled-wine-walls-and-spiral-cellars-43026.html

[4] Gov.uk, "Why the government believes that voting to remain in the EU is the best decision for the UK – with references." , Cabinet Office, 6th April 2016
https://www.gov.uk/government/publications/why-the-government-believes-that-voting-to-remain-in-the-european-union-is-the-best-decision-for-the-uk/why-the-government-believes-that-voting-to-remain-in-the-european-union-is-the-best-decision-for-the-uk

[5] The Guardian, "Why we need a second referendum. The consequences of Brexit are to grave.", David Lammy, 26th Jun 2016.
https://www.theguardian.com/politics/commentisfree/2016/jun/26/second-referendum-consequences-brexit-grave

[6] Independent, "Brexit petition: More than a million people demand change to EU referendum rules to force second vote.", Lizzie Dearden, 25th June 2016.
https://www.independent.co.uk/news/uk/politics/brexit-petition-latest-eu-referendum-rules-change-force-second-vote-poll-government-a7102486.html

[7] Public Policy Institute for Wales, "What will Brexit mean for Wales?", Ian Jones, 28th July 2016.
http://ppiw.org.uk/what-will-brexit-mean-for-wales/

[8] King's College London, "What sort of Brexit do the British people want? (2018)", Report 2017,
https://www.kcl.ac.uk/sspp/policy-institute/publications/what-sort-of-brexit-do-the-british-people-want-2018.pdf

[9] BBC News, "The new divide: Hard or soft Brexit?", Mark Mardell, 7th July 2016.
https://www.bbc.co.uk/news/uk-politics-36723220

[10] The Times, "Being a mother gives me edge on May - Leadsom.", Rachel Sylvester, 9th July 2016
https://www.thetimes.co.uk/edition/news/being-a-mother-gives-me-edge-on-may-leadsom-0t7bbm29x

[11] Independent, "Theresa May says 'Brexit means Brexit and we will make a success of it' in first speech as leader.", Adam Withnall and Caroline Mortimer, 11th July 2016.
https://www.independent.co.uk/news/uk/politics/andrea-leadsom-theresa-may-conservative-leadership-election-live-tory-latest-updates-next-prime-a7130671.html

Chapter Two
July 2018

6th July
The Government Announces the Chequers Deal

Today, Theresa May and her cabinet met at her Chequers estate to discuss plans for their Brexit White Paper. The plan was to create a Brexit plan that the EU might, reluctantly, accept. Brexiteers like Boris Johnson initially rejected but soon fell in line.

The negotiations have been going on for some time, and this Chequers session really has been the crunch moment for Brexit. It decides whether we get Brexit or not, and it looks like we probably won't.

Our cabinet seems to have agreed to a proposal, now known as the Chequers Deal. And it's not great. There are 12 points in the full document,[1] but four in particular did ring some alarm bells for me. The government's position, as outlined in the White Paper, are underlined below.

1. Free Movement

h. end free movement, giving the UK back control over how many people enter the country

So free movement is technically ending, but the PM has proposed a *'mobility framework so that UK and EU citizens can continue to travel to each other's territories and apply for study and work'*.

So free movement migration will technically end, but a framework is being put in place that – presumably – makes apply for work visas easier. This might depend on trade deals, and we'll have to see how this works out in the future. Who knows what this realistically will mean.

2. Customs

d. The UK and the EU would work together on the phased introduction of a new Facilitated Customs Arrangement that would remove the need for customs checks and controls between the UK and the EU as if a combined customs territory.

Ok, so let me explain the argument against the Customs Union.

It's a system that protects European industries that don't really affect the UK. Matthew Lynn expertly summed this up in the Spectator in April this year[2], explaining that in 2016 the Customs Union increased tariffs on citrus fruits from 3% to 16%. However, the UK grows so few oranges and lemons, it just meant that we had to pay more. Tariffs are imposed on products we purchase, but if we're *outside* the Customs Union, we'd be able to set our own tariffs or even remove them - and strike free trade deals on our own.

And this is what Theresa May is proposing: essentially a compromise to solve the Irish border issue. The system – if the EU even accepts it – would use new technology to track the movement of goods and determine where they're going, and if they're subject to tariffs.

This means the UK will set the tariffs on imported goods – and goods travelling to EU member states will have an EU tariff imposed that is charged in the UK and sent to Brussels.

Here's the problem with that. We want to sign free trade deals outside of Europe, and if we're stuck with EU level tariffs, then it makes agreeing to fair and reciprocal deals with non-EU countries much harder.

3. Law

f. ensure that in the future all laws in the UK would be legislated for by Parliament and the Devolved Administrations and subject to proper oversight and scrutiny

This means that Parliament can have 'oversight' whenever we adopt EU regulations into law. Essentially, the EU will write the rules, and then we just decide if we want them or not.

I struggle to believe there will be any situation in which our politicians won't take them. Our government is weak.

4. Common Rulebook

a. The UK and the EU would maintain a common rulebook for all goods including agri-food, with the UK making an upfront choice to commit by treaty to ongoing harmonisation with EU rules on goods, covering only those necessary to provide for frictionless trade at the border.

In short, it means the UK will stay aligned with EU regulations and maintain 'harmonisation' with their rules. So, we haven't escaped EU regulations and rules at all.

MPs will technically have the final say on whether the rules are changed, but if we change them, will the deal with the EU change? And will MPs even ever vote against them? Again, our government and politicians are weak. I doubt they ever will.

This could also affect future trade deals with the US. If we have common rules with the EU, then we can't accept the same standards as America to facilitate a deal. Ergo, trade deals are hard to make.

Take chlorinated chicken for example. I'm not so keen on the idea, but it explains the concept perfectly. The EU bans chlorinated chicken, and the US trades chlorinated chicken. We, therefore, cannot import it.

So those are the four that really concerned me, but in all honesty, the whole document is pretty terrible. This doesn't seem to be the Brexit we voted for, and Boris Johnson went into this knowing it wouldn't work out.

The Guardian reported[3] that Boris Johnson met David Cameron for a private meeting before he attended the Chequers summit, with the ex-PM allegedly agreeing with Johnson that the plans May was putting forward were the 'worst of all worlds'.

You know something's wrong when our Remainer former Prime Minister agrees the deal is terrible.

9th July
The Resignations Begin

Oh dear. Theresa has had only a mere day or two thanking her lucky stars that she managed to get the cabinet on board with her Brexit betrayal deal. That reality has come crashing down with the announcement today that David Davis is resigning from the cabinet.

Speaking to the BBC, Davis explained that he felt he was no longer the best person to deliver the Brexit plan because he simply didn't believe in it. Specifically, he explained:

> *"We are now proposing to use the same rulebook, or the same laws really, as the*

European Union. Not equivalent, not similar, but the same. And that will provide all sorts of problems when it comes to, if we want to diverge, do something different. So, the return of control to parliament is more illusory than it is real. Secondly, the customs arrangement: we will be collecting taxes effectively, tariffs for the European Union. They are bound to insist on the European Court having a say in that, and that will be a problem in terms of bringing back control of our laws, again, and our borders. And thirdly, the tactic: I am worried that what the European Union will do is simply take what we've offered and ask for more or wait for more. And I think this has got to be a time when we get a bit tougher with them. And this should have been the time."

Not good – and no doubt, a sign of more resignations to come. In fact, not long afterwards, Boris Johnson announced his resignation as well. Today has been absolute chaos. My favourite tweet I've seen about this was someone asking us to *"spare a thought for Terri who will be absolutely run off her feet today."*

If you've never watched The Thick of It, you probably won't get it. If that's you, then I urge you to put this book down for a little while and go watch it. It's a comedy series about life in Whitehall – and honestly, today feels like a real-life episode of that show. The resignations, the rolling news and the drama on Sky News. I've barely switched off the news today, eagerly awaiting the next bit of gossip. I'm not into sports, so *this* is my World Cup (or Super Bowl, for you Americans).

Chapter Two: July 2018

Boris Johnson's resignation came as a bit of a shock, actually. It was generally expected by pretty much every pundit on the television that if anyone was going to resign, it would have been him first. In fact, I expected Boris to be the first one to walk out of the Chequers summit and make his way home on foot. You might have seen the news that anyone who left the Chequers summit early would have had their ministerial cars stripped from them, prompting national news channels to offer ministers who quit a free ride home.

Davis was disappointed in Johnson's resignation, too. I suppose he was hoping his own resignation would have been enough to push May back in the right direction, and that Boris might have been his man on the inside. Not now.

I feel like Boris is probably kicking himself, wishing he'd done it first. He must already be angry that Gove stabbed him in the back and scuppered his leadership bid last time around. I'm sure he's still stewing over that and plotting his next bid to become the leader of the party. Make no mistake, this man has aspirations to become PM.

If you read Boris's resignation letter, you'll see it's particularly scathing. There's bad blood here, but I don't think he's being purposely destructive or rude to the Prime Minister. His claim that her deal effectively turns the UK into a colony of the European Union is right. He wrote:

> *"In that respect we are truly headed for the status of colony – and many will struggle to see the economic or political advantages of that particular arrangement".*

It's hard to argue against that, isn't it? Especially when you consider the fact that the deal Theresa May was supposed to be putting together with her cabinet had already been signed off by Angela Merkel beforehand. Seriously, that happened.

Charles Moore wrote in the Spectator[4] that at Chequers, he heard one of Theresa's responses to suggested changes in the deal was *"No, that's not possible, because I've already cleared it with Mrs Merkel".*

Start as you mean to go on, and all that. We're on our way to becoming a colony.

12th July
The DUP Rescues Brexit, Again

The Democratic Unionist Party have perhaps been a real blessing in disguise. When the Tories failed to secure a majority government in the 2017 general election, I was concerned. It's not that I like the Tories – I don't. But, I did believe they were the only party that at least gave us the POSSIBILITY of passing Brexit through the Commons.

But it turns out, the DUP have been holding Theresa's feet to the flame. They're the real conservatives from Northern Ireland who push back when the Tories start with their usual rubbish. Now, it looks like the DUP are once again stepping up to try and save Brexit.

The Belfast Telegraph reports[5] that the DUP is joining Brexit Tories to threaten rebellion against Theresa May. The news comes after Brexiteers in the Tories gave Theresa May one week[6] to drop the Chequers deal or face a vote of no confidence.

A rebellion threatened by the DUP could be enough to make May realise she simply doesn't have the support she needs in the Commons to pass the implementation bill this Autumn. If David Lidington's efforts to lobby Labour, SNP and Lib Dem MPs don't work, then she'll be faced with no choice than to either step down or change her plan.

Jacob Rees-Mogg is one of the leading Brexiters paving the way for a change to the Chequers plan. He's the head of the European Research Group, and he's put down four amendments to the Customs Bill that MPs might be asked to vote on next week.

The support of the DUP is very welcome in this process and could be the kick May needs to realise she must ask. At this point, she's stuck squarely between Brexiteers who could pass legislation through Parliament with the help of the Tory Party generally, or anti-Brexit campaigners in Labour, SNP and Lib Dems who could help her pass a soft Brexit.

Pick one, Mrs May.

16th July
The Government's Gone Quiet on Brexit

Is it just me, or has the government gone quiet on Brexit?

It might just be that I've had a weekend away from politics, or that the government is still getting over their traumatic experience welcoming Trump to the UK, but I feel like the government has gone quiet on Brexit.

There have of course been more resignations over the last few days. Tory MPs, ministers, and Parliamentary Private Secretaries appear to be dropping like flies. Robert Courts, the MP who replaced David Cameron as member for Witney, has said he would resign as Parliamentary Private Secretary to express his disapproval of the government's Brexit position. Conservative MP Scott Mann has also resigned[7] as a Parliamentary Private Secretary to the Treasury, over his concerns about a 'watered down Brexit'.

Chapter Two: July 2018

With an October deadline looming, I would have thought the government would be in full swing at this point – ready with a workable plan and telling the EU to accept it or face us leaving with no deal. But instead, Theresa May appears to be warning of the possibility of no Brexit at all.[8]

It seems that the Prime Minister is warning Members of Parliament that unless they back her Chequers deal, Brexit might not happen at all. And yes, that's a possibility – but it's only a possibility because that's what May will do if she doesn't get the support she wants. For her, it's Brexit Lite or no Brexit at all. That's her betrayal.

Amongst the turmoil and bickering, too, her new Brexit Secretary didn't even bother to turn up to EU talks[9]. The new Foreign Secretary Jeremy Hunt skipped the Foreign Affairs Council, and the new Brexit Secretary Dominic Raab did not attend the start of his first round of Brexit negotiations today, instead opting to attend a summer drunks event hosted by FREER, a free-market think tank.

Are these the priorities of our politicians? For once, the Labour Party is right when they tell Raab to 'rethink his priorities'.

All this happens while Justine Greening MP and former Prime Minister Tony Blair push for a second referendum with three options – including the option to cancel Brexit altogether.

I think this tells us something. The politicians have been gearing up for this scenario all along. Theresa May never intended to give us Brexit and has now landed us in a position whereby we might accept her Brexit Lite deal or face no Brexit at all. The small minority of Remainers in Parliament have very little power over her, and with her own Members of Parliament proposing that we ask people if they even want the Brexit negotiations to continue, I know the great betrayal started quite some time ago.

It seems to me that the government is, in fact, going quiet. They're either burying their heads in the sand and hoping something happens – perhaps May is expecting a leadership challenge and she's playing it cool – or they know that Parliament will vote down the Chequers deal and they're willing to let it happen.

27th July
May's Customs Arrangement Shot Down by Michel Barnier

On 6th July, the government announced the Chequers Plan[10] – the Brexit in Name Only plan that pushed Boris Johnson and David Davis to resign their front bench positions. In the plan, May outlined her vision of a future customs deal with the European Union that she called the 'Facilitated Customs Arrangement'.

The Chequers white paper explained:

> *"The UK and the EU would work together on the phased introduction of a new Facilitated Customs Arrangement that would remove the need for customs checks and controls between the UK and the EU as if a combined customs territory. The UK would apply the UK's tariffs and trade policy for goods intended for the UK, and the EU's tariffs and trade policy for goods intended for the EU - becoming operational in stages as both sides complete the necessary preparations. This would enable the UK to control its own tariffs for trade with the rest of the world and ensure businesses paid the right or no tariff - in the vast majority of*

cases upfront, and otherwise through a repayment mechanism."

This essentially means that the borders between the UK and the EU will remain open, with all goods coming from the EU entering the UK with no tariffs. If goods entering the UK from outside the EU are destined for the UK, they will pay UK tariffs – but if the goods received in the UK from outside the EU are destined **for** the EU, then the UK will arrange for EU tariffs to be collected and paid to the European Union.

I'm the first to admit that this is a tricky situation to solve, but by no means impossible. By starting the negotiations with a 'no deal', and working backwards from there, Theresa May would have found herself with a significantly stronger hand in these negotiations. But she didn't do that. She did quite the opposite, and that's why this Facilitated Customs Arrangement policy has today been knocked back by Michel Barnier.

At a news conference at the European Commission headquarters – the first time he appeared alongside our new Brexit Secretary Dominic Raab – Barnier made it clear he doesn't want the plan. And why would he? It might make trading easier, and they don't want to make this process simple. They want to punish the UK as much as possible – and make the negotiations as difficult for Theresa May as they can.

Specifically, Barnier explained:[11]

"The EU cannot, and the EU will not, delegate the application of its customs policy and rules, VAT and excise duty collection to a non-member who would not be subject to the EU's governance structures."

Well, duh. If other countries realised they could still trade with the EU, without being controlled by unelected commissioners and presidents, they'd all want in on the deal!

The rejection of this plan is sure to give May a headache over Northern Ireland, too. This plan wasn't just set out to make trade simpler, but it was a way of manoeuvring around the Northern Ireland issue. The Good Friday Agreement means there can't be a hard border between Northern Ireland and the Republic of Ireland, and this plan would have meant no border was necessary. Trade would remain seamless, meaning a lack of a hard border between the two Irelands – between the EU and the UK – wouldn't have been an issue.

Now we're back to square one…which isn't ideal given it's summer and the politicians are on their holidays. Barnier and Raab say they're hoping to finish the withdrawal treaty before October, but we're really up against it at this point. Negotiators won't be meeting for another two or three weeks.

All the while, the EU and the UK are preparing for a possible No Deal scenario. We've been told that sandwiches are under threat,[12] cheese is going to become a luxury,[13] and we should start stockpiling processed food[14]– in case we start starving, or something.

Great work, Theresa. You're really nailing this.

30th July
Project Fear is Out of Hand…and It's Working

Last Friday, the Head of Output for Channel 4 News and ITV, Oliver King, made an outrageous statement on Twitter.

He claimed:

> *"No insulin is made in the UK. It can't be by March. No deal Brexit threatens supply according to Medicines Regulator Sir Michael Rawlings. What are the government going to do to prevent type-1 diabetics dying?"* [15]

It's a serious thing to consider if it were true – but it's not. In fact, there are at least two manufacturing outfits in the UK that produce insulin – Wockhardt based in Wrexham,[16] and Eli Lilly in Basingstoke.[17] This isn't secret information, and nor is it difficult to find. This head of output for a major news channel in the UK could have found this information out with a cursory Google search – but he didn't.

This is how fake news operates, and it's symptomatic of a perpetually-outraged, and consistently untruthful media establishment that is engaging in Project Fear 2.0. The original Project Fear campaign ran throughout the Brexit referendum period in 2016, with politicians and big business warning of impending doom should we vote to leave the European Union. They thought it would work, but it didn't. We voted decisively to leave – and ever since, they've been upping their game.

Project Fear 2.0 is much more vicious, and it's stooped as low as scaring people into believing Brexit might kill them.

I've already mentioned the claims that Brexit will impact on our supply of sandwiches, and make cheese a luxury – but over the weekend, it was suggested in the national press that Brexit could lead to the spread of 'super gonorrhoea' and other diseases.

Chapter Two: July 2018

The story appeared[18] as a result of journalists conflating comments by Niall Dickson, the chief exec of the NHS Confederation, with the story of a man who contracted the world's worst Super Gonorrhoea and brought it back to the UK.

Dickson reasonably explained that diseases don't know any borders, and it's important for the UK to cooperate with the European Centre for Disease Prevention and Control. Combine the fearmongering suggestion that Brexit means Britain would be cut off from the rest of the world, with the story of a man who contracted super gonorrhoea, and you've got yourself one hell of a story – and one hell of a piece of propaganda.

It doesn't stop there, either. The Daily Mail reported[19] that Doctors were warning that delaying the transportation of radioactive medicines used to treat tumours could put cancer patients at risk. Once again, this depends on the ludicrous suggestion that Brexit means an inability to effectively trade with the rest of the world and Europe.

A Brexit negotiated by a *truly* strong and stable leader would not see any such problems. Once again, this is fearmongering and propaganda from a ramped-up Project Fear.

The government has even had to tell the press[20] that they are not, in fact, planning for the Armed Forces to maintain food and other supplies in the event of a No Deal Brexit – as if that was ever on the cards in the first place. This is propaganda that even Goebbels would be impressed by.

It's not just me that's noticing it, either. Even Tory MP Peter Bone spoke up about it, telling The Express:

> *"This tops it all. It's palpable nonsense.*
> *This is as stupid as the Project Fear stuff*

*in the referendum and it's all being done
for the same reason – to scare people in
the hope we will either agree to a Brexit in
name only, or stay in."*

And he's right. In fact, new polls show that the British people have been successfully scared away from Brexit.

A Sky Data poll[21] announced today shows that, in the event of a three-option second referendum, 58% would vote to Remain, 32% would vote to leave the EU with no deal, and 10% would vote to leave the EU with the government's deal.

It's fascinating that more would prefer no deal. In fact, it's somewhat comforting – but it's concerning we're losing the argument 42% to 58%.

We must also consider another couple of things here. First off, those who responded 'don't know' have been excluded from the data, and we'll never really know just how many shied away from providing their real opinion on the subject. The Shy Brexit vote won it for us last time, and maybe it would again. But this data remains unsettling.

The fearmongering in the press, combined with the unmitigated vitriol from politicians who have no idea what the life of normal people is like, is turning people away from the most positive political decision they have made in their lifetime. Working people who were brave enough to stand up to the Establishment and say "we're not happy with how you're running this country" and "we don't want to be ruled by foreign bureaucrats", are being forced to cower in the corner while the politicians just get on with ignoring their decision.

Labour Peer Lord Mandelson called Brexit voters[22] nationalists who 'hate foreigners'. Shadow Home Secretary Diane Abbott called Brexit voters 'racist'.[23]

This is how the politicians break down, subjugate, and silence the masses. They provide the illusion of choice at election times, and in the event of referenda going the wrong way, they'll collude to scupper the negotiating process and claim they tried their hardest to make it work. Their final step is to lie about the effects of implementing our decision, and hopefully give us another chance to make the right decision next time.

Project Fear is very much out of control, and I fear it's working.

31st July
81% of Tory Members Want May to Resign

A new survey shows that 81.12% of Tory members want Theresa May to resign....but should she?

It's a hard one for me to answer. On the one hand, there's the chance that we'll end up with a Brexit PM...but on the other hand, there's the possibility of Corbyn winning with a coalition of other left-wing parties.

We're stuck between a rock and a hard place!

The new survey by Conservative Home shows that a majority of members of the Conservative Party believe it's time for Theresa May to resign. Let's look at these figures.[24]

It found:

45% - Yes, now
36.12% - Yes, before the next election is due in 2022
17.31% - No
1.57% - Don't know

Chapter Two: July 2018

That means 81.12% of the Conservative Party believe that Theresa May should stop down as leader – and therefore, as Prime Minister – either now or before the next election in 2022.

And it's almost certainly because of Brexit. There's nothing else anybody really cares about right now.

Interestingly, Conservative Home notes that the 45% figure – people who want her to resign now – is more than double over last month's finding. They say:

> *"So this month's 45 per cent is more than double last month's – and is easily the worst finding for Downing Street since this survey question was first asked in the aftermath of last year's general election."*

Specifically, I think this is a reaction to Chequers. The Chequers White Paper is a disaster and that's why Tory voters are turning back to the barometer party UKIP – something which tends to keep the Tories in line.

Meanwhile, working-class voters are turning back to Labour out of habit. That's something that desperately needs changing in this country.

But I think the question here is…should Theresa May resign?

I'm not sure – because I don't think she would lose the leadership challenge. Most Tories are still remainers and I doubt they'd want total upheaval at this point. Once they come back from Summer recess, they'll have just months to negotiate and finalise this deal.

And if the No Deal propaganda I wrote about yesterday is anything to go by, then the politicians will do everything they can to stop a No Deal scenario.

Including taking a rubbish deal from the EU.

So the Tories want Theresa to resign. Three out of four voters think the government is doing a bad job on Brexit.[25]

Should she resign? I don't know. It's a tough one. I don't think I can give you an answer – YES, in that I would prefer somebody who actually intends to deliver Brexit. NO, in that I don't want to risk her being re-elected and delaying Brexit as a result, or even face a general election where Labour could gain seats and form a coalition with smaller parties.

May Government Planned to Scare Voters into Supporting the Chequers Deal

Just days ago, an anonymous Tory Member of Parliament, who described themselves as an 'ally' of Prime Minister Theresa May, told BBC Newsnight[26] that the government was intending to scare the voters so much that they embraced the wildly unpopular Chequers deal.

He said:

> *"We want to scare people witless so people will eventually embrace the Theresa May plan".*

It was claimed that the government's decision to release 70 official documents over the coming weeks, which outline measures the country would need to take to prepare for a No Deal scenario, was specifically made to build support for her Chequers deal.

May denied it, of course. She insisted that it was not her intention to alarm the public, but that she hoped instead, voters would 'take reassurance and comfort' in the knowledge that they had these measures in place. She told Channel Five:

> *"It's right that we say because we don't know what the outcome is going to be, we think it's going to be a good one, we're working for a good one but let's prepare for every eventuality".*

I'm not entirely sure that's even English.

What's interesting about this, is that it basically explains everything that's been happening recently – the Super Gonorrhoea talk. The stories about the Armed Forces on our streets, maintaining order and distributing rations. It all makes sense now.

The government has been planning to release more than 70 documents over the next few weeks, which will describe all the contingency plans in place that may come into effect in the event of a No Deal Brexit. Not only are the papers going mad over this, but they're reporting that it's an increasingly likely scenario.

After Barnier shot down her Facilitated Customs Arrangement plan, it looks like negotiation simply isn't going to work with the EU. And you know what, I and the rest of the working classes who voted for Brexit are cheering on a No Deal Brexit. Bring it on.

Sky News data keeps showing, over and over, that there's a lot of us out there who see through it all, and still want No Deal. One poll showed 27%[27] of the public cheering on a No Deal Brexit. Another claimed 41%.[28] That's a lot of people seeing through the tricks of the media and political establishment.

More people support a No Deal Brexit than Theresa May's Chequers deal…which would explain the derision and anger ever since it was claimed that it was the government's intentions to scare the voters. And now, according to Breitbart, the government is intending on releasing all the documents at once, on a single day in August.[29]

I can only imagine the stress behind the scenes at Number 10. Their secret is out, and their plan is scuppered. They wanted to scare us into thinking a No Deal Brexit was just around the corner, but it definitely is now. The Chequers deal does not have the support of the people, the EU and Barnier are not on board with any concessions and are happy to try and punish the UK or force us into cancelling the entire thing, and the voters are wising up to their tactics.

The more they try and mess with us, the more faith I have that we've done the right thing. We've thrown a hand grenade into Number 10 and we're watching Cabinet Ministers and the PM ducking and diving behind cabinets and desks before it goes off. We've changed the system and set a new narrative – and every attempt they make at reversing it has backfired. This grenade is going to go off – and if it turns out to be a No Deal Brexit, it's going to take out the entire government.

Once the electorate experiences a No Deal Brexit and doesn't catch Super Gonorrhoea, they'll never trust the main parties ever again.

In the meantime, let's wait and see if the No Deal propaganda dies down a bit. I wonder if they'll have the balls to keep trying to fool us, now we know their game.

References

[1] Gov.uk, "UK Government, "Statement from HM Government, Chequers"", 6th July 2018, https://assets.publishing.service.gov.uk/government/uploads/system/uploads/attachment_da ta/file/723460/CHEQUERS_STATEMENT_-_FINAL.PDF

[2] The Spectator, "Who is making the case for leaving the Customs Union?", Matthew Lynn, 23rd April 2018, https://blogs.spectator.co.uk/2018/04/who-is-making-the-case-for-leaving-the-customs-union/

[3] The Guardian, "Johnson met Cameron for private meeting before Chequers summit", Jessica Elgot, 6th July 2018, https://www.theguardian.com/politics/2018/jul/06/boris-johnson-david-cameron-meeting-chequers-summit-brexit

[4] The Spectator, " "Why did Theresa May 'clear' the EU deal with Merkel before consulting her colleagues?", Charles Moore, 14th July 2018, https://www.spectator.co.uk/2018/07/why-did-theresa-may-clear-the-eu-deal-with-merkel-before-consulting-her-colleagues/

[5] Belfast Telegraph, "DUP joins Brexit Tories to threaten rebellion against Theresa May.", Ashley Cowburn,12th July 2018, https://www.belfasttelegraph.co.uk/news/northern-ireland/dup-joins-brexit-tories-to-threaten-rebellion-against-theresa-may-37108380.html

[6] Politics Home, "Pro-Brexit Tories 'give Theresa May one week' to drop chequers plan or face no confidence vote.", Emilio Casalicchio, 11th July 2018, https://www.politicshome.com/news/uk/political-parties/conservative-party/theresa-may/news/96745/pro-brexit-tories-give-theresa

[7] Daily Star, "NINTH Tory MP resigns over fears of 'watered down Brexit' ahead of Commons showdowns.", Charlotte Ikonen, 16th July 2018, https://www.dailystar.co.uk/news/politics/716698/brexit-news-scott-mann-mp-resignation-tory-conservative-chequers-deal-cornwall-theresa-may

[8] Sky News, "Theresa May: 'We risk ending up with no Brexit at all'.", Tom Rayner, 25th July 2018, https://news.sky.com/story/theresa-may-back-my-chequers-plan-or-brexit-wont-happen-11437460

[9] Independent, "Theresa May's new Brexit and foreign ministers stay away from EU talks as Cabinet turmoil rages.", Jon Stone, 16th July 2018, https://www.independent.co.uk/news/uk/politics/theresa-may-brexit-eu-talks-firegin-ministers-cabinet-customs-bill-vote-conservatives-a8449226.html

[10] Gov.uk, "UK Government, "Statement from HM Government, Chequers"", 6th July 2018, https://assets.publishing.service.gov.uk/government/uploads/system/uploads/attachment_da ta/file/723460/CHEQUERS_STATEMENT_-_FINAL.PDF

[11] Independent, "Brexit: Michel Barnier rules out Theresa May's Chequers custom plan.", Jon Stone, 26th July 2018, https://www.independent.co.uk/news/uk/politics/brexit-barnier-rules-out-theresa-may-plan-customs-union-a8465341.html

[12] BBC News, "Brexit threats to sandwiches.", Simon Jack, 26th July 2018, https://www.bbc.co.uk/news/business-44960293

Chapter Two: July 2018

[13] *The Guardian, "Dairy products 'may become luxuries' after UK leaves EU.", Lisa O'Carroll, 18th July 2018,*
https://www.theguardian.com/politics/2018/jul/18/dairy-products-may-become-luxuries-after-uk-leaves-eu

[14] *The Guardian, "A no-deal Brexit survival guide: what food to stockpile.", Dale Berning Sawa, 12th July 2018,*
https://www.theguardian.com/politics/shortcuts/2018/jul/12/a-no-deal-brexit-survival-guide-what-food-to-stockpile

[15] *Twitter, "No insulin is made in the UK. It can't be by March. No deal Brexit threatens supply according to Medicines Regulator Sir Michael Rawlings. What are the government going to do to prevent type-1 diabetics dying ?", Oliver King, 27th July 2018,*
https://twitter.com/oliverjamesking/status/1022873025253978112

[16] *Wockhardt, "About Wockhardt",*
http://www.wockhardt.co.uk/about-wockhardt.aspx

[17] *Lilly, "Our Products",*
https://www.lilly.co.uk/en/products/index.aspx

[18] *Daily Star, "Brexit STD WARNING: Super gonorrhoea to spread more easily when UK leaves EU", Charlotte Ikonen, 30th July 2018,*
https://www.dailystar.co.uk/news/latest-news/719863/disease-warning-std-brexit-sex-infection-super-gonorrhoea-uk-eu-latest-news

[19] *Mail Online, "Doctors warn border delays could ruin medicines amid fears No-deal Brexit 'will put cancer patients at risk", Stephen Adams and Brendan Carlin, 29th July 2018,*
http://www.dailymail.co.uk/news/article-6003209/Doctors-warn-no-deal-Brexit-cancer-patients-risk.html

[20] *BBC News, "No 10 deny plan for Army role in "no deal' Brexit", BBC News, 20th July 2018,*
https://www.bbc.co.uk/news/uk-politics-45007787

[21] *Twitter, "UK, Sky Data poll: European Membership Referendum", Europe Elects, 20th July 2018,*
https://twitter.com/EuropeElects/status/1023845007768408064

[22] *Leading Britain's Conversation, "Lord Mandelson: Brextremists Are "Nationalists" Who "Hate Foreigners", not patriots", James O'Brien, 30th July 2018,*
https://www.lbc.co.uk/radio/presenters/james-obrien/mandelson-brextremists-nationalist-not-patriot/

[23] *HuffPost, "Diane Abbott Criticised Over BBC Question Time Comments About Brexit And Racism", Jasmin Gray, 7th April 2017,*
https://www.huffingtonpost.co.uk/entry/diane-abbott-bbc-question-time-brexit-racism_uk_58e7451ce4b05413bfe1a259

Chapter Two: July 2018

[24] ConservativeHome, "Our survey finds a record fall of confidence in May. Over two in five Party members want her out now.", Paul Goodman, 31st July 2018, https://www.conservativehome.com/thetorydiary/2018/07/our-survey-finds-a-record-fall-of-confidence-in-may-over-two-in-five-party-members-want-her-out-now.html

[25] Politico, "Poll:3 in 4 Brits think UK government doing 'bad job' on Brexit". Gabriela Galindo, 30th July 2018, https://www.politico.eu/article/poll-majority-brits-think-uk-government-theresa-may-doing-bad-job-on-brexit-second-referendum/

[26] Mail Online, "May 'plans to scare us witless' over No Deal: Stockpile warnings are aimed at building support for the PM's under-fire Brexit strategy, ally claims", John Steven, 26th July 2018, http://www.dailymail.co.uk/news/article-5993257/May-plans-scare-witless-No-Deal.html

[27] Twitter, "Sky Data poll: 78% think the government is doing a bad job on Brexit", @SkyData, 29th July 2018, https://twitter.com/SkyData/status/1023802467509837824

[28] Twitter, "If there were a referendum, would you vote...", @SkyData, 29th July 2018, https://twitter.com/SkyData/status/1023802897266618368

[29] Breitbart, "Cancel the Apocalypse: Govt Abandons Plan to 'Drip Feed' Negative Brexit Stories After Backlash", Jack Montgomery, 31st July 2018, https://www.breitbart.com/europe/2018/07/31/cancel-the-apocalypse-govt-abandons-plan-to-drip-feed-negative-brexit-stories-after-backlash/

Chapter Three
August 2018

1st August
'No Deal' Scaremongering Ignores WTO Trading Rules

I came across an interesting press release today, from the cross-party pro-Brexit campaign, Get Britain Out. Their press release focused on biased Brexit coverage from Sky News, specifically relating to a piece called 'Brexit Forensics', written by their political editor Faisal Islam.

In the piece,[1] Islam discussed a report released by Dover District Council about the implications of a No Deal Brexit – specifically, how the M20 motorway would turn into a 13-mile lorry park as a result of checks needing to be carried out on goods that enter the UK.

But Get Britain Out rightly points out that Sky News has completely avoided the immediate opportunity of trading under World Trade Organisation rules. It seems like Sky are in essence aiding the government in their plans to scare the people 'witless',[2] in hope that they'll support the Chequers Deal.

The press release outlines the reality of a No Deal Brexit that operates under World Trade Organisation rules:

> *"The UK will still be a member of the WTO after Brexit,* **meaning the EU will be unable to intentionally discriminate against UK products without just reasoning.** *Given the UK has committed to maintaining high standards after Brexit, Project Fear reports like this are*

far-fetched, and are only aimed at scaring the Great British Public.

The WTO's Agreement on Sanitary and Phytosanitary Measures, for example, ensures regulations and inspection procedures must only be applied to meet health and safety standards and must be removed if the scientific evidence is not sufficient.

The WTO's Trade Facilitation Agreement (TFA) is in place to ensure trade between neighbouring countries remains as frictionless as possible. *As both the UK and the EU are signatories to the TFA, this agreement commits both sides to coordinate their activities and facilities in such a way so as to promote cross-border trade."*

That's pretty conclusive, really. And it's handy to know if you didn't know already. The doomsday scenarios surrounding the No Deal Brexit scenario would be accurate if the European Union really did have free reign to punish us and discriminate – but they can't, and they won't.

First off, we know it's in their own interests to trade with the UK. Almost 14% of Irish exports went to the UK in 2015, along with 9% of the Netherlands' exports and 7.4% of Germany's exports.

And for a long time, the UK has been among the less-than-half of EU member states who were net contributors to the EU budget.

Consistently, the UK has proven to be one of the most important economic forces in Europe – and that's not about to change. For this reason – along with the fact that the

WTO wouldn't allow it – the EU is not going to be able to punish the UK in trade. They'll continue trading with us if they know what's good for them, and the queues down at Dover are unlikely to occur.

Are you getting sick of Project Fear 2.0, yet?

2nd August
May Cuts Holiday Short to Plead with Macron Over Brexit

After the government's doom mongering was exposed by an anonymous tip to Newsnight, Prime Minister Theresa May has cut her holiday short to plead with French President Emmanuel Macron over his Brexit stance.

The Times reported yesterday[3] that May has cut her summer holiday short to attend a summit in France, where she'll ask, beg, and plead with Macron to soften his stance on Brexit. OK, maybe I'm being a bit tough there – but let's be honest, May knows how rubbish her negotiations have been so far, and an ally in Europe is pretty much her only hope of pulling off some kind of Brexit by March.

May plans on attending a meeting on Friday, where she'll ask Macron to reconsider his objections to security cooperation once Britain leaves the EU. She'll also be asking France if they can provide reassurances that they'll assist Britain in securing a trade deal for the City of London, which has been resisted by Michel Barnier.

In April, Chief Brexit Negotiator for the EU, Michel Barnier, said that the EU doesn't need the City of London [4] and that he will not reward May's 'pleading' for a special deal.

At a meeting of finance ministers in Sofia, Bulgaria, Barnier explained:

Chapter Three: August 2018

> *"Some argue that the EU desperately needs the City of London, and that access to financing for EU27 business would be hampered – and economic growth undermined – without giving UK operators the same market access as today... This is not what we hear from market participants, and it is not the analysis that we have made ourselves."*

Ouch.

If May can't get Macron on board, then I can't see how Barnier's going to change his mind. If he wants to punish the UK, or get Brexit overturned, then he couldn't do much better than give majority-Remain-voting London angry over the lack of a trade deal.

The upcoming summit is part of a wider plot by May to go around the leaders of the EU, to take on the European Commission's hard line against her Chequers customs proposals.

It doesn't look like it'll work though. The Times says that a senior Élysée advisor explained that the PM shouldn't have high expectations from the summit. The newspaper was told:

> *"It is very difficult for Macron...It is not in his gift to offer compromises – only the commission can do that. He will stand firm with the commission".*

May isn't the first person from the cabinet to visit France in the hope of changing their minds, either. Business Secretary Greg Clark visited last Tuesday, and Chancellor Philip Hammond visited on Monday. On Tuesday, Foreign Secretary Jeremy Hunt visited Paris, and today the Brexit Secretary Dominic Raab will be paying his own visit. It seems like our struggling government sees France as the weakest link, but Europhile Macron seems unlikely to be interested in helping the EU knock down the first EU-exit domino.

It's embarrassing to know our government is scrambling to try and influence the weakest, instead of taking on the monsters in the EU head-on. Bring on No Deal.

Michael Gove's Secret Free Movement Plan

Michael Gove has long been considered a potential Brexit Prime Minister. Earlier last month,[5] a major Tory party donor warned that Gove should be installed as the new Conservative leader because May can't carry Brexit through.

He even ran in the Tory leadership contest and was said to have stabbed Boris in the back[6] by running and positioning himself as a Brexiteer candidate.

But it looks like the Tory Party's great Brexiteer hope has actually been discussing a secret plan with the EU that would maintain open borders.

The Express reported:[7]

> Brexit campaigner Mr Gove was talking with Tory MPs and peers at a dinner when the Conservative MP raised the scenario where the UK would remain in the European Economic Area (EEA), like Norway, so they could avoid the chaos of a disorderly 'no deal' exit.
>
> The cabinet minister was speaking at a private dinner of the Green Chip group,

which was set up in support of David Cameron during his time as Prime Minister, with about 20 Tory MPs and peers on June 25.

According to the Financial Times, one MP at the dinner said: "He was steering the conversation towards the EEA idea.

"There's no doubt about that."

But others say that he isn't advocating the EEA option, at all.

The Express also reported that an ally of Gove explained:

"He's totally behind the prime minister's Chequers strategy. He's not considering any other option. He likes discussing things."

OK, so this is the reality here. Michael Gove (once considered the Brexit Prime Minister) is either in support of Theresa May's Chequers Plan, or he's happy to go with the Norway model (staying in the European Economic Area) which would maintain open borders for the UK.

The fact that Michael Gove even considered the possibility of the UK staying in the European Economic Area – something which by definition requires the free movement of persons, goods, services, and capital – shows that the Tories cannot be trusted on Brexit.

If we can't trust Gove, then who can we trust?

3rd August
EU Judges Can 'Interpret' Withdrawal Bill However They Like

The Express reported[8] four days ago that UK officials are planning on giving EU judges the final say on crucial Brexit decisions – and this isn't overhyped fearmongering. It's literally the case.

The British government has agreed to give the European Court of Justice the final say to break the deadlock in troublesome negotiations regarding the Withdrawal Agreement. This means that judges from the ECJ (European Court of Justice) will have the final say on the Irish backstop, assuming that the final deal on trade between the UK and Brussels results in checks on the Irish border.

If you're still unclear on the 'backstop', think of it as a safety net. The term is actually a reference to baseball, where the 'backstop' refers to a fence behind the catcher which stops the ball leaving the field.

The backstop is essentially a fall-back option if negotiations don't go well – and on June 7th, the government published a policy paper[9] entitled 'Technical note on temporary customs agreement'. In it, they explain:

"The UK's proposal is that in the circumstances in which the backstop is agreed to apply, a temporary customs arrangement should exist between the UK and the EU".

The temporary customs arrangement would be put in place to avoid a backstop that would apply only to Northern Ireland – effectively splitting Ireland in two. The backstop would, instead, apply to the whole of the UK – meaning a temporary customs arrangement would be put in place on the whole country if they can't negotiate a proper deal.

This is a measure to stop any hard border between Northern Ireland and the Republic, which is forbidden under the Good Friday Agreement. So if the whole of the UK leaves the European Union without a trade deal or any kind of security agreements, there won't be any border checks between Northern Ireland and the Republic.

The backstop would be implemented at the end of the transition period, which should be December 2020, if the UK has not negotiated a deal with the European Union. Prime Minister Theresa May has stressed many times over that she doesn't intend for the backstop to even come into effect, but I'm not so confident in her ability to negotiate a beneficial deal for our future relationship with the EU by the end of the transition period.

Therefore, the news that the government is giving the ECJ the final say on the backstop is serious – and further down the line, the ECJ will be able to make rulings about the final Withdrawal Agreement. The EU may also be given the power to decide that we should stay within the backstop indefinitely. Given the final agreement will become EU law, the ECJ will be able to make rulings about the interpretation of the agreement. So the UK might resist, and we may well technically leave the EU, but they'll still be there. Over our shoulder. Watching.

My friend Anne Marie Waters is right when she says that we'll never be free of the European Union until it dies. As long as the EU exists, they'll exert some kind of control over us. They'll come back and reinterpret our final deal, put pressure on us to avoid being too competitive, and ultimately do everything they can to make life difficult for us.

7th August
May Returns to UK, Tail Between Legs, After Failing to Win Over Macron

I thought that summer recess would mean fewer interesting stories to write about every day, but the weekend has been crazy.

On Saturday, my suspicions that Macron would not be interested in the slightest in helping Theresa May get the EU to budge were proven right. The Mail reported that Macron refused to help break the Brexit deadlock, telling Mrs May that he stands behind the EU's negotiators.

He warned May that he refused to break ranks over Brexit, despite May's warnings that Brussels faces a 'Chequers deal or no deal'. Yikes, is that Theresa trying to be down with the kids? If so, I guess it's slightly better than openly admitting she likes NCIS (which she did, during a recent question and answer session in the North East).

Downing Street was intending to use the meeting with Macron at Fort Bregancon as a way of winning over the French President and having him help soften Barnier's hard-line stance. But it hasn't worked.

In non-Brexit news, The Daily Telegraph reported yesterday[10] that trauma surgeons are warning that Britain's knife crime epidemic is putting the NHS under strain. Figures revealed a 57% increase in knife offences in England and Wales over the figures from 2014.

And today, the knives are out for May. She's been blamed for preparations for a No Deal Brexit ramping up, with a row breaking out in Whitehall about how to advise businesses to prepare for the possibility.

The Telegraph reports[11] that civil servants have been ordered to start compiling the 70 documents I've previously mentioned, called 'technical notices', by the end of August to explain to businesses and self-employed individuals on what they need to do to prepare if it happens. Ministers are saying, however, that they weren't consulted before the PM made the announcement about technical notices.

And Corbyn isn't safe, either. Both leaders are extremely unpopular right now. The Mail reported today that Labour 'moderates' (basically, not anti-Semites) are allegedly plotting to oust Jeremy Corbyn, and they're being branded 'traitors' and threatened with deselection by Corbyn supporters in the party.

It's said that the coup is being organised by Liz Kendall, Stephen Kinnock, Chuka Umunna and others., and that they've been plotting in a £144-a-night farmhouse in Sussex. Alright for some.

We'll see how well that goes because it looks like the only thing going for Corbyn is the huge number of socialists, students, and morons who joined the Labour Party in recent years. The *public* hates him.

Polls released today[12] by Ipsos MORI show that 46% of the public think the Tories should change their leader before the next general election, and 55% of the people think Labour should change their leader before the next election. 27% wanted Corbyn to stay, compared to 31% who wanted May to stay. May beats him – sort of – but I wouldn't call it a win by any stretch.

Given how useless Theresa has been in the negotiation process, and the fact she just came back with her tail between her legs after unsuccessfully trying to convince Macron to change his position, Corbyn should be smashing her in the polls.

And, to top things off for the day, we've got more doom and gloom news about Brexit. The papers are running a story[13] about how the UK would 'run out of food a year from now' if we reach a No Deal Brexit. I suppose it's technically true – the National Farmers' Union has made the claim – but in order for this to happen, there would have to be a catastrophic scenario where Britain is somehow unable to trade at all.

That's obviously not going to happen, so don't go stockpiling tinned carrots just yet.

8th August
New Poll Says Most Brits – Even Remainers – Want the Government to Get on with Brexit

Theresa May is continuing her embarrassing trips to meet foreign leaders. Well, sort of – this time she's crossed the border to Scotland, visiting Edinburgh to attend the Edinburgh International Festival and the Fringe Festival. She was immediately met by protestors[14] at Edinburgh's Assembly Hall, with hecklers asking: "any plans for when the government collapses, Theresa?".

Even one of the comics performing at the festival, Jane Godley, shouted "Theresa, are you coming in for the show? We've got a food bank".

And, while the visit is underway, a Scottish political commentator has claimed that the PM's relationship with Scottish First Minister Nicola Sturgeon has hit 'rock bottom'.

Ian Macwhirter claimed that the two leaders should now try and build a constructive relationship, based on the similar experiences they've had as women in male-dominated professions.

He told The Express:[15]

"I think they actually had quite a lot in common and quite a lot to talk about…But that relationship has certainly deteriorated over the subsequent years and is now at rock bottom, mainly because of this controversy over the so-called power grab which is the powers that are repatriated from Brussels going directly to Westminster and not going to Scotland in devolved areas".

Meanwhile, British voters are telling the pollsters that they want the PM to just hurry it up and get on with Brexit, regardless of what the deal is.

A survey by Deltapoll[16] found that 60% of the British public agreed to the question "Right now, I no longer care how or when we leave the European Union, I just want it all over and done with'.

That's quite substantial. It's certainly higher than the 52% that originally voted for Brexit. Even 48% of Remainers agreed with the question. Interestingly though, 75% of Leavers agreed with the statement. I suppose that 25 % actually just mean that they do care about the deal – with maybe a few percentage points having changed their mind about Brexit since.

75% of Labour Leavers want her to get on with the job as well, and a sizeable chunk – some 42% - of Labour Remainers want her to get on with it.

It seems pretty obvious to me that the British public wants Brexit, but with the way our Parliamentarians are behaving, you'd think there had been some major change in public opinion.

I think I've found out why, though. Reports today[17] explain that there has been an increase of incidents where large lumps of stonework are falling off from the Parliament building, as it undergoes much-needed repair works. The politicians must have experienced a fair few bonks to the head if so many of them are acting this crazy over Brexit.

9th August
EU Could Let UK Stay in Single Market without Free Movement

The Express reports today[18] that the EU might be preparing to let the UK stay in the Single Market without accepting free movement – breaking the EU's four freedoms. These are the free movement of goods, services, capital and persons, which are required for access to their internal market, as per the Single European Act.

It's an interesting new move but all might not be as it seems.

It's suggested that member states of the EU might be willing to cross this 'red line', but only if Theresa May is willing to make a few concessions. A deal is allegedly on the table that will be discussed during a special meeting of all 28 EU leaders in Austria next month – something I wouldn't have expected to happen given that Michel Barnier had previously said any such proposal would undermine the Single Market.

So what will May have to give up? Well, it seems like her Facilitated Customs Arrangement would have to be scrapped. It hasn't been popular with the people in Britain, and the EU wasn't keen on it, either.

The Mail reports[19] that the EU might also demand that the UK sticks to their social and environmental rules following Brexit, which would mark not just a retreat from

Brexit but a total betrayal of the result of the referendum. It would seriously hamper our ability to strike trade deals with the rest of the world if we're stuck with EU regulation.

However, according to other reports,[20] Mrs May might be stalling negotiations and plotting to push negotiations as far back as possible so that they become more lenient as time runs out. The idea is this: European leaders want a 'united front' against Trump at the G20 summit in November, and ideally want the Brexit negotiations out of the way by then.

Negotiations start up again after the summer break next week, and British officials will be heading out to Brussels to try and nail down some final parts of the withdrawal deal. One EU Commission official, however, told the Express that they believe it would be 'highly unlikely' anything could be finalised next week.

This doesn't really strike me as a strong negotiating tactic. Delaying? Really? If the EU has to battle Trump and the UK at the same time then I reckon they'll do it – and delaying until the last minute might just mean the UK has to make even more concessions. If it turns out to be true that the EU might let us stay in the Single Market without free movement, as long as the UK makes concessions, then what's to stop the British government making even *more* concessions?

Imagine you're negotiating a deal over a used car and you've only got 60 seconds to do it. One side wants to charge as much as possible but knows there are other buyers if it all goes wrong. The other side is desperate for a car because he promised his wife a new car. Get down to those last ten seconds and you're probably going to be willing to pay a lot more than you originally planned. You've got to keep the missus happy.

Let's face it – the EU doesn't care if May betrays her people or not. So why would they be willing to help her out?

And, by the way, don't go thinking we won't end up with free movement. I think all bets are off right now. As I've explained in a previous entry, Theresa May won't be stopping free movement to the UK. She's just renamed it and jiggled the process around a bit. The Chequers deal outlines a method of ensuring people can come in and out of Britain from the European Union almost as easily as they can do now.

10th August
The People's Vote is Taking to the Road

Guess what, guys – the People's Vote roadshow is coming to a town near you![21] Are you excited? Lib Dem leader Sir Vince Cable is definitely just a normal guy like you, and he's taking his People's Vote campaign on the road with fellow normal people Stephen Doughty and Sarah Wollaston.

They'll be speaking tomorrow at an event in Bristol, where tickets have sold out. That should come as no surprise to anybody who has been to Bristol, before. The last time I was there I saw Antifa stickers plastered all over the city centre, and I felt uncomfortable in any bar I visited. It's enemy territory, and I feel sorry for the normal, sane people who live there.

The decision to take the People's Vote campaign on the road is obviously an attempt to show that it isn't run by out of touch elites. They'll be going to Edinburgh, Newcastle, Cambridge, Cardiff, and ultimately Liverpool where they will be holding an event alongside the Labour Party national conference.

These people are delusional, and they can't see it. In a rare moment of sanity, Owen Jones actually admitted that a second referendum could be potentially disastrous for his side. He believes that the Leave campaign would win it by an even bigger margin,[22] and I suspect he's right. After all the fearmongering and the betrayal by our politicians – including a coordinated campaign to force people to change their minds and admit their vote was ill-informed – I think it's perfectly reasonable to expect the voters to turn out in even greater numbers and tell the establishment to *do one*.

13th August
CBI Suggests Scrapping Migration Targets

I think it's entirely accurate to say that business controls government. In fact, I'd say it was true across a lot of the Western world. That's the problem with our system – the government is in the pockets of big business, bending at will to their demands in hope that the economy doesn't crash.

If fascism relies on government and business being closely linked, then I think there's an argument to suggest our current system is – at least – similar to fascism. But I digress.

My claim that government is too closely linked with business, and that big business in effect tells the government what to do, is proven today with the report that the Confederation of British Industry is advising the government to scrap their net migration targets.

And they're being clever about it.

So let's start with the net migration targets. For years, the government has claimed they intend to bring immigration down from hundreds of thousands every year, to tens of thousands. Since 2010, however, the Tories have failed to deliver. Eight years seems like plenty of time to achieve something even close to the goal, but we're still in the multiple hundreds of thousands.

And so, now, the CBI is saying[23] that the government should scrap their net migration targets and instead replace it with a system that ensures those who come to the UK make a positive impact on the economy.

Nice try.

The CBI has a history of digging its heels in over Brexit, and they're not quiet about their opinion on freedom of movement. The CBI's deputy director general, Josh Hardie, has said that immigration must be 'put on the table' in trade talks to give us a better deal. Specifically, he wrote:[24]

> *"For Global Britain to succeed, the UK must send the right signals that show it remains open and welcoming to the world. That means putting migration on the table in trade talks to get us a better deal, first with the EU and then other countries where it is clear existing visa restrictions inhibit trade and foreign direct investment."*

Free movement. He's talking about free movement, in a different name. Their own recommendations on the CBI website say they intend to *'Replace free movement with an open and controlled immigration system for EU workers'.*

An open and controlled system for workers only in the EU is the equivalent of free movement with Europe. Otherwise, what's the point?

I won't be fooled by this, and I won't trust big business to tell me what's good for my country. When the CBI tells us that immigration proves time and time again to have a net economic benefit for the UK, I have to ask...for who? For the worker, or for the business owner? Because looking at towns neglected in the north – my home town, places in the northeast like Hartlepool and Sunderland, large parts of Yorkshire and Lancashire – I can't help but think the CBI is either lying or being economical with the truth. Immigrants do offer quick and cheap labour, yes, but that doesn't benefit the people of Britain. It benefits big business.

I'm sure cheap labour is nice for them, but it's not so handy for the mother of four who is unable to find a low-skilled position in Sunderland that pays fairly.

I'm not fooled by the CBI. Let's not forget that they wanted the UK to join the Euro. They have a history of making bad judgements and predictions, and I don't think the accuracy or reliability of their predictions has changed.

13th August
EU Commission Warns 'No Deal' Brexit Could Harm the EU More than Britain...and is There a Coup to Replace Theresa May with David Davis?

So there are a few interesting Brexit developments today. There's the news that EU officials have warned that the European Union could, in fact, be left worse off than Britain in the event of a No Deal Brexit...confirming something we knew all along.

There's also the story of the CBI, the Confederation of British Industry, advising the government to scrap net migration targets after Brexit, and even some news on who our next Prime Minister might be. Hint – it's David Davis!

I'll touch on the CBI story on a separate piece for today, so let's take a look at the No Deal story first.

A 15-page document has been issued to the EU27 – the 27 remaining member states – which warns of the consequences of a No Deal Brexit. It suggests that everything from animal health and pharmaceuticals, to customs and financial services, could all be hit hard by a hard, No Deal exit.

The Express reports[25] that the European Commissions' secretary general, Martin Selmayr, is preparing for a No Deal situation and implementing a planning task force. The concern, however, is that this new task force would require the member states to agree on decisions made, making it difficult to implement any of their preparations. There's also the question of whether each decision they make is in alignment with European treaties.

It looks like all that bureaucracy is coming back to bit them on the arse.

Oh, and don't forget the European parliamentary elections coming in May 2019. The current set of MEPs will leave Parliament three weeks before Brexit is implemented, and the new set of MEPs (which could be vastly different and even more Eurosceptic this time), won't come back until July. That leaves a big gap.

And you know what this tells me? It tells me that Britain is in a great negotiating position here. If only Theresa May had the balls – if you'll excuse the phrase – to take on the EU head on. It's time to get tough with these people, recognise their weaknesses, and start negotiating a better deal. It'd be nice to avoid a No Deal Brexit, and we could certainly achieve something if someone with any will to do it was in power.

I almost wrote that perhaps we could achieve something meaningful and worthwhile, but I wouldn't go quite that far. I think that as long as the EU exists, it will be impossible to achieve any kind of worthwhile deal – but hey, while it's still limping on its last good leg, why not try and make the best of a bad situation?

Interestingly though, it looks like we could be getting all that we've hoped for. Maybe, anyway. There's talk that Tory MPs might be urging Boris Johnson to push back his leadership bid and team up with David Davis. The idea is this:

A full leadership contest makes the party unstable, and the comments Boris made about the burqa recently could potentially plunge the party into a civil war at the worst possible time. So instead, the party could oust Theresa May and replace her with David Davis, who would act as interim leader and interim Prime Minister. Kind of like the way UKIP installed Gerard Batten as an interim leader following the Henry Bolton fiasco, in order to avoid a full leadership contest.

The Mail on Sunday reports[26] that the plot is underway and could result in May being removed as early as October. Should that happen, there will be very little time to change the EU deal – but it may just be possible. An EU summit will take place on the 18th and 19th October, and it's during this meeting that we should expect a final agreement on Brexit to be agreed. If May is replaced on the 1st October, that gives the government just a matter of weeks to negotiate a new deal.

Failing that, they'll move to an emergency EU summit in November. This has always been on the cards, as a last-minute opportunity to finalise the divorce if an agreement hadn't been made in October. Beyond November, however, all cards are on the table. The last possible date to seal the Article 50 divorce agreement – or at least, the most practical – would be during the last European Council of 2018. That takes place between December 13th and 14th.

So who knows? Perhaps the tide is turning. There's a month or so to go until the parties come back from their summer hols – and if the coup gains steam, May might be removed shortly after. That'll make for an embarrassing party conference.

14th August
Is This the Start of the Davis Revolution?

The papers are reporting that while the UK foreign secretary Jeremy Hunt is urging the EU to strike a 'strategic' Brexit deal, Rees-Mogg and co are still plotting for a hard Brexit.

Politico reports[28] that Jeremy Hunt will today urge EU counterparts to make 'strategic choices' to strike a Brexit deal during a three-day tour in Europe where he'll meet Dutch, Danish, Latvian, and Finnish foreign ministers.

The Foreign Office released official comments before the three days of meetings begin, explaining how Hunt intends to 'safeguard our operational capacity as we leave the EU'. The foreign office says they have put forward 'precise' and 'credible' proposals, and that they intend to take this opportunity to 'achieve a deal that works in our mutual interests'. Nothing new here really, but if Theresa May's recent trip to France is anything to go by, not much is going to come from this.

Over in Brexiteer territory, at camp ERG (European Research Group), work has said to have begun on a policy paper that is due to be published next month. The Times reports that the policy paper will outline the advantages of Britain leaving the EU and trading on World Trade Organisation rules. Apparently, the report will be backed by up to 80 Conservative MPs, and will potentially put serious pressure on the PM before their party's conference in Birmingham.

Jacob Rees-Mogg is the architect behind the paper. He's working with Steve Baker to create an 'alternative view' to the government's Chequers White Paper.

What could this mean, though? Well, with talk of Tory MPs plotting to install David Davis as an interim PM, it could be the spark that gets it all going. Senior ERG figures believe that the Chequers deal will be rejected by Brussels anyway, making this alternative view an important step in changing our direction on Brexit.

This could be the start of the Davis revolution.

15th August
Officials Dismiss Possibility of Direct Talks with EU27

Remember I wrote a few days ago that I don't believe our government will be successful with any further attempts to sweet talk European leaders over Brexit? Well, I was right. I'd say I hate to say 'I told you so', but I don't. It was obvious, right?

The Guardian reports today that European officials have slashed May's hopes that she could sweet talk EU27 leaders in an attempt to break current deadlocks. Diplomatic sources, the Guardian claims, are rejecting suggestions that the Prime Minister could hold talks with the 27 EU heads of government and state next month in Salzburg.

A senior source told The Guardian:[29]

> *"That is completely ridiculous, that is complete overspin of Salzburg…It would mean that we ditch our negotiating approach of the last two years and*

*discuss at 28 instead of 27 to one, and I
don't see why this would happen".*

But who knows? Brexit talks start up again later this
week in Brussels, and lots have changed since. It's public
knowledge that the EU is getting worried about the potential
of a No Deal Brexit, and time's ticking. Somebody's going
to have to buckle...I just fear it'll be Mrs May. That is,
assuming she's still leader in the coming weeks.

And I think she will be. Tory insiders tell me that the
reports in the papers about David Davis being installed as
an interim PM appear to be little more than fantasy. They
inform me that there is little talk about this inside the party,
and the constitutional questions of whether it's even
technically doable would cause a whole world of chaos in
itself. So perhaps this really is all talk – rumours and stories
from the press.

Can you imagine if Theresa really remains PM
throughout this whole process? Until March? It's a
harrowing thought.

16th August
EU Negotiators Trying to Stop 'No Deal' Behind the Scenes

Things are getting pretty weird in Brexit world now.
Talks resumed today, and we appear to be in the same old
stalemate - but the latest news is that Brussels won't deny
reports that Brexit negotiators on the continent fear their
talks are being bugged by British spies.

ITV reports[30] that the deputy chief Brexit negotiator for
the EU, Sabine Weyand, told officials at a European
Council party on exit talks that they couldn't exclude the
possibility that UK intelligence services had been
penetrating their meetings. It's believed that British

negotiators somehow found a copy of a presentation that outlined negative economic assessments of the UK staying in a Single Market for goods. Mere hours after the presentation was given, the UK began lobbying at the 'highest level' to stop the slideshow files from being published, according to the Daily Telegraph.

The content of the slides – an analysis of the Chequers White Paper's proposals on trade – were due to be published the day after the presentation was given. It appears the files weren't published so that the British government could maintain its credibility, help avoid a No Deal scenario, and cause chaos. But it's not just a British scandal – a senior EU official told the Express[31] that member states, and members of Barnier's team, were told to welcome the Chequers White Paper 'with open arms' and to avoid killing it off completely.

So perhaps there has been more cooperation behind the scenes than we've been led to believe. The EU's weakness is showing. They know that May's government is weak, and should it collapse over the disastrous Chequers proposals, it increases the likelihood of a No Deal scenario.

Are you following? I hope you are. It's all very smoke and mirrors – exactly the kind of thing that gives politicians a bad name. However, knowing what we do now, it's evident that the EU is willing to negotiate. It's quite obvious that they don't want a No Deal Brexit, and it's time that May started taking advantage of that.

Fine – Let's Have a Proper "People's Vote"

I was scrolling through Twitter today when I saw yet another photo of a left-wing activist holding a 'People's Vote' sign outside of Westminster. For some reason, it really got on my nerves. It's not like I'm not used to seeing this stuff, and I've definitely written about it before.

Chapter Three: August 2018

Today though, the lies and the disingenuous nature of this campaign made my blood boil...and it got me thinking. You know what? Fine. Let's do it. Let's have another People's Vote. But let's do it right.

I've said before that the People's Vote idea is a scam – that's literally what it is. It's a scam set up by the people who don't want Brexit, and who have enough influence in Parliament to make it look like Brexit won't work. Then they put it to another vote, after having made the entire process terrifying, and hope to get their preferred result the second time around. It's a fairly simple con but it seems like it could work.

Now, if the People's Vote was really about ensuring maximum democracy – which is what they're claiming, right? – then they would be doing it in a way that respects the outcome of our first referendum. If this was *really* just about ensuring we have a say on the final deal, then the second referendum would not include an option to remain in the European Union. This is meant to be a referendum on the deal for *leaving* the European Union, isn't it?

So maybe we should do what the left is asking for. That'd shut them up.

Here's how I propose this could work:

There should be two options. One option to leave the European Union on the deal agreed upon by the government and the European Union, and one option to leave the European Union without a deal, and begin trading on World Trade Organisation rules.

And that's that. It's a People's Vote on the final deal, and nothing more. It's not an attempt to reverse the decision we made in 2016, and it gives the people a chance to reverse Theresa's betrayal.

If the left has been honest with us all along – if they really are concerned about democracy and whether we have a say on the final deal – then this should keep them satisfied.

Come on Mrs May – let's do it! Give us a People's Vote! Your deal, or no deal!

17th August
Nigel Farage is Back

When Nigel Farage abandoned ship and stepped down as leader of UKIP following the successful Brexit referendum campaign, he plunged the party into chaos. I didn't lose any sleep over it. I've never been a fan of UKIP, and Nigel is no fan of mine. I don't like that he has brushed aside people like me for years, branding us racists for voicing our concerns about Brexit. Regardless of my opinions of the man, he's without a question one of the most prominent voices and representatives of the Brexit movement.

Trump called him Mr Brexit. It's hard to argue with. So, when he returns to the forefront of politics, you know it's a big deal. Today, he announced his return – but it's not as leader of UKIP. He might well not do that until March next year when current leader Gerard Batten steps down and retires. Until then, he'll be heading up the Leave Means Leave campaign group.

Farage is still an MEP, and in between his trips to New York and Australia, he's occasionally popped into the Parliament chambers to fight for Brexit. Now, he'll be on tour, pressuring the politicians not to betray the decision we made in 2016. And you know what – I welcome the move.

The left is behaving like the referendum campaign never came to an end, so we should be out there too. If the

People's Vote campaign is out there and lying to people, we need to be out there and telling people about those lies.

This is weird, isn't it? We voted on this over two years ago, but it feels like the campaign is starting all over again – except, this time, we're trying to convince the politicians to make the right decision and not the electorate.

20th August
Celebrities Prove the Brexit Battle is Globalists vs Normal People

Over the weekend, the celebrities have stepped in and joined the People's Vote cause. Combine that with the news that SuperDry – the brand of clothes for people with no personality - is pumping a million pounds into the anti-Brexit campaign, and it's clearer than ever to the average person that the People's Vote, is a matter of globalism vs regular people.

It's a battle between the establishment and the people, celebrities and the peasants, the elite and the oppressed.

The Standard[32] reported how a multitude of other BBC characters have come out in favour of a second referendum. Some are predictable – of course, Gary Lineker has already been rightfully questioned about his support for a second referendum. Apparently, senior figures in the BBC didn't like his political affiliations but issued a statement explaining that because he isn't involved in political output, his personal views don't affect the BBC's impartiality. Sure…

Others, however, surprised me. Tracey Ullman, for instance. She's the amazing impressionist who impersonates Nicola Sturgeon perfectly and has ripped Jeremy Corbyn a new one over his anti-Semitism. I'm really surprised by her, but she's lent her support to the People's

Vote campaign alongside Armando Iannucci (the writer of The Thick of It, one of my favourite shows), Steve Coogan of Alan Partridge fame, and even Duncan Bannatyne and Deborah Meaden.

Surely this is enough for the people to see the con. I think the average voter already knows what's going on at this point, but if the message isn't clear enough, these people help drive that home. If Nigel Farage wants a new campaign idea, then perhaps he should consider this: plaster the faces of these wealthy brats on a billboard and remind the people who is in favour of Brexit and who isn't.

Include SuperDry, too – run by left-wing multi-millionaire Julian Dunkerton, who has been accused of selling products made by factory workers in India who are paid 28 pence per hour. Dunkerton loves his cheap labour, which is why he just pumped a million quid into the People's Vote campaign.

He's not even subtle about his intentions, either. This isn't about improving democracy or giving people a voice – it's about reversing the decision we made in 2016. The BBC reported[33] that he was backing the campaign because "we have a genuine chance to turn this around".

With the news that Nigel Farage is back and working on the Leave Means Leave campaign, that Jacob Rees Mogg is warning the Prime Minister she won't have sufficient support in the Commons to back her Chequers plan, and the celebrities coming out en masse to support the People's Vote tour, it feels like we're in the referendum campaign again.

You wouldn't think we'd done this all before, would you? The politicians and the celebrities are shamelessly acting as if the question was never asked, and they think they're going to get away with it. By now, though, they should have learned – we won the Brexit vote *because* we didn't trust the establishment and the celebrities. And we'll win it again if we have to.

21st August
Gov's Scaremongering 'No Deal' Documents Edited to Reflect Reality

I've been talking about the upcoming release of around 70 documents that outline the UK's plans for leaving the EU on World Trade Organisation trading rules. Now we're closer to that day – this Thursday – and it appears there will, in fact, be 84 documents in total.

Originally, these documents were going to be used to scare the British public, the press, and business into thinking a No Deal Brexit would cause the sky to fall in. But that plot was exposed. Remember? A government insider told Newsnight that May's cabinet was planning to scare people witless?[34]

Now, sources have told the Telegraph[35] that the tone of many of the documents from the treasury – run by Chancellor Philip Hammond – have been a cause for concern. The paper reports that sections of a document that claimed the implications of a No Deal Brexit could be 'negative'.

So let's translate that: the government is exposed as wanting to scare people. The government denied it. The government changes the documents before release to prove that they aren't trying to scare people over a No Deal Brexit.

Are we really meant to believe that Chancellor Hammond, who supported Remain during the referendum, is being totally honest about this?

Well, let's see. The documents will be released in two days. If No Deal is played down, then great – but we'll know they've been lying.

22nd August
The October EU Agreement Deadline is Over

As I've discussed previously, October is expected to be the month where negotiations end. If we go beyond then, a multitude of issues will make further negotiations inconvenient and difficult. It's for this reason that it's in our best interests to pressure Theresa May to do the right thing *now*, and if there *is* going to be a leadership challenge in the party, it must also happen *now*. It's almost September, and we don't have much time.

Interestingly, Barnier thinks that we'll miss it[36] – but not by much. During a press conference yesterday, 21st August, the chief EU Brexit negotiator told the media that he expects to come to an agreement with the UK by early November. He explained:

> *"If you count backwards from that date, March 30 2019, the day on which the UK will no longer be a member of the European Union – while remaining for 21 months, if we reach an agreement, in the Single Market, Customs Union and European policies – the countdown backwards from there has to take account of the time which is necessary for ratification.*
>
> *"That is a given, it will take a certain amount of time to ratify the agreement – on the UK side and the European side.*

"That takes us for a final agreement on the Withdrawal Agreement and political declaration well before the end of the year – I'm not going to say October, a few days here, the beginning of November, but not much later than that."

But, he also said that the EU shouldn't be blamed[37] if there isn't a Brexit deal at all. We already know that the European Union is concerned about a No Deal Brexit hurting their political project more than the UK, but they're already making their excuses in case it does happen.

During the same press conference, Barnier said that Brussels would not accept the blame if an agreement couldn't be struck. And you know what, that's fine. We know it's their fault so they can deny it all they like – and I still believe that as long as the EU even exists, we won't get a decent deal anyway.

Dominic Raab is doing his best, though...I think. At least, he's going through the motions and putting on a brave face. He has vowed to 'negotiate continuously' in order to meet the deadline, or at least not let it go beyond November.

23rd August
Brexit Papers Released: New Cigarette Packet Photos, Sperm Crisis

The infamous planning papers have been released today. Well, 25 of them have. Brexit Secretary Dominic Raab confirmed the release of papers that advise on safeguards for the nuclear industry, state aid rules, and provides guidance for businesses who will face extra paperwork when moving products across the border.

Chapter Three: August 2018

One of the stories the papers has picked up on is the possibility of Britons facing extra credit card charges when in the EU. The papers explain that the cost of card payments between the EU and UK will 'likely increase' – which is, of course, causing meltdown online. Is this the best they have?

The documents also outline that businesses trading with the EU should start planning for new customs checks (which is fair and to be expected), low-value parcels coming to the UK from the EU won't be VAT-free, and we'll have to replace the picture warnings on cigarette packets because the EU owns the copyright on the current ones.

Well, that's a relief. I was getting bored with the images of a baby smoking a cigarette, and a man crying on his bed because smoking stopped his male parts from working. I mean, come ON, is this all they have?

One thing did stand out to me, though – and that's the claim that Britons who live in the European Union would lose access[38] to their UK banks and pension services unless the EU acts. So let's pretend we're a Remainer for a moment, and assume that leaving the EU means that Brussels won't act on this issue, and will stop pensioners living in Europe from accessing their bank and pension.

That would make those in charge pretty nasty, vengeful people, wouldn't it? I mean, jeez, why did we ever join a union with these monsters in the first place?

Give it a rest. The EU might be wicked and terrible, but if Barnier, Merkel and co want to maintain their union, they're not going to deny British pensioners access to their money. Can you imagine the PR crisis they'd have on their hands if old British retirees were out on the streets begging?

Other parts of the documents[39] suggest that there won't be any need for hospitals, GPs or pharmacies to stockpile medicine, as pharmaceutical companies should have six-week supplies ready in case there are queues at the border. So that's another scare done away with. I suspect that this might be one of the things recently changed in the documents. I explained yesterday that after the government's plan to scare people witless was revealed, changes started to be made to make the documents more 'realistic'.

So let's break this down:

- New medicines will need UK approval. Sounds easy enough.
- Credit card costs will increase. Big whoop.
- Businesses should start planning for new customs checks. Well, obviously.
- Britons in the EU could lose access to pensions. No, they won't.
- We'll need new nuclear safeguards. Sounds doable.
- We'll get some lovely new graphic images on our cigarette packets.

Reading these documents and contrasting it with the fear mongering of the press is a great exercise in learning how the establishment controls us. They'll scare us into thinking cancer patients will die, there won't be enough drugs, and that we might even run out of sandwiches. Perhaps the most ludicrous of all is the claim by a spokesman for the Best for Britain campaign. Speaking to Politics Home[40], the spokesman explained how a No Deal Brexit could mean heartache for couples, owing to a shortage of sperm in commercial sperm banks.

They do all of this without any shame whatsoever. In fact, I think many of them are so deluded they think they're doing the right thing.

Chapter Three: August 2018

In Other Brexit News:

- Ribble Valley MP Nigel Evans accurately points out on[41] Twitter that there is no such thing as 'no deal'. There is, of course, the WTO option, which the UK uses to trade with other parts of the world.

- Vince Cable appears on Sky News[42] telling the usual porkies, suggesting that the No Deal scenario is 'a pretty horrible outcome and worse than a bad deal' – while David Davis tells Ann Widdecombe[43] that No Deal is better than a bad deal. Ann Widdecombe, eh! Whatever happened to her? I've always had a soft spot for her.

- Oh, and former UKIP donor Arron Banks has joined the Tories, believe it or not! Well, he technically did. He announced on Twitter that he'd joined and received an acceptance letter, but the party have rejected his membership[44].

    This is all part of a new campaign by Leave.EU to encourage people to join the Conservatives. They're being called 'Blue Momentum', as they're using the same tactics Momentum used when they elected Corbyn. That reminds me of my time assisting Anne Marie Waters' campaign for UKIP leadership. We got thousands of people to join UKIP in anticipation of her standing, only for UKIP to pull the rug underneath our feet and ban those members from voting. The press was calling us 'Fascist Momentum' at the time.

    I wonder what will happen now Arron has been rejected. He's got thousands of Leave.EU and UKIP supporters to sign up to the Tories in anticipation of a leadership election, and I doubt the Conservative Party is going to kick all of those out.

I guess William Hague is right to be scared about this. He wrote a piece the other day expressing his concern about a takeover of the Conservative Party, and that definitely looks possible.

All interesting stuff. Perhaps Blue Momentum can save Brexit by electing a new Tory leader, but they certainly won't save the country in terms of immigration and cultural issues. The Tories will never tackle it.

24th August
Chancellor Hammond's Doomsday Letter Divides Government

Chancellor of the Exchequer Philip Hammond has sparked division and anger in the Conservative Party by claiming in a letter that borrowing would be £80 billion per year higher as a result of a No Deal Brexit. In his letter to Nicky Morgan MP[45], he explained:

> *This January provisional analysis estimated that in a no deal/WTO scenario GDP would be 7.7% lower (range 5.0%-10.3%) relative to a status quo baseline. This represents the potential expected static state around 15 years out from the exit point. The analysis did not estimate the path the economy and different sectors might take under no deal and the potential for short-term disruption.*

And:

> *GDP impacts of this magnitude, were they to arise, would have large fiscal consequences. The January analysis*

estimated that borrowing would be around £80 billion a year higher under a no deal/WTO scenario by 2033-34, in the absence of mitigating adjustments to spending and/or taxation, relative to a status quo baseline. This is because any direct financial savings are outweighed by the indirect fiscal consequences of a smaller economy.

Certainly not ideal, if it were true, but not all his Westminster colleagues are on board. Tory MP Marcus Fysh has claimed[46] it's just 'another instalment of dodgy project fear', and Jacob Rees Mogg so eloquently explained that it would not be as 'absurdly frightening as the Chancellor of the Exchequer thinks it may be', and:

"As a dog returneth to his vomit, so a fool returneth to his folly".

He also explained that Hammond was reminding people why nobody believes the politicised forecasts of the Treasury any more. These are fighting words. A Tory Member of Parliament has explicitly called the Treasury 'desperate to stop Brexit', and suggested that their forecasts should be treated with a pinch of salt.

That's where independent forecasting comes in. We can't trust everything the government says, and we can't consider everything the Treasury says to be gospel. It's not. There is a political motive here, and the Treasury has proven to be wrong in the past. As has the CBI.

This divide between reality and scaremongering has been revealed at a deeper level of government, too. Mogg is a backbench MP, but there are two governmental departments that appear to be giving out different messages. Sky News says[47] that the Treasury told them the Brexit Secretary was shown Hammond's letter two weeks ago and agreed for it to be published today – but sources over at the Department for Exiting the EU (DEXEU) categorically deny the claim.

Philip Hammond has made it perfectly clear that there is a divide within the party and within the government – and I suspect that whichever way Brexit goes, the party will remain divided. If we leave on WTO terms, the Anna Soubry types will scream bloody murder. If we leave under the Chequers deal, there'll be a Jacob Rees Mogg or Boris Johnson-inspired rebellion within the Tories. And they'll have the members they need to support them in ousting Theresa, thanks to Leave.EU's recently trojan horse operation. Thousands of Aaron Banks and UKIP-supporting activists have joined the party in the last few days, and that's likely to deepen the cracks in this rift, and ultimately sign a death warrant for Remain MPs in the Tories.

28th August
New Trade Deal with South Africa Won't Work if the Farmers are Dead

Theresa May sealed the first post-Brexit trade deal with Africa today, and she did a little jig to celebrate. Seriously, she's been all over the news after showing off her dancing skills when she was greeted in South Africa by dancing school children.

I felt a bit bad for her – the mockery has been pretty intense. The school children were dancing, and so were the African delegates around her. So she waved a leg around, moved her arms a bit, and even did the Robot at one point. It was all very sweet and innocent, and I found myself relating to her awkwardness...but then she went and opened her mouth.

Commenting on land expropriation in South Africa – where the government takes land from white owners –

Theresa said that Britain supports the policy as long as it's 'legal' and 'democratic'.

I feel truly ashamed of my country's government after this, and I suppose May is hoping the fact that she secured a trade deal with Africa will help us forget all about it. She signed a free trade agreement that is said to be worth about £10 billion a year[48] – meaning we'll be buying South African tea, fruit, and wine. Well, that is, assuming all the farmers aren't killed first. At this rate, it isn't looking good.

She couldn't escape Brexit while she was out in Africa, either. She's been challenged about Philip Hammond's warnings about a No Deal Brexit, and she reconfirmed that no deal would be better than a bad deal. She also said that a No Deal Brexit 'wouldn't be the end of the world'[49], which is always refreshing to hear.

However, when asked out-right[50] whether she would vote Leave in a second referendum – and whether she thinks Britain would be better off after Brexit – she simply refused to say it. That's because she doesn't believe it.

I remember when this was first done to her during an LBC interview. I felt bad for her. I thought 'Well, maybe she doesn't believe it, but at least she's doing it!'. Now, I can't help but think she doesn't believe it and she's actively working to stop it happening, too.

29th August
The EU Backs Down (Sort Of)

Well, I never. The EU has finally backed down,[51] it seems – or at least, they're preparing to back down. The news today is that the EU is suggesting they will offer the UK a post-Brexit deal 'unlike any it has given another country'.

Chapter Three: August 2018

The European Union would fare worse than the UK in a No Deal Brexit, and it seems like they really know it.

Michel Barnier has said that the EU is willing to offer Britain a trade deal unlike any it has offered any other country while reiterating that the bloc would not divide or change the Single Market for Britain. So this leaves me wondering. If they won't be changing the Single Market, and don't suggest they'll be changing the fundamental 'freedoms' the EU requires in order for countries to be within the Single Market, then what exactly are they going to back down on?

Does this mean, instead, that the EU will simply be willing to offer a deal along the lines of the Chequers Plan, that keeps these 'freedoms' in place under another name? After all, if freedom of movement is maintained under a different name, it doesn't really affect the EU all that much at all. Other than some possible administration work to facilitate the trickery, it wouldn't change very much for them.

Barnier warned: "We respect Britain's red lines scrupulously. In return, they must respect what we are".

So don't go thinking this is the EU doing us a favour. In fact, I think this is a warning sign. If the EU is willing to accept this deal, then in all likelihood, it won't represent the Brexit we voted for.

Chapter Three: August 2018

References

[1] *Sky News, " Government's 'no deal' Brexit plans lost on M20 motorway", Faisal Islam, 3rd August 2018,*
https://news.sky.com/story/long-read-governments-no-deal-brexit-plans-lost-on-m20-motorway-11454929

[2] *Breitbart, "Project Fear 2.0 – May Plans to 'Scare People Witless' to Win Support for Soft Brexit, MP Reveals", Jack Montgomery, 27th July 2018,*
https://www.breitbart.com/london/2018/07/27/theresa-may-scare-people-witless-no-deal-brexit-support-soft-chequers/

[3] *The Times, "Theresa May to plead with Emmanuel Macron to ease Brexit stance", Sam Coates, Bruno Waterfield, Adam Sage, Catherine Philp, 1st August 2018,*
https://www.thetimes.co.uk/article/theresa-may-s-brexit-plea-to-president-macron-qbvxggx03

[4] *The Telegraph, "Michel Barnier deals blow to City of London's Brexit hopes", James Crisp, 26th April 2018,*
https://www.telegraph.co.uk/politics/2018/04/26/michel-barnier-deals-blow-city-londons-brexit-hopes/

[5] *The Guardian, "Replace May with Gove to sort out Brexit, Tory donor urges", Michael Savage, 3rd June 2018,*
https://www.theguardian.com/politics/2018/jun/02/replace-theresa-may-with-michael-gove-tory-donor-says-brexit-uk-news

[6] *The Guardian, "Michael Gove denies stabbing Boris Johnson in the back", Jessica Elgot, 25th October 2018,*
https://www.theguardian.com/politics/2016/oct/25/michael-gove-denies-stabbing-boris-johnson-back-conservative-leadership-campaign

[7] *Express, "What on EARTH? Michael Gove in shock talks to keep UK IN EU Single Market to AVOID no deal", Laura Mowat, 2nd August 2018,*
https://www.express.co.uk/news/politics/997861/Brexit-news-michael-gove-no-deal-hard-brexit-eea-Norway

[8] *Express, "Fury as UK officials plan on giving EU judges the FINAL say on vital Brexit decisions", Joe Barnes, 30th July 2018,*
https://www.express.co.uk/news/uk/996178/Brexit-news-UK-EU-withdrawal-agreement-negotiations-European-Court-of-Justice-latest

[9] *Gov.uk, "Technical note on temporary customs arrangement", Cabinet Office, 7th June 2018,*
https://www.gov.uk/government/publications/technical-note-on-temporary-customs-arrangement?utm_source=2ee1e4f1-35e9-4abd-911e-a64bb2616a3e&utm_medium=email&utm_campaign=govuk-notifications&utm_content=immediate

[10] *The Telegraph, "Knife crime is now at record highs - but what is driving the increase?", Ashely Kirk, 3rd August 2018,*
https://www.telegraph.co.uk/news/0/knife-crime-now-record-highs-driving-increase/

[11] *The Telegraph, "Theresa May blamed for 'chaotic' no deal Brexit preparations as row breaks out in Whitehall", Gordon Rayner, 7th August 2018,*
https://www.telegraph.co.uk/politics/2018/08/06/theresa-may-blamed-chaotic-no-deal-brexit-preparations-row-breaks/

Chapter Three: August 2018

[12] Guido Fawkes, "Public want May and Corbyn gone before next election", tweet by @britianelects , 7th August 2018,
https://order-order.com/2018/08/07/public-want-may-and-corbyn-gone-by-next-election/

[13] The Guardian, "UK could run out of food a year from now with no-deal Brexit, NFU warns", Lisa O'Carroll, 7th August 2018,
https://www.theguardian.com/politics/2018/aug/07/uk-run-out-of-food-no-deal-brexit-national-farmers-union

[14] The New European, "Theresa May visits Edinburgh and is heckled by protesters", Jonathon Read, 8th August 2018,
https://www.theneweuropean.co.uk/top-stories/theresa-may-visits-edinburgh-and-is-booed-by-protesters-1-5643427

[15] Express, "Theresa May's relationship with Nicola Sturgeon hits 'ROCK BOTTOM after Brexit power grab'", Thomas Hunt, 8th August 2018,
https://www.express.co.uk/news/uk/1000274/Theresa-May-Nicola-Sturgeon-relationship-Scotland-video-live-speech-Brexit

[16] Mail Online, "Just get on with it! Poll reveals most British voters no longer care how or when we leave the EU, as 48 per cent of Remainers admit they 'just want Brexit over and done with'", John Steven, 8th August 2018,
http://www.dailymail.co.uk/news/article-6037411/Poll-reveals-British-voters-no-longer-care-leave-EU-want-Brexit-over.html

[17] Express, "'DEATHTRAP PARLIAMENT': Terrified MPs demand action as crumbling Parliament risks injury", Alison little, 8th August 2018,
https://www.express.co.uk/news/politics/1000388/parliament-house-of-commons-refurbishment-big-ben

[18] Express, "How May is plotting to EXPLOIT Trump trade spat: UK will help EU in return for best Brexit", Joe Barnes, 8th August 2018,
https://www.express.co.uk/news/uk/1000613/Brexit-news-Theresa-May-UK-EU-deal-Donald-Trump-trade-exploit

[19] Mail Online, "Brussels 'prepares a Brexit climbdown and is set to agree the UK can stay in the EU Single Market for goods without having to accept free movement", Kate Ferguson, 9th August 2018,
http://www.dailymail.co.uk/news/article-6042765/EU-offer-UK-stay-single-market-goods-without-free-movement.html

[20] Express, "How May is plotting to EXPLOIT Trump trade spat: UK will help EU in return for best Brexit", Joe Barnes, 8th August 2018,
https://www.express.co.uk/news/uk/1000613/Brexit-news-Theresa-May-UK-EU-deal-Donald-Trump-trade-exploit

[21] The Guardian, "Campaign for second Brexit vote seeks support beyond capital", Dan Sabbagh, 10th August 2018,
https://www.theguardian.com/politics/2018/aug/10/campaign-for-second-brexit-vote-seeks-support-beyond-capital

[22] Express, "'Remain would lose even worse!' Owen Jones FEARS second referendum would UNITE Brexiteers", Thomas Hunt, 7th August 2018,
https://www.express.co.uk/news/uk/999723/Brexit-news-Owen-Jones-second-Brexit-referendum-video-live-Tony-Blair-Peoples-Vote

[23] BBC News, "Immigration: Scrap targets after Brexit, CBI urges", BBC News, 10th August 2018,
https://www.bbc.co.uk/news/business-45136390

[24] CBI, "Open and controlled - recommendations for a new approach to immigration", CBI Press Team, 9th August 2018,

Chapter Three: August 2018

http://www.cbi.org.uk/news/open-and-controlled-recommendations-for-a-new-approach-to-immigration/

[25] Express, "EU WILL PAY: Brussels PANICS no-deal Brexit will hit Europe much HARDER than UK", Joe Barnes, 13th August 2018,
https://www.express.co.uk/news/uk/1002606/Brexit-news-UK-EU-no-deal-hit-Brussels-harder-latest-Theresa-May

[26] Mail Online, "Revealed: Secret plot to oust Theresa May in Brexiteer putsch and install David Davis as 'interim' PM with Boris Johnson urged to delay his leadership bid until after Brexit", Glen Owen and Brendan Carlin, 12th August 2018,
http://www.dailymail.co.uk/news/brexit/article-6051043/Plot-oust-Theresa-David-Davis-interim-PM-Boris-Johnson-urged-delay-bid.htm

[27] BBC News, "Westminster car crash: Man arrested on suspicion of terror offences", BBC News, 14th August 2018,
https://www.bbc.co.uk/news/uk-45180120

[28] Politico, "UK foreign secretary to urge counterparts to strike 'strategic' Brexit deal", Annabelle Dickson, 14th August 2018,
https://www.politico.eu/article/uk-foreign-secretary-to-urge-counterparts-to-strike-strategic-brexit-deal/

[29] The Guardian, "EU rebuffs idea of escalating Brexit talks to leaders' summit", Jennifer Rankin, 15th August 2018,
https://www.theguardian.com/politics/2018/aug/15/brussels-rebuffs-idea-of-escalating-brexit-talks-to-leaders-summit

[30] ITV, "EU officials 'fear UK is bugging Brexit talks'", ITV Report, 16th August 2018,
http://www.itv.com/news/2018-08-16/eu-officials-fear-uk-is-bugging-brexit-talks/

[31] Express, "BREXIT BOMBSHELL: Brussels kept White Paper demolition documents TOP SECRET to save May", Joe Barnes, 16th August 2018,
https://www.express.co.uk/news/uk/1004089/Brexit-news-UK-EU-Michel-Barnier-document-secret-Theresa-May-White-Paper-Chequers-plan

[32] Evening Standard, "The Londoner: BBC stars flock to the People's Vote", Evening Standard, 16th August 2018,
https://www.standard.co.uk/news/londoners-diary/the-londoner-bbc-stars-flock-to-the-peoples-vote-a3913156.html

[33] BBC News, "Brexit vote campaign gets £1m from Superdry co-founder", BBC News, 19th August 2018,
https://www.bbc.co.uk/news/uk-politics-45235655

[34] Mail Online, "May 'plans to scare us witless' over No Deal: Stockpile warnings are aimed at building support for the PM's under-fire Brexit strategy, ally claims", John Stevens, 26th July 2018,
http://www.dailymail.co.uk/news/article-5993257/May-plans-scare-witless-No-Deal.html

[35] The Telegraph, "Philip Hammond 'forced to tone down' no-deal plans that were likened to Project Fear", Steven Swinford, 20th August 2018,
https://www.telegraph.co.uk/politics/2018/08/20/philip-hammond-forced-tone-no-deal-plans-likened-project-fear/

[36] The Sun, "Michel Barnier officially rips up October deadline for a Brexit deal – as Dominic Raab admits 'still some significant issues to overcome'", Harry Cole and Nick Gutteridge, 22nd August 2018,
https://www.thesun.co.uk/news/7068597/michel-barnier-officially-rips-up-october-deadline-for-a-brexit-deal-as-dominic-raab-admits-still-some-significant-issues-to-overcome/

Chapter Three: August 2018

[37] The Telegraph, "EU should not be blamed if there is no Brexit deal, Michel Barnier says", James Crisp and James Rothwell, 21st August 2018, https://www.telegraph.co.uk/news/2018/08/21/dominic-raab-michel-barnier-give-update-brexit-talks/

[38] BBC News, "UK's 'no-deal' Brexit plans warn of credit card fees", BBC News, 23rd August 2018, https://www.bbc.co.uk/news/uk-politics-45274972

[39] BBC News, "What do the government's Brexit "no-deal" papers reveal?", BBC News, 23rd August 2018, https://www.bbc.co.uk/news/uk-politics-45284855

[40] Politics Home, "No-deal Brexit 'could leave couples with heartbreak' due to sperm shortage risk", Emilio Casalicchio, 23rd August 2018, https://www.politicshome.com/news/uk/foreign-affairs/brexit/news/97763/no-deal-brexit-could-leave-couples-heartbreak-due-sperm

[41] Twitter, "Memo to Govt.....", Nigel Evans, 22nd August 2018, https://twitter.com/nigelmp/status/1032500330544746496

[42] Twitter, "'The no deal scenario is a pretty horrible outcome and worse than a bad deal'", Sky News, 23rd August 2018, https://twitter.com/SkyNews/status/1032567089641521152

[43] Talk Radio, "David Davis tells Ann Widdecombe a no-deal is 'better' than remaining in the EU", James Hingle, 23rd August 2018, http://talkradio.co.uk/news/david-davis-tells-ann-widdecombe-no-deal-better-remaining-eu-18082327622

[44] Sky News, "Conservative party reject membership of Leave.EU founder Arron Banks", David Mercer and Greg Heffer, 23rd August 2018, https://news.sky.com/story/conservative-party-reject-membership-of-leaveeu-founder-arron-banks-11480346

[45] "Chancellor Philip Hammond, HM Treasury letter to Rt Hon Nicky Morgan MP", 23rd August 2018, https://assets.publishing.service.gov.uk/government/uploads/system/uploads/attachment_data/file/735881/180823_CX_to_Chair_of_TSC_Nicky_Morgan_.pdf

[46] BBC News, "Brexit: Conservative anger at Philip Hammond's 'dodgy project fear'", BBC News, 24th August 2018, https://www.bbc.co.uk/news/uk-politics-45292025

[47] Sky News, "Tory divisions exposed by Hammond letter as Sky Data poll reveals shift against Brexit", Jason Farrell, 24th August 2018, https://news.sky.com/story/tory-divisions-exposed-by-hammond-letter-as-sky-data-poll-reveals-shift-against-brexit-11480562

[48] The Times, "Theresa May seals first post-Brexit trade deal with Africa pact and £4bn investment pledge", Esther Webber, Francis Elliott and Jane Flanagan, 28th August 2018, https://www.thetimes.co.uk/article/theresa-may-seals-first-post-brexit-trade-deal-with-africa-pact-and-4bn-investment-pledge-k6bvdvnmq

[49] CNN, "Theresa May says no-deal Brexit 'wouldn't be end of the world'", James Masters, 28th August 2018, https://edition.cnn.com/2018/08/28/uk/theresa-may-brexit-africa-trip-intl/index.html

[50] The Sun, "Theresa May refuses six times to say if Britain will better off after Brexit", Hugo Gye, 28th August 2018, https://www.thesun.co.uk/news/7120764/theresa-may-brexit-better-off-second-referendum/

Chapter Three: August 2018

---

[51] *Independent, "EU says it will offer UK post-Brexit deal 'unlike any it has given another country'", Jon Stone, 29th August 2018,*
https://www.independent.co.uk/news/uk/politics/brexit-latest-barnier-raab-lidington-no-deal-eu-berlin-pound-sterling-spike-jump-a8513226.html

Chapter Four
September 2018

4th September
Poll Finds Brexit Voters Not Deterred by Project Fear

Project Fear might still be pounding the drum for a second referendum and fabricating scare stories, but it isn't working on Brexit voters. A poll commissioned by LBC[1] has found that 70% of those who voted Brexit are happy to leave the European Union even if it means long queues at border control, and a majority would still leave even if it means the cost of food increases.

This tells us something really important. It confirms that people voted to leave the European Union not necessarily because they thought it would bring us major economic gains, but instead as a way of rejecting mainstream politics. Brexit voters, much like Trump voters in America, wanted to destroy a system that they believe disadvantages regular people – and I'd agree with them. I *am* one of them.

The poll even showed us that Brexit voters are willing to enter a recession for the sake of Brexit.

The results are significant as Project Fear has already claimed that hundreds of thousands of jobs could be lost, diabetics would lose access to insulin and cancer patients would die waiting for treatment. Despite the scare tactics, Brexit voters are steadfast – they want Brexit, they want to regain power from bureaucrats in Brussels, and they're even willing to make a few sacrifices for it.

I'm happy to admit that my concerns in politics are largely cultural. The economy is important, and I'd like to see a smaller government with lower taxes, but my priority is ensuring a stable cultural footing for our country first. And apparently, I'm not the only one.

It's worth mentioning, however, that I think most respondents to this poll knew what was really going on with the question. I doubt that most Brexit voters believe the country would slip into a recession after Brexit anyway, but regardless, they're happy to take it on the chin if it does.

So, Gina Miller can continue her campaign if she likes. She can carry on appearing on national television claiming that a No Deal Brexit would "literally destroy the UK",[2] or even cause riots that the Armed Forces would have to control. The people aren't listening to her – and when she's proven wrong, I hope she never shows her face in politics again. The same goes for the rest of the disgraceful Project Fear operation.

6th September
'Operation Yellowhammer' Revealed in Leaked Gov Document

Yesterday I was in London, meeting Brexiter campaigners who wanted to block Theresa May's entrance to Parliament for the first Prime Minister's Question Time (PMQs) since the summer recess. The organiser of the event, David Clews, informed me that unfortunately Theresa May just left half an hour early...which I suppose was to be expected. But what I found interesting about the day was that everyone there agreed entirely that a) Project Fear was baseless nonsense and b) a short-term recession would be worth it, for Brexit.

I thought that was really interesting. I, just like them, voted for Brexit knowing that there may well be short term costs to the divorce. We've seen that already with the ridiculous £39 billion divorce bill (which we don't technically even need to pay). I accepted the possibility that the markets and the economy would need a little time to calibrate and settle, and everyone there agreed with me. I don't think there will be any long-term damage; in fact, I think Britain will thrive once we're out. Good things come to those who wait!

During my time out reporting on the event, I kept up to date with what was happening inside the House of Commons. I read that Theresa May had explained how more than 6,000 civil servants were currently working to prepare for the possibility of a No Deal Brexit – and today, some more details about it have been carelessly leaked into the public sphere. So carelessly, that it seems convenient.

Political editor for the BBC, Laura Kuenssberg, tweeted out a photograph of a document that appeared to be peeking out of the bag of a Downing Street aide...but it wasn't an aide. We've since found out that it was actually John Glen, Treasury Minister. Either he's in a lot of trouble tonight, or he's trying to show the world that the government is prepared.

The photograph clearly shows[3] the front page of a briefing document which is titled 'Operation Yellow Hammer: no deal contingency planning'.

Juicy!

But what does it reveal? Well first of all, it reveals that government departments are being advised to begin making cuts and to begin 'internal reprioritisation'. The document also explains that the government must 'maintain confidence in the event of contingency plans being triggered', which they say is 'particularly important for financial services".

Nothing in it appears all that terrible. If the prospects of No Deal were so terrifying, I'd have expected much more to have been revealed – but Operation Yellowhammer appears to be a pretty mundane and bog-standard plan of action. It tells of a two-day workshop that reviewed departmental plans and shows that the government is properly planning to prepare for us to begin trading on WTO rules and leaving the EU without a deal.

With Operation Yellowhammer revealed, and Theresa May's announcement that thousands of civil servants are working to prepare, could it be that the Prime Minister is finally realising the EU doesn't want her Chequers deal?

7th September
Vince Cable Will Stand Down as Lib Dem Leader

When Tim Farron resigned as leader of the Liberal Democrats, the party didn't have many people to choose from to replace him. Under the current party's rules, the leader needs to be a Member of Parliament – and with just 12, the race was a tough one. I guess that's why Lib Dem veteran Vince Cable ended up taking up the reigns, at the age of 74. He'd been the leader of the Lib Dems previously, so he was certainly the most experienced candidate...but after Nick Clegg lied to Britain's youth about university fees, and Tim Farron was attacked by the left for his Christian faith, he was hardly the inspiring new face they needed.

Now, it looks like Cable's finally had enough – and has announced, he'll be standing down[4] as Lib Dem leader next year. He's done his best to give the party a new lease of life, and I suppose he's been reasonably successful. Unlike Nick Clegg, who steered the party into what he considered a 'middle-ground' direction that picked up votes from either side of the political spectrum, Clegg steered the party down a strictly anti-Brexit line. This wasn't a liberal party any more, it was a pro-EU party that aimed to pick up as many votes as possible from the large minority who voted to Remain.

Cable once rightly pointed out that the Liberal Democrats are winning by-elections most Thursdays in the UK, and it's true – but I don't think it's just a result of his pro-EU message. The party has historically been very talented at winning local elections. They promise local people the world (and never deliver) and attack the big parties in power.

That's why they boom and bust. When the big parties are screwing up, the Lib Dems position themselves as the reasonable guys and they do well in local elections and maybe gain some Parliamentary seats. When the Lib Dems have any level of influence, as they did following the 2010 election, they're held to account and they go bust again. It's a cycle, as you can see in the next diagram.

Chapter Four: September 2018

Here's another attempt at showing how GB councillors have changed over the past 11 months. Scales are equal (but at different levels!), includes defections and suspensions.

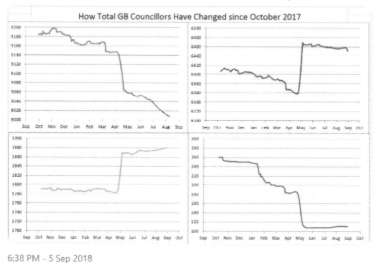

How Total GB Councillors Have Changed since October 2017

6:38 PM – 5 Sep 2018

Council Data from OpenCouncilData.co.uk [5]

I think the UK is a three-party system, not a two-party system. This third party always plays a role in British politics, but always ends up with the worst deal. Cable knows he needs to break free from this cycle, which is why he's announced that he'll be stepping down next year and changing rules to allow non-MPs to become leader.

In a speech, Cable explained that he wanted to transform his party into a 'movement for moderates'. He's noticed the chaos in the Labour Party with the anti-Semitism crisis, and he's realised there are lots of pro-EU Tories to be won over. He's planning to allow people to join the party as 'supporters', for free, and give those people some decision-making ability.

He wants to continue campaigning for a second EU referendum, and to reinvigorate the party with fresh blood – but Gina Miller doesn't want in. The anti-Brexit firebrand who has brought legal cases[6] against the government, demanding a vote on the Brexit process in Parliament, has ruled out a bid to lead the party. She's booked to address the Lib Dem conference later this month, but she told BBC News[7] that, while flattering, she isn't interested in becoming leader.

So who is there?

I don't think Vince knows, and I don't think the party knows. The only thing they *do* know is that poor old Vince is just too much of a stale, pale, straight-white-male.

10th September
Two Tribes Go to War in the Tory Party

Today marks 200 days to go until the official Brexit day – and things are still as uncertain as ever. Interestingly, Steve Baker (ERG and former Brexit Minister) has marked the day by announcing as many as 80 MPs would be willing to vote against Chequers in the Commons.

That's around 20 more MPs than Mogg and others originally claimed to have on their side. That's significant – very significant. In fact, it's probably enough to bring the plan to a sudden halt in the Commons. That'd be a major defeat for Theresa, and potentially the spark that's needed to cause a leadership challenge.

He also told the BBC that there could be a 'catastrophic split' if the Conservative Party was unable to negotiate a more flexible arrangement.

But, I don't think Baker is planning a leadership coup. He has insisted that he isn't seeking a change in Tory leadership, but instead a change in policy. He told the BBC:[8]

> *"We want to change the policy and we would be delighted to unite behind Theresa May with a different policy. The Conservative Party must come together to deliver Brexit behind a policy and the policy we are arguing for is the one the EU has offered us in March."*

Baker works with Jacob Rees Mogg in the European Research Group, so I honestly wouldn't be surprised if this was an honest effort to change Theresa May's mind. I don't think Mogg has any aspirations to become Prime Minister, and I do genuinely believe he wants to see Theresa May pull off Brexit successfully. So, whether this move is successful or not is beside the point – I think Baker is being honest when he says he'd like to unite behind Theresa May with a new Brexit plan.

It still is a threat, though. Along with the very real possibility of 80 Tory MPs blocking Chequers – meaning May might have to rely on votes from Labour and the Lib Dems to get it passed – the ERG is planning to release its own alternative plan for Brexit at the Tory Party Conference at the end of the month.

On the other side of the Tories...

Things look quite different in the Remain camp in the Parliamentary Conservative Party. A senior Tory has been quoted in the Daily Mail[9] yesterday that roughly a dozen Remain-supporting Tory MPs would refuse to work in the Conservative Party under Boris Johnson as leader.

With the possibility of Boris taking over from Mrs May becoming more likely by the day, that means the Tories could be rid of Remain nuisances quite soon. It also means, however, that the government could collapse. With no majority in Parliament, and by relying on the DUP to prop up their votes in Parliament, the Tories might be forced to hold another general election.

So here's how things could play out:

1. Theresa May listens to the ERG and changes the Brexit plan. The Remainers might not be happy, but they may just stay in the Tories under Theresa May.
2. Theresa May ignores the ERG (and the people), goes ahead with Chequers, and gets tripped up last minute by Boris. If that happens, I see no way that Boris could legitimately hold the reins and keep a stable government together without holding another general election.

This month could get turbulent. I wonder if we'll have any interesting announcements at the conference? I suspect the break off sessions and hotel room press conferences will be far more interesting than the speeches on the main stage.

12th September
Could May be Gone in a Matter of Days?

Just a few days ago we learned that as many as 80 Tory MPs were willing to vote against Chequers in the Commons – and now it seems like Theresa May could be facing a coup within a matter of days. I wouldn't hold my breath on this one right now – I've heard this a few times before – but it's certainly an interesting development.

Chris Hope, Chief Political Correspondent for The Daily Telegraph, has tweeted that an 'informed source' has told him at least 35 letters have been submitted to the chairman of the 1922 Committee, Sir Graham Brady. These letters call for a vote of no confidence against Theresa May – and should another 13 be delivered, that vote will take place.

This has happened before, with the number of letters falling short by just single figures. Maybe this is just a re-run of that.

Tory MP Andrew Bridgen spoke to ITV News[10] after a dinner at Number 10, responding 'we'll have to see' when asked if this was a coup against Theresa. He also insisted that the PM take on board the comments given to her, chuck Chequers, and get on with a Super Canada trade deal.

That could be on the cards, too. Mrs May knows her job is on the line here and the threat of a coup is very real, so the 'Plan B' appears to be in consideration right now. No10 is said to have two escape options[11] if the European Union rejects her Chequers deal, with a plan to 'pivot' away from her soft Brexit plan last minute.

The upcoming EU summit in Salzburg could potentially be make or break for the Chequers deal, so a plan is being formulated to pivot away and get back to business. It's funny that the PM seems willing to consider cleaner Brexit deals only if her soft Brexit betrayal doesn't work first, isn't it?

One option is to simply stall – the Chequers deal will be kept on hold until talks resume following the official Brexit day. The second option is to completely scrap Chequers and go for a Canada style agreement that Bridgen and Rees-Mogg appear to be calling for.

So let's hope the EU holds out and scraps Chequers *for us.*

13th September
Steven Woolfe Joins the Tories...and Gets Rejected

As part of Arron Bank's 'Blue Wave' project – which is attempting to bring in ex-UKIP and pro-Brexiteer supporters into the Conservative Party – former UKIP MEP Steven Woolfe joined the Tories. He also became the president of Blue Wave, which will attempt to command enough grassroots support to replace Theresa May with a Brexiteer candidate in the event of a leadership challenge.

But all is not going to plan. Just like Arron Banks, Woolfe has had his Tory party membership application rejected.[12]

This surprised me. Arron Banks, I understand – he's a provocateur and has been plenty critical of the Tories...but Woolfe? He's a former UKIP MEP who left the party to become an independent. He seems like an ideal candidate for a new Tory Party member. He could have helped the Tories consolidate Brexit support and grow their membership, but they're obviously too spooked by the Blue Wave.

The fear surrounding Woolfe makes me think the Tories really are concerned about the prospects of a leadership challenge. Kicking out Banks might simply have been an issue of revenge or spite – but Woolfe really means something. They just kicked out a real asset, and it's probably because May is so weak.

14th September
The EU Gets Spiteful

It's only been a matter of days since we were told that the UK and the EU were just six weeks away from a deal – but EU diplomats are now rejecting[13] the claim that we're closing in on an agreement. EU officials are reportedly surprised by the Brexit Secretary Dominic Raab's claim that they're 'closing in' on a solution to the Irish border issue, after a half-hour discussion with Michel Barnier.

Yesterday, Raab suggested[14] that Britain might withhold the £39 billion divorce bill in the event of a No Deal Brexit, but that he was looking forward to continuing the negotiation process the next day. But, today, the two men spoke on the phone for just 30 minutes. Raab believed the conversation meant a deal was almost ready – but the EU doesn't agree. Diplomats have suggested that his claims that their teams were 'closing in on workable solutions to the outstanding issues in the Withdrawal Agreement' are untrue. Instead, they say there was an impasse on the issue of a backstop solution in Ireland.

I feel like games are being played here. After Barnier seemed to suggest that he was willing to give Britain a deal like no other country had ever been given, we seem to have come full circle and the scaremongering has started all over again.

As well as stabbing Raab in the back, we're now hearing that the Eurostar won't run if there's No Deal...and that our driving licences won't be valid. I mean, really, is there any need?

A French Minister has warned[15] that Eurostar trains will be turned back from Europe if Britain leaves with No Deal. He even said that planes from the UK would be barred[16] from entering Europe if we can't reach an agreement. I'd love to hear the argument for this. This hurts both our economies and seems like a 'cut your nose to spite your face' kind of situation.

I also suspect that this is greatly exaggerated. We know about Operation Yellowhammer, and the government is clearly planning for a No Deal exit. I can't imagine thousands of people having flights cancelled, cargo stuck in UK airports, and countless airlines stuck and wondering how to properly compensate ticketholders. It's just not going to happen, is it?

So perhaps the news about our driving licences is exaggerated too – though, I fear it may not be. The government tells us that after March next year, our driving licence 'may no longer be valid by itself' in the European Union. That is, according to the most recent No Deal planning papers. Published on 13th September, the report[17] is titled *'Driving in the EU if there's no Brexit deal',* and it explains:

> *If there is no deal with the EU, you may need to obtain an International Driving Permit (IDP) to drive in the EU. An IDP is a document which when carried with your driving licence means you would be able to drive outside of the UK including in EU countries. There are different types of IDP. Which one you need depends on which country you are driving in.*

> *If you currently drive outside the EU, for example in some states of the USA and countries including Japan, you may already be used to obtaining an IDP.*
>
> *You may be turned away at the border or face other enforcement action, for example fines, if you don't have the correct IDP.*
> *You may also need an IDP to hire a vehicle when you are abroad.*

I mean, come on. The permits only cost about a fiver, so it's hardly a significant issue – but that's the point, isn't it? Is this necessary? Is there *really* nothing that the Europeans can do to change that?

The National Audit Office believes that between 100,000 and 7,000,000 of these permits would need to be issued in the first year. That's a lot of people. Many people in Britain drive to Europe – we are lucky enough to be very close to the continent – and I think the spiteful EU bureaucrats know that.

That's all this is. Pure spite. The closer they get, the more confused they become. I do wonder whether the news that Theresa May is planning a 'pivot' if the Chequers deal is rejected might have prompted this. Perhaps the EU is fighting back and undermining our Brexit minister because they know we're preparing other options if they don't want to offer us a deal.

17th September
IMF Predicts the Sky Will Fall in Post-Brexit

The International Monetary Fund is at it again, predicting the sky will fall in and Britain's economy will incur 'substantial costs' in the event of a No Deal Brexit. The IMF has said that all Brexit scenarios – even soft Brexit that essentially changes nothing – would 'entail costs'. They believe, however, that a No Deal Brexit would be a 'significantly worse outcome'.

The IMF believes[18] Britain's economy will grow by 1.5% in 2018 and 2019 if a 'broad' Brexit agreement is made. But, in the event of a No Deal exit, the IMF's Managing Director Christine Lagarde says we'll experience an increased deficit, depreciation of our currency, and reduced growth – all meaning the UK economy would contract.

Let's assume it's true…would you take it? I've spoken to a lot of people about this recently, and the consensus among Brexiteers appears to be that they're willing to accept a short-term hit to the economy for the sake of the country. I'd agree with them. So what if there's a short-term hit? We know that in the long run we'll be fine – in fact, we'll thrive, and we'll be free of European dictators.

Freedom isn't free, and the world isn't perfect. Scaremongering in the press changes nothing. We are still being ruled by dictators and bureaucrats, and as a lady told me outside Westminster the other day, "I'll accept a few less pounds in the short term if it means being free of these monsters".

Here's the thing, though: the IMF has been wrong before. In fact, they've been wrong a lot. In their 2016 report, the IMF told us[19] that Brexit with trigger a recession, hit living standards in Britain, cause inflation and reduce the GDP by up to 5.5%. They even claimed it'd cause a stock market and house price crash.[20]

So why should we believe them this time?

18th September
What the MAC Migration Report Gets Right and Wrong

A new report has been released today[21] by the Migration Advisory Committee, specifically focusing on EU migration. It advises the government that there should be no preference given to EU nationals for visas following Brexit – a blow to Theresa May's renamed version of Free Movement.

The Chequers Deal specifically references a system whereby EU nationals would be given easier access to the UK. This is just another nail in the coffin for the deal…or at least, I hope it is. Mrs May seems resilient. Kudos to her for hanging onto her job so well. It seems to me that she's hanging over a cliff, clinging on with her fingernails, while a mob of far-left and pro-Brexit activists take their turns stamping on her fingers. But she's hanging in there, and the Chequers deal is clutching onto her ankles for dear life.

The report has also suggested the government should make it easier for higher-skilled workers to migrate to the UK, and to scrap a limit on those highly-skilled workers coming to the country.

I do take some comfort in the fact that the report has stated that there is no need for low-skilled workers[22] following Brexit. It's good to hear some sanity, and the MAC has said that immigration has specifically hurt low wage workers. But, they have also said that the immigration of higher-skilled workers is neither good nor bad and that the government should lift the cap and make it easier for those people to come here.

Don't get me wrong, that's a nicer option – but I still don't think it's perfect. Would you agree with me that what Britain needs, right now, is a programme of education and training of young British people – either those out of work or those in pointless gender studies university courses – to fill the roles that we're currently giving away to immigrant workers?

Why aren't we trying to fill those gaps with our own people rather than importing talented workers from all over the world? There's almost an imperialist feeling to this, I think. We're taking the most skilled workers from developing countries that desperately need them at home. Isn't that wrong?

Interestingly, though, the report also said that there was no evidence that increase migration has damaged life in the UK. I wonder where they get this? I wonder where the discrepancy comes from – because the reality is very different in working-class communities. I don't come from the most impoverished working-class town – there are many much, much worse places than where I'm from – but even we saw the effect of EU migration. It would be hard to try and state an exact percentage of the Polish workforce in my town, but from local workers and family, I know it's quite large.

I grew up in an area with lots of Polish workers and they are exactly that – workers. They're exceptionally motivated, and just last year the Office for National Statistics reported[23] that 80% of Britain's 1.4 million Eastern European residents were in work. But this can impact work availability for young British people who require unskilled or low-skilled work – and the MAC report does acknowledge this to some extent.

Whether it's the IMF, the government, or an advisory committee – it seems like the elite and the working people of this country are living in two different worlds.

Chapter Four: September 2018

19th September
EU Chief: May's Brexit Plan Must Be Reworked

Donald Tusk, President of the European Council, has put a dampener on Theresa May's day. He's announced today that her Chequers Brexit plan will need to be 'reworked' in some key areas – meaning, if the plan goes ahead, it'll be even worse for the British people than originally planned. It looks like we're going to need to make even more concessions to the EU if May is to pass the Chequers deal.

Ahead of a European Council meeting in Salzburg, the EU Chief said that May's compromises did show a 'positive evolution of the UK's approach' and a willingness to attempt to minimise what he called the 'negative impacts of Brexit'. In plain speak, that means that May's compromises give more to the EU and make greater sacrifices for Britain. It essentially fits Merkel's vision[24] of the UK suffering 'a little bit' during the negotiation process.

Tusk tweeted[25] about his thoughts on the negotiation process, explaining:

"Today there is perhaps more hope but there is surely less and less time. On the Irish question and the framework for economic cooperation the UK's proposal needs to be reworked".

His comment 'less and less time' of course refers to the reality of an emergency summit that looks to be held in the middle of November to try and agree on the final deal.

20th September
All 27 EU Leaders Say Chequers Trade Plan Won't Work

Theresa May attended a summit in Salzburg, Austria, today. The EU leaders met to discuss the Brexit deal that remains up in the air – and it's bad news for Theresa. Every single EU leader, according to Donald Tusk, believes that her trade plan simply "will not work."[26]

At the end of the summit, Tusk told the press that the emergency summit in November might not even happen and that the European Council would decide next month "whether conditions are there to call an extra summit."

The issue appears to be that EU leaders refuse to accept any deal that would split the UK into two customs territories – whereby Northern Ireland would have different customs rules to Great Britain. This was the first opportunity for all EU member states to consider the trade proposals in the Chequers plan, primarily because they consider it as undermining the Single Market.

May is digging her heels in though. She once admitted she was a 'bloody difficult woman' and I don't doubt that. I just wish she would be a bloody difficult woman and fight for the Brexit we voted for. She has said that the Chewers deal is the 'only plan'[27] on the table, pushing back against the EU and potentially making No Deal more likely. Doesn't sound so bad, really, does it?

She's even suggested that the EU's criticism of her plan is merely a 'negotiating tactic', so she's definitely upping her game in the negotiations. Can you imagine if she'd been working this hard all along, and doing it with Brexit in mind?

I wonder whether the stories about her last minute 'pivot' are true. If the EU really isn't bluffing over her trade plans, then what would Theresa prefer? A Canada Plus deal, or no deal?

21st September
Theresa May Grows a Backbone (Sort Of)

After being embarrassed by pretty much every single EU leader yesterday in Salzburg, Theresa May's come back swinging[28]. I know she isn't respecting the results of the referendum – despite how often she says she does – but I can't help but respect her a little bit. She thinks she's doing the right thing by the British people and she's fighting back after being shown zero respect by European leaders, yesterday.

Tusk and others should be happy they're dealing with Theresa and not Boris or Jacob. Or me. If they were dealing with us then they'd be experiencing hell right now. At least Theresa is trying to respect their desire to protect their Union.

In a speech today[29], May said that the EU must respect the UK in Brexit negotiations. She also said that it is unacceptable for either side to ask the other side to do something unacceptable – specifically, to ask one side to hurt or divide their union.

May is specifically referring to Northern Ireland. In her speech, she explained how the two options on the table with the EU are remaining in the EEA (which would tie us to all EU rules and stop us making other trade deals) or having a Free Trade Agreement which would see a customs border down the Irish Sea, effectively separating Northern Ireland from the rest of the UK. May said this is unacceptable and she won't be made to divide her country, and I respect that. She also reaffirmed her belief that no deal is better than a bad deal, which is great. I just wish her version of a bad deal was the same as mine. Everything on the table right now is pretty abysmal.

The Prime Minister also addressed the statement by Tusk made yesterday, suggesting that the Chequers agreement is a non-starter. She said:

> *"At this late stage in the negotiations, it is not acceptable to simply reject the other side's proposals without a detailed explanation and counter proposals. So we now need to hear from the EU what the real issues are and what their alternative is so we can discuss them. Until we do, we cannot make progress."*

Fair enough, Mrs May.

You know, I'm glad she did this. Regardless of who our Prime Minister is, I don't like seeing dictators and bureaucrats trying to make a mockery of our leader and our country.

Donald Tusk is no rude, disrespectful and childish that he used his Instagram account to mock the Prime Minister[30]. He showed a picture of him offering the Prime Minister a cake – but apologised 'Sorry, no cherries'. A reference to May's 'cherry picking'.

I don't like that. And I suspect that's what made Mrs May fight back.

So come on, Theresa. Go get 'em. And tell them it's time for them to pluck up their ideas or deal with us leaving without a deal and becoming the most competitive country on the continent.

It's good to see this side of the Prime Minister come out. She occasionally comes out with some fantastic,

Thatcher-esque corkers during PMQs with Corbyn. I wish we got to see that in her more often, and I hope it comes out again. Soon.

24th September
The Chequers Alternative Has Arrived

We've known for a whole that Jacob Rees Mogg and co were working on an alternative to the Chequers plan, and today we finally saw it. Named "Plan A+", the proposal was announced by the Institute of Economic Affairs and was launched by cross-bench, pro-Leave MPs – including David Davis, Jacob Rees Mogg, and Gisela Stuart.

It's already gaining support, with Tory Remain MP Greg Hands tweeting his support for the plan. He explained that Plan A+ was the kind of free trade agreement he'd like to see. This is the perfect time for it, too. The EU has made it perfectly clear that they don't want the Chequers deal, and the political elite has made it equally clear that they don't want No Deal. So in comes Jacob Rees-Mogg to save the day.

The new plan is essentially a free trade deal with the European Union – which the EU, by the way, has already offered it. The only reason we haven't already taken the free trade deal option with the EU is because Theresa May doesn't really want Brexit, and doesn't want to divide the United Kingdom. Fair enough – but Rees-Mogg has long said that splitting off Northern Ireland from the rest of the UK isn't necessary, and his Plan A+ outlines how.

The report suggests that the UK should call for a more advanced free trade agreement with the EU which uses technology to prevent a hard border. I suppose they're talking cameras and other monitoring equipment at the border that allows us to track who comes and does. I'm sure it could work in terms of the movement of goods, but I remain concerned about the prospects of illegal migration by third world immigrants with EU passports.

A few days ago I would have said I think we're moving towards a No Deal Brexit, but things seem very different now. Theresa May is desperately trying[31] to unite the Cabinet and tell the public that they're all on board with her Chequers deal – but The Telegraph says otherwise. In a report today, the Telegraph said that the majority of the Cabinet now supports a Canada-style trade deal (a la Plan A+), meaning the Prime Minister might be the last and only person on board with Chequers. That's a good sign for us.

According to the report, Foreign Secretary Jeremy Hunt is even on board. I'm really quite impressed by all of this. A Tory insider told me not that long ago that there really wasn't a desire for a leadership challenge within the party, and that instead, the Eurosceptic lot in the Tories wanted to push the Cabinet to do the right thing on Brexit. And it looks like it's worked.

Jacob Rees-Mogg is doing important work showing support for his version of Brexit across all parties, with the Labour Leave campaign. Inside the government, the likes of Jeremy Hunt are pushing the Prime Minister to do the right thing. It's quite possible that if the EU keeps on knocking back Chequers, May well be left with the choice between a free trade deal and No Deal. The only way she'll choose No Deal is if she really is desperate to keep us in the EU. It would have to be a deliberate act of sabotage, and while I don't trust Mrs May all that much, I'd be surprised if she went that far.

Suddenly, the future feels all that bit brighter.

25th September
Theresa May Rejects Plan A+

Well, I guess my dreams of Theresa adopting Rees-Moggs Plan A+ have just been slashed. At the United Nations summit today,[32] the Prime Minister has said that a No Deal Brexit would be better for Britain than a Canada-style deal.

I suppose it's not the worst thing in the world, but it does seem like an unnecessary setback. A free trade agreement along the lines set out by Rees-Mogg and others could be hugely beneficial for the UK. Perhaps this is Theresa cutting her nose to spite her face. Her deal didn't work, and she'll be damned if she lets the Brexiteers in her party do better than her.

Her appearance at the UN summit in New York was her first chance to get the Brexit narrative moving again, following her scathing speech demanding respect from the rest of the EU. She's making it clearer than ever that it's her deal or no deal.

She claims that the free trade agreement plan proposed by Brexiteers in her party would require a hard border in Ireland. We know that's not true – so what's really going on her, Theresa? Do you think the EU will buckle and take your Chequers deal?

Labour's Fighting Over a Second Referendum Policy

Nobody knows what Labour's stance on Brexit is. They just used their conference in Liverpool over the weekend to try and clarify it, but I still don't have a bloody clue what they stand for.

Some of the leadership is pro-Brexit, but secretly. Much of the leadership is pro-Remain, openly. Many of the members are pro-Remain, many of the members are so pro-Remain they want a second referendum that includes the option to cancel Brexit, and even some of their membership now want a second referendum that focuses only on the *kind* of Brexit we have. Confused yet? Well, consider the fact that most of their voters – who make up a large proportion of the 52% who voted Brexit back in 2016 – are quite openly pro-Brexit, and it all gets even more confusing.

This party doesn't know what it stands for, and it's clear there is a great divide. Dennis Skinner was visibly displeased when Keir Starmer, Shadow Secretary of State for Exiting the European Union, said that he wouldn't rule out the possibility of remaining in the European Union.

Dennis Skinner looks visibly displeased. [33]

Skinner is one of the most principled Labour Members of Parliament they've ever had, and he shows how this party has become so disconnected from the working class.

Starmer received a standing ovation[34] from the Labour Party conference when he said 'nobody is ruling out remain'. This is serious, too – Starmer isn't a nobody. He would be in charge of the Brexit negotiations if a general election were held and Labour won. Something that, amazingly, isn't entirely impossible.

There seems to also be a disconnect between the Labour Party and the unions. Can they get anything right? Just the other day, Len McCluskey, the Unite general secretary, supported the idea of a second referendum that excluded an option[35] to remain in the EU. Steve Turner, assistant general secretary from Unite, reconfirmed this after Starmer's speech, saying a referendum must just be a vote 'on the terms of our departure'.

Can Labour make up its mind?

I think Starmer knows this is a sensitive issue, too. He knew that when he got up on the stage, but he also knew he didn't have any choice. He wants us to stay and he must act now, as a No Deal Brexit looks more likely than ever. He even chickened out[36] of defending himself on Good Morning Britain with Piers Morgan.

God, I wish I could get on that show. I was invited previously, about a year ago. I was due to go on the day after Tommy Robinson – but after Tommy completely showed Piers up, they called up and cancelled my appearance. Such is life, I suppose.

But, back to the point - Corbyn and co could well end up bound by the will of its members, who are overwhelmingly pro-Remain. That would mean endorsing a second referendum.

And you know what – if that happens, I suspect it might be the straw that broke the camel's back. There is a huge untapped market out there for a political party that represents the working class, and if Labour turns its back on the working classes who voted for Brexit then they might not be able to regain that vote. It will go somewhere else.

It could be UKIP, but I suspect that boat has sailed at this point. Something new is coming, I'm sure, and Labour is about to speed up that change. If the party wants to survive, they must realise that their party and its elected representatives have a duty to the country and not just to its far-left membership.

26th September
The EU Steps Up 'No Deal' Preparation

Remember how last month I was writing about how Barnier seemed willing to give the UK an offer he'd previously given no other country? Well, that's all gone Pete Tong!

In fact, with the mockery being made of Theresa May in recent weeks, it looks to me that the EU has given up on us. They seem, to me, to be willing to just accept defeat and work around the UK. They'll suffer, but maybe they think it's worth it.

A leaked document revealed today has shown that the EU has begun intensifying its preparations for No Deal, suggesting that they haven't responded to May's call for respect. The document is said to have been circulated among ambassadors in Brussels before a meeting goes ahead later, where the prospect of Labour MPs and Tory rebels working together to kill off any possible deal will be discussed.

The Guardian reports[37] that the document says:

> *"Preparedness work has to intensify in the months ahead at national as well as EU level, as uncertainty remains about the outcome of the negotiations and the ratification of a possible deal."*

The fear of Labour MPs trying to scupper a deal might be justified, too – as Corbyn is set to meet Barnier tomorrow[38]. Corbyn used his speech at the Labour conference to demand May to 'step aside' (she doesn't have a majority of seats in Parliament so technically COULD step aside for Corbyn…but won't). I'm not entirely sure what the leader of the opposition has to do with this, and why he's getting involved, but it's not a good sign.

During his conference speech, he demanded that any agreement in Brussels delivers 'exactly the same benefits' as membership of the EU – which is pretty terrifying. The man's an old school Brexiteer, so corrupted by his party and a new generation of far-left activists that he's going back on the work of a lifetime and calling for Brexit to be delivered in name only.

Remember – Corbyn's idea of 'benefits' is very different from our idea of benefits. He and his mates think importing half the world through the EU is a huge benefit, and under Labour, that'd be a key part of any Brexit deal.

And while the EU would like to maintain control over the UK, I doubt they'll be much more responsive to Corbyn calling for 'exactly the same benefits' as membership. Remember – the EU doesn't want to give anything away without total control being handed over in return.

27th September
Project Fear Exposed: EU-Bound Planes WON'T Be Banned After No Deal

Remember when I reported that Project Fear was telling us how EU-bound planes from the UK would be grounded in the event of a No Deal Brexit? Well, it turns out we were right to laugh it off. Today, a senior EU diplomat has told the press that in the event of No Deal, the EU and the UK will, in fact, make lots of deals that ensure life goes on as normal.

That means there's no need for stockpiling food, and you're not going to be stopped from going on your holidays. I suspect the Eurostar won't grind to a halt, either.

Reuters reports[39] that a senior EU diplomat has explained they will be we waiting for "if and when the negotiations with Britain officially fail to kickstart more open work among the 27 on preparing for a no-deal". The same diplomat also confirmed they have given themselves until November to agree on a deal – specifically, November 17th and 18th when a summit expected to take place.

The diplomat went on:

> *"There are areas where we need to act to have something in place on March 2th no matter what....That's a lot of deals assumed on the British side for a no-deal scenario...but it's probably true that for some areas like air traffic we will have to make sure we go on".*

And there you have it, people! The lie exposed.

The issue of customs is pretty much a legitimate concern – but again, not something I imagine the EU will want to dillydally on. I suspect they'll extend existing rules for a short period while a new deal is worked out – meaning that, in the event of No Deal, there will, in fact, be a deal.

The talk of chaos is not just wrong, it's a lie.

28th September
David Davis: Merkel and Macron Trying to Make Britain Suffer

To nobody's surprise, David Davis revealed in an interview with the Evening Standard[40] that Angela Merkel is leading moves in the EU to stop it appearing like Britain has 'succeeded' with Brexit. During the interview, former Brexit Secretary Davis also said that Emmanuel Macron, French President, is the only one who wants Britain to fail more than Merkel does.

He explained:

> "Other than Macron, Merkel is the most emphatic in Europe about us not being seen to succeed".

He also made a point that I and others have been saying for a while – and that is how we won't experience easy times with the EU any time soon.

He said that Chequers "is a toothache", but not a crisis – and that we've had a toothache with Europe for 30 years, and "we'll have it for another 20".

I'd agree – but I'd go further and say that for as long as the EU exists, I can't see any peace or easy cooperation at all. If Merkel and Macron have it in for us now, imagine how nasty and spiteful they'll be once we've actually left. They'll be the spiteful ex-girlfriend following every step we make, looking at every future trade deal we make, and doing everything they can to destroy our new relationships. They'll continue failing and blaming everyone else for their failures.

I do wonder if Davis and other Brexiteers in the Tories realise this. They're good on free trade deals, and they've been quite clever with coming up with Northern Ireland solutions – but do they realise that the EU is more than just a bad deal, but an authoritarian monster?

The fact that the leaders of France and Germany want our country to fail is significant. It's even more significant when one considers the fact that our leaders are weak. If we had a Trump-esque leader who would stand up to these bullies, as the US president did at the United Nation the other day, then things might be different.

If you didn't see the United Nations speech[41], then you must. Trump stood up in front of the world's leaders, calling out Iran's corrupt regime, and China's attempt to meddle in America's mid-term elections. This is the only kind of leadership that counteracts the wicked and malicious attempts by Merkel and co to make an example of Britain.

It's time for May to stand up to these bullies or make way for someone else who will.

References

[1] *Leading Britain's Conversation, "Brexiteers Happy For UK To Go Into Recession In Order To Leave EU", Nick Ferrari, 3rd September 2018,*
https://www.lbc.co.uk/radio/presenters/nick-ferrari/brexiteers-happy-for-uk-to-go-into-recession-poll/

[2] *Express, "'The Army is on ALERT' – Gina Miller warns no-deal Brexit is 'recipe for DISASTER'", Mat Drake, 4th September 2018,*
https://www.express.co.uk/news/politics/1012401/brexit-news-gina-miller-no-deal-brexit-uk-eu

[3] *Twitter, "Operation Yellowhammer...", Laura Kuenssberg, 6th September 2018,*
https://twitter.com/bbclaurak/status/1037661665142206465

[4] *BBC News, "Vince Cable could stand down as Lib Dem leader next year", BBC News, 7th September 2018,*
https://www.bbc.co.uk/news/uk-politics-45438907

[5] *Twitter, "Here's another attempt at showing how ...", Council Data UK, 5th September 2018,*
https://twitter.com/CouncilDataUK/status/1037394487989989377

[6] *BBC News, "Brexit court case: Who is Gina Miller?", BBC News, 24th January 2017,*
https://www.bbc.co.uk/news/uk-politics-37861888

[7] *BBC News, "Gina Miller rules out Lib Dem leadership bid", BBC News, 29th August 2018,*
https://www.bbc.co.uk/news/uk-politics-45344197

[8] *BBC News, "Brexit plan: 80 MPs will reject Chequers deal, says ex-minister", BBC News, 10th September 2018,*
https://www.bbc.co.uk/news/uk-45468544

[9] *Mail Online, "Boris triggers Tory civil war: 12 MPs vow to quit to stop him getting into Number 10 after his 'suicide vest' jibe following scandal over 'fling' with spin doctor - as he shows strain of wife branding him an 'adulterer' in divorce", Jason Groves, 9th September 2018,*
https://www.dailymail.co.uk/news/article-6149099/MPs-vow-quit-stop-Boris-getting-number-10-suicide-vest-jibe.html

[10] *Twitter, "Is a Tory coup on the cards? Here's what Conservative MPs Andrew Bridgen and John Baron had to say after a Downing Street dinner on Tuesday night.", ITV News, 11th September 2018,*
https://twitter.com/itvnews/status/1039628783379259393?ref_src=twsrc%5Etfw%7Ctwcamp%5Etweetembed%7Ctwterm%5E1039628783379259393%7Ctwgr%5E373939313b636f6e74726f6c&ref_url=https%3A%2F%2Fwww.westmonster.com%2Fmay-faces-brexiteer-coup-within-days12%2F

[11] *The Sun, "Downing Street is drawing up secret plans to dump Theresa May's Chequers Brexit proposal if EU leaders reject it", Tom Newton Dunn, Harry Cole and Nick Gutteridge, 12th September 2018,*
https://www.thesun.co.uk/news/7234952/plans-dump-chequers-brexit-proposal/

Chapter Four: September 2018

[12] Breitbart, "Former UKIP MEP Woolfe Blocked from Joining Tories", Liam Deacon, 13th September 2018,
https://www.breitbart.com/london/2018/09/13/former-ukip-mep-woolfe-blocked-joining-tories/
[13] The Guardian, "EU diplomats reject Raab claim that Brexit talks are 'closing in' on deal", Daniel Boffey, 14th September 2018,
https://www.theguardian.com/politics/2018/sep/14/eu-officials-refute-raab-claim-that-brexit-talks-are-closing-in-on-deal

[14] Euronews, "Raab - Brexit deal attainable, but no deal means no EU payment: Telegraph", Reuters, 13rd September 2018,
http://www.euronews.com/2018/09/13/raab-brexit-deal-attainable-but-no-deal-means-no-eu-payment-telegraph

[15] Independent, "Eurostar will not run if there is a no-deal Brexit, French Europe minister warns", Rob Merrick, 13rd September 2018,
https://www.independent.co.uk/news/uk/politics/eurostar-trains-brexit-no-deal-uk-eu-london-paris-nathalie-louiseau-a8536316.html

[16] The Guardian, "France may stop trains and planes from UK under no-deal Brexit", Patrick Wintour and Dan Sabbagh, 13th September 2018,
https://www.theguardian.com/politics/2018/sep/13/france-may-stop-trains-and-planes-from-uk-under-no-deal-brexit

[17] Gov.uk, "Driving in the EU if there's no Brexit deal", Department for Transport, 13th September 2018,
https://www.gov.uk/government/publications/driving-in-the-eu-if-theres-no-brexit-deal/driving-in-the-eu-if-theres-no-brexit-deal

[18] BBC News, "No-deal Brexit would hit UK economy, says IMF", BBC News, 17th September 2018,
https://www.bbc.co.uk/news/business-45546785

[19] The Guardian, "IMF says Brexit would trigger UK recession", Katie Allen, 18th June 2016,
https://www.theguardian.com/business/2016/jun/18/imf-says-brexit-would-trigger-uk-recession-eu-referendum

[20] News Locker, "Brexit would prompt stock market and house price crash, says IMF", Via The Guardian - Phillip Inman, 13th May 2016,
http://www.newslocker.com/en-au/news/economic-news-australia/brexit-would-prompt-stock-market-and-house-price-crash-says-imf/

[21] Migration Advisory Committee, "EEA migration in the UK: Final report", September 2018,
https://assets.publishing.service.gov.uk/government/uploads/system/uploads/attachment_data/file/741926/Final_EEA_report.PDF

[22] The Times, "Britain set for tough new curbs on low-skilled immigrants", Sam Coates and Philip Aldrick, 19th September 2018,
https://www.thetimes.co.uk/article/no-need-for-low-skilled-workers-after-brexit-says-migration-report-jhvsj87b2

[23] The Guardian, "80% of Britain's 1.4m eastern European residents are in work", Alan Travis, 10th July 2017,
https://www.theguardian.com/world/2017/jul/10/majority-of-britain-eastern-european-residents-are-in-work

[24] Express, "'UK must SUFFER!' Angela Merkel makes shocking Brexit attack", Martina Bet, 18th September 2018,

Chapter Four: September 2018

https://www.express.co.uk/news/uk/1019030/Brexit-news-Angela-Merkel-EU-UK-negotiations-Chequers-BBC-Newsnight

[25] Twitter, "Today there is perhaps more hope but there is surely less and less time.", Donald Tusk, 19th September 2018,
https://twitter.com/eucopresident/status/1042398469674229765

[26] Independent, "All 27 EU leaders believe Theresa May's Brexit trade plan 'will not work'", Jon Stone, 20th September 2018,
https://www.independent.co.uk/news/uk/politics/brexit-talks-latest-eu-no-deal-chequers-plan-theresa-may-emmanuel-macron-edited-a8547076.htmls

[27] The Guardian, "Brexit: May says Chequers 'only plan' on table after EU calls it unacceptable - as it happened", Andrew Sparrow, 20th September 2018,
https://www.theguardian.com/politics/blog/live/2018/sep/20/salzburg-eu-summit-brexit-theresa-may-polite-doing-her-job-eu-chiefs-non-committal-verdict-on-mays-brexit-appeal-at-salzburg-politics-live?page=with:block-5ba3a8c1e4b0b62144347a78

[28] BBC News, "Theresa May: EU must respect UK in Brexit talks", BBC News, 21st September 2018,
https://www.bbc.co.uk/news/uk-politics-45603192

[29] YouTube, "Theresa May makes a statement on Brexit negotiations – watch live", Guardian News, 21st September 2018,
https://www.youtube.com/watch?v=wUnAGAakzt4

[30] "Donald Tusk posts a picture with Theresa May captioned with a sly putdown about Brexit cherry-picking", ITV Report, 20th September 2018,
http://www.itv.com/news/2018-09-20/sorry-no-cherries-donald-tusk-posts-a-picture-offering-theresa-may-a-cake-captioned-with-a-sly-putdown/

[31] BBC News, "Brexit: No 10 says cabinet 'fully behind' PM's plan", BBC News, 24th September 2018,
https://www.bbc.co.uk/news/uk-politics-45624789

[32] The Guardian, "No-deal Brexit better than Canada-style deal, says Theresa May", 24th September 2018,
https://www.theguardian.com/politics/2018/sep/25/no-deal-brexit-better-than-canada-style-deal-theresa-may

[33] Figure , Twitter, "I think it's fair to say Dennis Skinner was unimpressed by Sir Keir Starmer's talk of the option of Remaining in the EU...", Jonathan Isaby, 25th September 2018,
https://twitter.com/isaby/status/1044544069828071425

[34] Huffpost, "Standing Ovation For Keir Starmer After He Tells Labour Another Referendum Could Stop Brexit", Ned Simons, 25th September 2018,
https://www.huffingtonpost.co.uk/entry/standing-ovation-for-keir-starmer-after-tells-labour-another-referendum-could-stop-brexit_uk_5baa1172e4b069d5f9d62a4c

[35] The Independent, "Brexit: New referendum must exclude any option to remain in EU, says Len McCluskey", Joe Watts, 23rd September 2018,
https://www.independent.co.uk/news/uk/politics/brexit-second-referendum-options-choice-exclude-remain-eu-len-mccluskey-labour-a8551086.html

[36] Twitter, "Hi @Keir_Starmer - sorry you didn't have the balls to come on @GMB today because...", Piers Morgan, 24th September 2018,
https://twitter.com/piersmorgan/status/1044474188956930049

Chapter Four: September 2018

[37] *The Guardian, "EU steps up plans for no-deal Brexit as Labour stance alarms capitals", Daniel Boffey, 27th September 2018, https://www.theguardian.com/world/2018/sep/26/eu-steps-up-no-deal-brexit-preparations-as-labour-alarms-capitals*

[38] *Mail Online, "Corbyn to meet EU negotiator Barnier after demanding Theresa May stand aside if she cannot get her Brexit deal through Parliament", Tim Sculthorpe, 26th September 2018, https://www.dailymail.co.uk/news/article-6210223/Corbyn-meet-EU-negotiator-Barnier-Brussels.html*

[39] *Reuters, "EU accepts no-deal Brexit would still include some deals - diplomats", Gabriela Baczynska, 27th September 2018, https://uk.reuters.com/article/uk-britain-eu-no-deal/eu-grudgingly-accepts-no-deal-brexit-would-still-include-some-deals-idUKKCN1M71E9*

[40] *Evening Standard, "David Davis: We've had a toothache with Europe for 30 years, we'll have it for another 20 more", Charlotte Edwards, 28th September 2018, https://www.standard.co.uk/news/politics/david-davis-weve-had-a-toothache-with-europe-for-30-years-well-have-it-for-another-20-more-a3948456.html*

[41] *Abc News, "'They do not want me or us to win': Trump slams China for trying to meddle in upcoming midterms", Conor Finnegan and Meghan Keneally, 26th September 2018, https://abcnews.go.com/Politics/trump-administration-turns-ire-iran-alienating-allies/story?id=58079785*

Chapter Five
October 2018

1st October
Brussels Refuses to Break Brexit Deadlock

We've been in a Brexit deadlock ever since the Salzburg summit, where Theresa May was mocked by EU leaders. She then demanded respect from the EU and left it there, stating that it was now down to the EU to make the next move and break the Brexit deadlock. The EU doesn't want the Chequers deal, and Mrs May said it's either Chequers or No Deal.

Today, the EU has finally responded – and it seems like it's No Deal. That is, presuming Mrs May doesn't cave. EU diplomats have rejected May's pitch that it was now down to Brussels to break the negotiations deadlock.

Jean-Claude Juncker, President of the EU Commission, told a German audience today that he believes the British voters had not been properly informed about the scale of the problems that Brexit would cause, before the referendum.

Who does this man think he is? He said:[1]

> *"What I really regret is there was no real Brexit campaign in terms of actual information...In Great Britain the people are finding out now, also British ministers and ministers on the continent, they're finding out now how many questions it actually poses, all the things that we need to resolve".*

This is how these tyrants operate. They lie right to our faces. The tell mistruths without flinching. They're master operators. To suggest that there was a lack of information is a blatant lie – the British people knew exactly what we were voting for. Not only that, but to claim that we naively walked into Brexit not realising the plethora of inevitable problems, is disingenuous too. These problems aren't inevitable – they weren't always going to happen. They were, instead, created by these monsters on the continent who want to punish us.

So I'm not surprised at all that they've rejected May's call for them to break the deadlock. They were never going to do it. They don't care how tough Theresa May acts if they know very well that she's scared of No Deal. She might stand on stage and say that No Deal is better than a bad deal, but nobody believes her. We don't believe her because we know she doesn't want No Deal. She wants Chequers…and she might just be willing to do whatever the EU tells her, to get it.

They also reiterated the fact that they won't accept the economic deal set out in the Chequers plan, suggesting it would benefit British businesses and make us too competitive.

So we know the EU doesn't want to have to compete, we know they want to give us the worst deal possible, and I fully expect Theresa May to go crawling back to the EU and break the deadlock herself.

Though I'm hoping I'm proven wrong. Come on Mrs May…surprise me.

2nd October
Boris Rips into Chequers at Conference Speech

Boris Johnson has caused a stir at the Conservative Party Conference – though I suspect there would have been an equal amount of drama if he hadn't even turned up. Multiple Brexit events and breakout sessions at the conference have been left with standing room only and queues out the door, while May and her governmental colleagues put on a brave face and told the crowds that everything is just fine.

Johnson ripped into the Chequers plan during his speech at the conference today, pleading with the Tory government to implement a new plan based on 'one nation' Conservative values. He said that the only winners from a Chequers-style deal with the European Union would be the far right and far left of politics – suggesting that getting Brexit wrong would unleash the extremes of politics into the mainstream. Of course, we know he's talking about people like me when he says that. He thinks that anyone who dares to talk about our traditional culture and values, and who wants to dramatically change our immigration policy, is far right. That's the standard Tory position – but, he's also kind of right.

If Brexit isn't delivered, then it will fuel the extremes of politics. The working-class Brits who were ignored for decades will have been ignored again, and I don't doubt that it will result in some people lurching to the real far right. It'll also empower the far left under Corbyn.

He said:[2]

> *"If we get it wrong, if we bottle Brexit now, believe me, the people of this country will find it hard to forgive...If we get it wrong, if we proceed with this undemocratic*

solution, if we remain half in, half out, we will protract this toxic tedious business that is frankly so off-putting to sensible middle-of-the-road people who want us to get on with their priorities".

It certainly didn't go down well with Mrs May. In an interview with the BBC[3], May reminded the British public that Boris originally signed up to the Chequers plan before resigning. When told that Boris is directly challenging her authority, she simply stated that her government is putting the national interest first, both in what they do on Brexit but also on their domestic agenda. Nice pivot, Mrs May.

But she couldn't escape the questions, and admitted:

"There are one or two things that Boris said that I am cross about".

She also said Boris was trying to tear up her guarantee to Northern Ireland, which isn't exactly true.

Don't underestimate how serious this is. In the last few days, Boris has staged a photograph of himself running through a field of wheat[4], mocking Theresa May's response to a question about the naughtiest thing she ever did. Today, he completely tore apart the Chequers deal and riled up Tory party activists and members. He's staging a rebellion, and it could work...presuming he can get the party behind him.

Mrs May needs her party and Parliament behind her to get Chequers passed. It's unlikely that Labour will vote it through Parliament, her own party is turning to Boris, and now even the DUP is threatening to topple May's government by withdrawing the votes[5] supplied to the Tories on their Confidence and Supply deal.

It's hard to believe that the Tories would vote to put Boris on a final leadership ballot put to the members, but it's harder to believe at this point that the Tories are united enough to vote for the Chequers deal.

3rd October
Theresa May's Big Conference Speech Shows Her PC Credentials

I just watched Theresa May's speech at the Tory conference. She ended days of chaos with a speech designed to unite the party, and I found myself almost respecting her. Here's the thing: I recognise she's weak on immigrant and religious extremists, she's doing a terrible job on Brexit, and she'd probably call me a far-right extremist. But she's so awkwardly loveable, I wish I could like her.

She even walked onto the stage to 'Dancing Queen' by ABBA, throwing some shapes and basically doing the robot as she walked to her podium. I thought it was clever and admirable. She's awkward and she's embracing it in front of the world's press. They can't attack her if she's making fun herself.

But when it comes to the nitty gritty, her speech just confirmed her PC credentials. She proudly praised our multicultural society, referencing how the son of a Pakistani migrant could become Home Secretary, and a pregnant lesbian woman could become the leader of the Scottish Conservatives. That's all very nice and all, but this didn't inspire the normal people of Britain – and it completely ignored the fact that her Brexit proposals are practically impossible to pass in Parliament.

Farage chimed in[6] on Twitter saying that her speech sounded like the relaunch of the Social Democratic Party, and that it was 'politically correct beyond belief'. I'd agree –

May's speech went further than Cameron ever did with his rebranding of the Tories.

She even defended Diane Abbott from the mean trolls online, completely ignoring the fact that Abbott is mocked because of her disdain for democracy, her attacks against Brexiteers, and for her total ineptitude. Not her skin colour. She called for an end[7] to "the bitterness and bile which is poisoning our politics". Well, that might end if the main parties stopped calling decent working people 'far right' – and that goes for Boris Johnson, too.

Interestingly, Mrs May also rebranded her Chequers deal as a 'free trade' deal. She stole a line from Boris and responded no doubt to party donor Michael Spencer's words a few days ago, stating that she will 'back' business.

No amount of deception will work, and no amount of distraction will work. May can praise the virtues of our multicultural society all she likes, and try and present her Chequers deal in a new way – but it doesn't change the fact that the EU doesn't want the deal, Parliament doesn't want the deal, and the British people don't want this deal. If it happens, May is toast.

4th October
Here Comes Chequers 2.0

Reuters reports that a source close to the Brexit talks have said that new plans are coming from Britain, which take a 'step in the right direction' and 'make finding a compromise possible'.

Mrs May told the EU to break the deadlock, the EU said no, and now Mrs May is backing down. That's not quite what some people have been predicting. I even thought for a while that Mrs May might be heading towards No Deal if the

EU refused to compromise, but if these claims by Reuters are true, it shows just how spineless she really is.

EU diplomats claim that the new proposal would involve Britain agreeing to an indefinite backstop solution for Ireland – but that if a backstop is triggered post Brexit, then the entirety of the UK would remain in the Customs Union and not just Northern Ireland. That means we'll have the same trade situation as NI, and we'll be united in that way...but we'll essentially be in the EU. This is a terrible plan. It's also not Brexit.

According to EU sources, the proposal would mean that there would be no need for customs checks on goods in Ireland – but again, I must reiterate...it's not Brexit.

This isn't just a compromise. It's a concession made on an existing, terrible compromise. This is even worse than what Boris Johnson predicted when he says Chequers makes the UK a vassal state.[8]

Today, the Irish Prime Minister Leo Varadkar will be meeting with Donald Tusk, Michel Barnier and Guy Verhofstadt in hope that a deal can be made over the next couple of months. November is getting closer, and we appear to be no closer to a deal.

If he's meeting Verfhofstadt, then I expect nothing but stalling, delays, and manipulation. This is a man who has railed against Brexit from the beginning, mocked Boris Johnson,[9] and said explicitly that he refuses to compromise[10] EU 'principles' to rescue the Tories from Brexit.

This isn't looking good people. Mrs May acted tough, the EU called her bluff, and now she's backing down.

10th October
Juncker's Got Moves Like May

At the Conservative Party Conference last week, Theresa May walked on stage doing the dance moves that made her famous during her trip to Africa. She walked onto the stage to 'Dancing Queen', and while the media mocked and the Brexiteers laughed, I thought it was pretty clever.

You can't be mocked if you're making fun of yourself! It made me want to like the Prime Minister again, but as soon as she finished her awkward, robotic dancing, I remember just how terrible she's been on Brexit.

And on the 9th October, during a speech in Brussels, Jean-Claude Druncker (Sorry, Juncker...) did a little shimmy on the stage.[11] His arms were spaced out in the same robotic way as Theresa's, and he had a big grin on his face as he did it. He looked like your dad when he's drunk on the dance floor at a Christening. Juncker knew exactly what he was doing – it was yet another dig at our Prime Minister.

We're allowed to do it, but I'll be damned if we let Eurocrats get away with it, too.

Amazingly, though – the European Commission claims[12] he wasn't mocking Mrs May at all. The Commission's chief spokesman, Margaritis Schinas, says that Juncker's dance was 'not directed at anyone' and was simply an 'improvisation'.

OK, sure.

This reeks to me as an authoritarian institution desperately trying to defend the honour of its drunk leader. It's also disturbing how they're willing to lie so easily. This is 1984 IN 2018. Left is right, up is down, right is wrong, and Juncker's dancing isn't mocking Theresa May. Ok...

11th October
Theresa May Set to Brief Ministers During DUP Crisis

Oh, the DUP. They've saved Brexit before, and they might well be doing it again. The party's 10 Westminster MPs who are currently propping up the Tory government are planning to vote down the Budget[13] later on this month if they aren't happy with the Brexit plans. Mrs May relies on these votes in the House of Commons, and if she can't strike a deal that stops barriers being made between Great Britain and Northern Ireland, then she could struggle to pass anything through Parliament at all.

The new Budget will take place on 29th October, and if the DUP vote it down, it could lead to a vote of no confidence in the Prime Minister. Did someone say Prime Minister Boris Johnson?

Theresa May is set to brief ministers amidst this tension, and just before a summit takes place in Brussels next week. The EU doesn't like her plan, the DUP doesn't like her plan, the Tories don't like her plan, and Labour doesn't like her plan. Does anyone?

The Prime Minister has called a meeting of cabinet ministers to discuss the problem, which according to Ben Wright of the BBC[14], is an attempt to 'bind ministers into Number 10's approach'.

Unless she has something new up her sleeve, I don't see why or how Tory ministers would get on board now if they already haven't. And, in order for anything to change, we'll need to see a new deal on how to manage border checks between Northern Ireland and the Republic of Ireland, and a new plan for the divide between NI and GB. I'm not confident, are you?

12th October
Mrs May Has Until Monday to Stop Cabinet Walkouts Over Brexit

I've been saying it for a while; the cabinet doesn't like Mrs May's Brexit plans, the EU doesn't like them, Labour doesn't like them, and the voters don't like them. Now, it's finally catching up with the Prime Minister, and she's just been given the weekend to change her Brexit plans to avoid a Cabinet walkout. Of course, she may choose not to make any changes – she is a 'bloody difficult woman' after all – but who knows what new hell that would bring to her doorstep?

A senior Cabinet source has told Business Insider[15] that the Prime Minister is now facing a 'killer moment' in the Brexit talks, and that Brexiteers within the Cabinet are not happy with her refusal to put a definite end-point on her plans for the backstop. The fear being, of course, that Britain might be stuck in the Customs Union for the foreseeable future while the UK and the EU battle it out over trade deals for goodness knows how long.

But Downing Street has insisted already[16] that the government is not going to sign any deal with the EU that would keep the UK in its Customs Union indefinitely – a start for Mrs May in her attempt at keeping her Cabinet together.

The national press is reporting that British negotiators over in Brussels have been planning to sign up to a new backstop option that would keep the whole of the UK in the Customs Union to stop Britain being divided from Northern Ireland. So it's not clear who to believe right now – all we know is that the Prime Minister has two days to sort out this mess that could have been solved a long time ago.

Jacob Rees-Mogg and the European Research Group have already put forward plans for a Canada+ deal that could solve these issues, but it remains unclear whether

May will eventually concede it's the best option we have. The Canada+ deal is an expansion of the current Comprehensive Economic and Trade Agreement (CETA) that integrated EU and Canadian markets. The '+' element refers to the greater liberalisation of the trade in services, and the inclusion of financial services within the agreement. This boosts the British economy, puts us on a good footing on the world economic stage, and could even solve the NI/GB issue. Mogg and his colleagues at the ERG propose a technological solution at the NI/Republic border that could make the CETA+ option extremely desirable for Britain.

It all depends on how stubborn Mrs May is feeling. It seems like she saves her stubbornness for the British people, rather than the Eurocrats who are knocking back every proposal that she offers. That surely won't go down well with her Cabinet, and if she makes the wrong decision, they could be gone by Monday.

Meanwhile, the October UK/EU summit is around the corner – and it's looking increasingly likely that there'll be an emergency summit in November to finalise whatever deal the government manages to scrape together.

15th October
After a Weekend of Plotting, Ireland is Still the Brexit Sticking Point

Theresa May was given the weekend to solve some major Brexit issues, or risk a Cabinet walkout. The weekend has been and gone and we don't seem to have moved. Mrs May today gave a speech to the Commons, outlining how she believes that a deal is still achievable. She gave the House an update before Wednesday's summit with the European Union, explaining:[17]

> *"We are entering the final stages of these negotiations. This is the time for cool,*

calm heads to prevail, and it's the time for
a clear-eyed focus on the few remaining
but critical issues that are still to be
agreed."

She was met with much heckling and laughter, of course – before explaining how on Sunday, the Secretary of State for Exiting the European Union, Dominic Raab, went for further talks with Michel Barnier. She said there has been a great deal of inaccurate speculation about the meeting, and that in fact, great progress on both the Withdrawal Agreement and the political declaration our future relationship with the EU.

But have we? Really? It feels like we're still where we were a few months ago – still stuck on the Ireland border issue.[18] We have been bouncing back and forth over the backstop issue. Mrs May wants a backstop solution that keeps the entire UK in the Customs Union and Single Market. Brexiteers, obviously, don't want that. Nor will we accept it.

If the backstop includes Northern Ireland only, then it creates a border down the Irish Sea between GB and NI. That divides the United Kingdom, and still, the question remains…how long will the backstop be in place? Brexiteers want to know when the end of the backstop will be, and how much time we will offer to allow negotiations to continue. The European Union, however, would prefer the backstop have no such deadline, so they can effectively keep Northern Ireland in the European Union. I hope this is making sense to you.

There must be a border in Ireland somewhere. If one half of Ireland is staying in the European Union, and the other half isn't, then the border needs to go somewhere. If it goes between Northern Ireland and the Republic, then that contravenes the Good Friday Agreement. If it goes down the Irish Sea, then it divides Northern Ireland and Great Britain…and the DUP won't let that happen.

That's perhaps why Mrs May is considering ditching the DUP. The religious, conservative, Irish defenders of Brexit were originally the kingmakers after the 2017 election, giving the Tories the last few votes they needed in a Confidence and Supply deal. Now, they might be kicked to the curb.

The Express reports[19] that the Prime Minister is ready to dump the DUP and gamble on her plan for Brexit being voted through Parliament without their support. Somehow, I guess, she thinks she might be able to get enough of Labour on board to vote for her Brexit 'compromise'. It's a bold move, and one that could potentially let her have her own way on Brexit.

So far, though, things aren't looking good. Number 10 sources claim[20] that the talks with the EU are now actually stuck in an impasse, because the EU wants to implement a 'backstop to the backstop'. Their idea is to keep Northern Ireland in the Customs Union permanently. But Mrs May, being the bloody difficult woman she is, has said she won't settle for it. So there we are. I suppose we need to wait until later this week when the Prime Minister meets her counterparts in Brussels to try and talk over the final deal.

This is all getting rather repetitive, isn't it?

17th October
Mrs May is Back in Brussels, with Nothing to Show for Herself

There have already been so many 'crunch days' for Brexit, but today really is important. Today, Theresa May is holding meetings with key figures across the EU, before leaving to let the European leaders discuss over dinner what they plan to do next. She's on the continent in the hope that she can win over European Council President Donald Tusk, Irish premiere Leo Varadkar, and President of the European Commission Jean-Claude Juncker.

Mrs May told the press that she believes 'intensive' work[21] is needed now to overcome the differences over the Irish border situation, but that she still thinks a deal is possible. You have to hand it to her – she's at least determined to get her **own** deal through.

The summit today was a big occasion. The leaders of the remaining 27 EU member states were going to give the go-ahead for an emergency summit to be held in November, where the terms of Britain's withdrawal from the EU would be finalised. This was meant to happen this month, but alas, the can is still being kicked down the road. It remains to be seen whether the go-ahead will be given. It all depends on how much progress Mrs May has made today over the Northern Ireland border issue. I suspect, however, that no such progress will be made. Michel Barnier, the EU's chief Brexit negotiator, is expected to say today that the talks have not resulted in the 'decisive progress' that the EU wanted to see before agreeing to a new, emergency summit in November.

This is the moment that any decent leader would back out, but Mrs May is clinging on there. You know that really tacky poster you used to see in offices years ago, of the cat hanging on to a washing line, which read 'Hang in there, baby!' at the bottom? That's Theresa. She's a cat clinging onto a washing line, being poked with a stick by pesky local kids, while her other feline mates should from the sidelines that it's time to let go and chase the kids that have been poking her. The EU is taking advantage of us, and we don't have to take it.

So what happens if Mrs May just refuses to let go, refuses to abandon the talks, and refuses to change her

Chequers proposal? Well, the EU might simply reject a summit in November…and that causes serious problems. We're heading towards new European Parliament elections, which is going to take up a lot of the EU's time. The year is almost over, and we have to leave by March next year. If the summit is pushed back even further, we're looking at a couple of options – either No Deal, or Theresa caves and we get the worst deal possible.

But until later this evening, we won't know. Who knows, perhaps Mrs May has something up her sleeve. But I wouldn't hold your breath.

18th October
EU Prepared to Extend Post-Brexit Transition Period

After all this drama over the last few days, with Theresa May meeting EU officials in Brussels and trying to thrash out the final parts of the deal and come to an agreement about a November summit, we've come back to just kicking the can down the road. Mrs May finally came to a brick wall at the end of the road, but she's knocked right through it and carried on kicking the can through the gardens and alleyways behind it.

The Prime Minister has repeatedly said during press conferences today and yesterday that she doesn't *intend* to extend the transition period, but that it is an *option*. That option, it seems, might be exactly what's about to happen.

During a press conference today, she said:[22]

> *"I'm not standing here proposing an extension to the implementation period. What has now emerged is the idea that an option to extend the implementation period could be a further solution to this*

issue of the backstop in Northern Ireland,"

Mrs May today announced in a press conference that the current 21-month deal might be extended by 'a few months' if necessary. She proposed this as an option that would help her government and the EU come to an agreement about the areas they agree on, and have more time to solve issues they didn't agree on – namely, the Irish backstop issue. According to an EU source who spoke to the BBC[23], however, there would have to be 'financial implications' if the UK did decide to extend this transition period. So we could be in for yet another hefty bill.

There are some other theories about why the Prime Minister is doing this, however. Tom Newton Dunn, the Political Editor for The Sun, tweeted today:[24]

"Why would the PM appear to commit near political suicide by flaunting a transition extension? Because, I'm told, she thinks it may be the only way to re-engage Barnier. Appears No10 are now v worried that EU27 are close to pulling the plug entirely, and ready to go for no deal".

And that really could be it. A few weeks ago when Mrs May demanded respect from the EU and told them the ball was in their court, the EU responded by saying...well, nothing. Perhaps this is Theresa trying to provoke them into reacting again. It may have worked, too.

At the end of the summit, Donald Tusk told journalists that while there was no major breakthrough on the Ireland border issue, he was in a 'much better mood' than the previous summit in Salzburg.

Jean-Claude Juncker also publicly stated that the extension of the Brexit transition period 'probably will happen'[25], and that a 'No Deal' scenario would be dangerous for both Britain and the EU. Translation: bad for the EU. So it could well be that by the time of the next summit in November, there could be some kind of process in place for us to leave in March. But it could mean that the UK is tied to EU rules for longer, and that the next few months will remain turbulent and uncertain.

Merkel even thinks that a Brexit deal might be possible, stating that she had left the dinner table after the summit yesterday 'neither more pessimistic nor more optimistic' than before. She even said "where there is a will, there is a way, that is usually the case" – and we all know that there is, secretly, a will within the EU to strike a deal. They know they need us, and there's only so long they can keep on bluffing. Time is ticking and they know it's in their interests to make some kind of deal. If we leave without a deal, we're able to become as competitive as we like, and we know they don't want that.

Yesterday and today were meant to be pivotal moments for Brexit, but yet again, we've been let down and misled. Nothing has happened, *still*, and I'm getting tired of it. So is every other Brexiteer and regular person in this country who just want the politicians to listen to them.

That's why Boris Johnson and David Davis have reminded Theresa May that the British people will not forgive them if there is a Brexit surrender. The two Brexiteer Tories issued their first joint intervention[26] since they both left the cabinet, writing an open letter to Theresa May that reminds her why getting on with Brexit is important. They stated that the Chequers plan is 'less popular with the public than the poll tax' and she should 'reset' the negotiations and begin negotiating a Canada-style free trade deal.

Interventions at this stage, however, seem futile to me.

19th October
Could David Davis be PM as Early as Next Week?

Just a few months ago, I reported that David Davis could be installed as an interim Prime Minister to see the government through the Brexit process, and everyone I mentioned it to scoffed. Most thought it was ludicrous, that it wouldn't even be constitutional, and that something so dramatic surely wouldn't happen. But, it might.

After returning from Brussels without making any substantial progress, the Prime Minister has faced substantial criticism from both Remain and Leave MPs and campaigners – and now, more letters of no confidence are being submitted to the chairman of the 1922 Committee this week. Two more letters are reported to have been sent[27], increasing Mrs May's chances of being ousted in the coming weeks or months.

The Sunday Times reports[28] that between 42 and 44 letters of no confidence have now been submitted, meaning as little as four more letters could be needed to trigger a vote of no confidence. It could be as quick as a week before she's gone.

Boris Johnson's friends in the Tory Party are claiming that Boris is struggle to build a large enough support base of MPs to put him on the ballot paper in a leadership contest, too – which is something I've been talking about for a while. In the event of a Tory leadership contest, Tory MPs will vote for two candidates to be put on a ballot that would be sent to members. I see no way that enough Tory MPs would vote for Boris – but Davis? Davis, maybe.

The Mail on Sunday says that Davis is the Brexiteer 'candidate of choice', and I find it hard to disagree with. Johnson is polarising, and Rees-Mogg is so visibly posh that he'd struggle to get the support of the working class.

That is, unless he went full Enoch Powell. Davis is the only choice, and I think he'd be a steady pair of hands in these negotiations.

The question is, though, whether Davis would run in a leadership election or whether Tory MPs would be happy to have him installed as an interim leader. I suspect the latter would be the best option. There's no time for an election, with Brexit looming.

21st October
Another Rocky Weekend for Mrs May

It's been another rocky weekend for the Prime Minister, so far. Mrs May is facing a Cabinet revolt, after a conference call with her ministers that lasted 90 minutes. She was once again trying to keep her Cabinet on board while she plans to tell the public on Monday that the Brexit deal is 95% done. But a no confidence vote is lingering and closer than ever.

While the Prime Minister plays a game of chicken with the European Union, her job is literally on the line – and so is the future of this country. She seems perfectly willing to gamble it all.

She will still hold Cabinet as usual on Tuesday, but Wednesday looks to be another dramatic day with her Tory Members of Parliament. Her next Brexit cabinet meeting will be held on Thursday, but at this point, I wouldn't be surprised if the final four Members of Parliament needed to trigger a vote of no confidence are impelled to write those last few letters. I wrote last week that David Davis could be PM by next week, and I don't think it's off the cards. He'd need to be installed as an interim PM rather than going through the lengthier leadership contest – but with Brexit around the corner, Parliamentary Tories would be wise to make that decision.

22nd October
The Operation to Oust May is Well and Truly Underway

ITV journalist Robert Peston, writing on Facebook, has claimed that there is an operation currently in progress by Tory Brexiteers to encourage more backbenchers to write letters to the chair of the 1922 Committee.

He writes:[29]

> *There is an operation in progress by Tory Brexiters to persuade fellow backbenchers to write to Graham Brady, chair of the 1922 backbench committee, calling for a vote of no confidence in Theresa May as leader of their party.*
>
> *This is what one of them told me:*
>
> *"I'm campaigning myself. We need 60-70 letters, not 48...I know people who are putting letters in today. I think we are the closest ever to her going and I think, thank God, this could be it".*
> *The reference to 48 letters is the threshold for triggering the vote. But this MP wants a comfortable margin above that, so that the PM can see that a sizeable number of her colleagues want her to go.*
>
> *This is not an exquisitely centralised and coordinated campaign against her. It is an emotional outpouring, largely by Brexiters, that May's version of Brexit betrays what they see as the most important prize of leaving the EU, namely "taking back control".*

Referencing the idea of David Davis being an interim PM, he explained how Davis has become 'Brexit marmite', and that many Tory 'centrist' MPs have said that they wouldn't vote for him. But that begs the question...who would they vote for? Would the majority of the Tories who are 'centrist' and even Remain actually vote for another Remainer as leader? Would they be that masochistic, or even suicidal?

Revolt is definitely in the air, though – and Peston isn't the only one to say it. Over the weekend, unnamed Conservatives told the Sunday papers that 'assassination is in the air' and Theresa May is entering 'the killing zone'. A former Tory minister even said:

> "The moment is coming when the knife gets heated, stuck in her front and twisted. She'll be dead soon".

The graphic language has, of course, been denounced by some. The tragic murder of Jo Cox has been dragged into it, with Sarah Wollaston, the chair of the Health and Social Care Committee, stating:[30]

> *"Totally unacceptable. Have they learned nothing following the assassination of Jo Cox?"*

I mean, come on. Things are getting heated, but I don't think Mrs May is under any physical threat from her Tory colleagues. They want her out, but they don't literally want her dead. But of course, there's now a campaign to unveil the MPs who used the language, and everyone is getting on board the Offended Express. Yvette Cooper MP of the Labour Party has even gotten on board, slamming the 'vile and dehumanising language'[31]. Which is funny...I don't remember Cooper speaking up when Ken Clarke called UKIP voters 'racists' and 'clowns'[32], or any other time working class people have been smeared by the Westminster elite. This is just a clever and convenient way to distract the media and scare MPs who might want to send a letter to the 1922 Committee. I can see right through this.

One thing that's for certain, however, is that the operation to oust her is quite evidently underway. Cooper is getting involved with this campaign against Tory Brexiteers who said hurty words about Mrs May simply because she's fearful of the Brexit revolt that's coming within the Tory Party. And, this language wouldn't be used if Parliamentarians weren't passionate, and didn't believe her when she says a deal is right around the corner.

In Other News…

Owen Paterson (MP for North Shropshire), Iain Duncan Smith, and Lord Trimble met Michel Barnier today[33]. They had a 'long and constructive' meeting where they discussed the European Research Groups' solution to the Northern Ireland border, which includes using technology to manage and process crossings between the Republic of Ireland and Northern Ireland.

Some say this simply went behind the Prime Minister's back. Maybe they did – but regardless, it's good to see the ERG speaking directly to the European Union and outlining alternative proposals that are no doubt more attractive.

Speaking to reporters, Owen Paterson explained:

> *"Further to my letter to my letter Michel Barnier back in September, when we published our European Research Group paper on how we can help resolve issues around all of the UK's papers, with particular reference to Northern Ireland, and we believe using existing techniques, existing processes and all within existing*

> *EU law we can continue to trade pretty much seamlessly across all borders without breaching the integrity of the European Customs Union and Single Market, which is obviously fundamental to them.*
> *"We had a long and constructive meeting with Mr Barnier, and his staff, and we are going to go back and report the details to our colleagues and our own Government.*
> *"I'm afraid we can't negotiate in public and we are not negotiating on behalf of our Government."*

23rd October
Theresa May's 4-Point-Plan to Make Break the Brexit Deadlock

Amidst turmoil in her party, and reports that 48 letters have now been submitted[34] to the 1922 committee calling for a vote of confidence, the Prime Minister is today briefing her cabinet that Brexit is '95% done' and that her four-point-plan could unlock further Brexit talks.

Mrs May has been stuck in a deadlock with the European Union essentially since the Salzburg summit, and no matter how much she speaks positively about her most recent summit, the fact remains that nothing has changed in terms of the UK/EU disagreement on the Northern Ireland border and backstop issue.

So the Prime Minister is pushing her new four-point plan that she believes will unblock further Brexit talks in Brussels. The plan was revealed in a statement to the House of Commons, and one proposal includes the possibility of an extended Brexit 'transition' period that goes right up to 2021.

Another point refers to a new backstop solution that would be built on a 'commitment to a temporary UK-EU joint customs territory' if no trade deal agreement can be made. This means the backstop solution applies to the whole of the UK rather than just Northern Ireland, meaning that Britain won't be separated from Ireland...but the United Kingdom also won't be separated from the EU. So yes, you can be sure that this is another Brexit betrayal.

Mrs May also says[35] that the government will ensure that full access for Northern Ireland businesses to Great Britain must be guaranteed in the deal, and that the UK must always reserve the right to leave the EU at will, and not be locked into any arrangements. Those final two sound perfectly good, but she's missing the mark on a simple requirement of Brexit in her earlier points. Brexit must entail the United Kingdom leaving the European Union.

How exactly this new four-point plan will unblock talks, however...I don't know. It seems like Barnier and the EU have been against all of this from the start, so I'm not sure how the Prime Minister thinks things will change now.

Reports Suggest 48 Letters Have Been Submitted: Will May Now be Removed?

An unnamed source has told Paul Waugh of the Huffington Post that the 48 letters required to trigger a vote of no confidence in Theresa May have now been sent. Waugh wrote on Twitter:

> *"Today's #WaughZone is in your inbox folks. One source tells me the 48 letters threshold, needed for a vote of confidence in Theresa May, has been passed. Only Sir Graham Brady knows for sure".*

145

Honestly, I believed it was technically possible, but that no Tory MP would want to be responsible for handing in those final four letters that would essentially get Mrs May removed from her role. But it might just have happened. An anonymous Tory MP told The Sun[36] that he and two of his colleagues would be sending in letters yesterday – and as we know, at the beginning of this week, we were waiting on four final letters. I wonder who handed in that final one? That must have felt good. Or terrifying.

The Prime Minister knew this was coming. Two days ago, she wrote for The Sun[37] that she vowed to do Brexit her way, and continue with her Brexit plan even if it meant losing her job. As a politician, she should have been aware and mindful of the fact that politicians tend to lose their job when they go against the will of the people. She claims to be making the 'right choices, not the easy ones' – but if the whole country is against her, shouldn't that tell her she's doing something wrong?

Mrs May should expect roughly half the country to be disappointed with her plan. That would be representative of the 2016 referendum results. If almost the entire country is against you, you should know you've taken a wrong turn.

So, the next step is that the chairman of the 1922 Committee must check the number of letters and go from there. We've read before that the aim is to provide significantly more than 48 letters to show the Prime Minister that those who now oppose her leadership are not a small minority. Whether more people are encouraged to come forward now they won't technically be responsible for crossing the threshold, I don't know.

24th October
Bad News: Theresa May Survives the 1922 Committee

So it happened. The number of letters submitted to the 1922 Committee from Tory MPs reached 50 – two more than the 48 required to trigger a vote of confidence. And so, Theresa May today met with rebel MPs to discuss her future and their concerns. This should be the beginning of a confidence vote in the House of Commons, but amazingly, it looks like the rebels have chickened out.

We learned a couple of days ago that Number 10 planted decoy letters to the 1922 Committee, which would have alerted the Prime Minister to an incoming threat. The theory is that when Sir Graham, the chair of the 1922 Committee, receives the required 48 letters, he would go back to those who submitted the letters and ask them to confirm they have not changed their mind. When the decoy MPs receive this notice from Sir Graham, they can inform the Prime Minister that they are close to reaching the required number of letters and action can be taken.

The Evening Standard received the news[38] that as many as eight letters from MPs loyal to the Prime Minister had been submitted, meaning that over the last few days it was possible we weren't as close to achieving the 48 we needed after all. But today changed everything.

We reached 50 letters[39]. That meant Theresa May had to face the 1922 Committee earlier today to answer for herself and hear from Members of Parliament who are unhappy with her leadership and direction.

I wish I had better news to report, but it appears that those who submitted the letters have lost their backbone. Not only are we being betrayed by Tory Remainers, but it seems that Tory Brexiteers have lost their backbones too. Theresa May has survived the 1922 Committee meeting.

Every single Member of Parliament in that meeting agreed with the Prime Minister that they need to remain united, and she needs to stay in her position.

Jessica Elgot of The Guardian tweeted:[40]

> *One MP leaves declaring "outbreak of unity... not a single dissenting voice" at the 1922. Is she safe? "Well, you look over the cliff, consider the alternative, and then think, hmmmm, perhaps not."*

The reports in the press sound like the meeting ended with a very happy bunch of MPs with a new-found confidence in the Prime Minister. Tory MP for Torridge and West Devon, Geoffrey Cox, claimed the Prime Minister's speech was 'very good'[41].

Sky News reported Alan McGuinness tweeted:[42]

> *"Very happy. All good" smiles one MP as they stride out of the committee room.*

McGuinness also claimed[43] that former Home Secretary Amber Rudd even claimed that the Prime Minister is in a "stronger position" than before the meeting, and that she "spoke emotionally and personally". MPs in turn reassured her that they will condemn any further violent language about her.

But that's not what this is about, and it never has been. This was supposed to be the crunch meeting that resulted in an ousting. Those 50 people signed those letters to say they were unhappy with May's leadership – but somehow, the Prime Minister has walked out having gained sympathy points, and the backing of rebel MPs who have shown they have absolutely no backbone.

I'm sorry to say, but it looks like Mrs May is sticking this one out. I briefly had some faith in rebel Tories. Now I'm back to being my usual cynical self. There is literally nobody in Parliament that can be trusted. Not one.

We are being betrayed not just by the Remainers, but by the Tories who claim to be standing up for Brexit. What a scam.

25th October
78% Think May Will Fail on Brexit

A poll by Ipsos MORI for the Evening Standard found that 78% of Brits think May won't get a good Brexit deal.

The new poll revealed by the Evening Standard is pretty devastating for the Prime Minister. It reveals that confidence in Theresa May is lower than ever.

The Standard reports:[44]

> *Confidence in the Prime Minister to get a good deal in the Brexit negotiations has fallen to its lowest level yet. Just 19 per cent - fewer than a fifth - of Britons think she can pull it off, a figure that has plunged from 28 per cent last month. Some 78 per cent think she will fail, up eight points in a month.*
>
> *Some 43 per cent think they will personally be worse off after Brexit, which has shot up from 36 per cent a year ago. Only 18 per cent think their standard of living will rise, despite the Brexiteer promises of prosperity outside the EU's giant trade bloc, which is down two*

points. One in three thinks Brexit will make no difference.

Almost half the country, 49 per cent, feel the negotiations are going worse than expected.

I mean, when Theresa has negotiated Brexit this badly, is it any wonder people might be thinking negatively about Brexit? Theresa May took an amazing opportunity and she ruined it.

And just when we thought we might be fighting back, and we might be able to change course last minute, the Prime Minister managed to survive a 1922 Committee meeting.

We exceeded the 48-letter minimum required to push a vote of confidence in the Prime Minister. 50 letters were submitted to the chair of the 1922 committee, and the Prime Minister was made to face Members of Parliament who have lost faith in her leadership.

Somehow, though, she survived the meeting. This shocked me. Why on earth would those people submit the letters in the first place if they were only going to back down last minute and support her when they met face-to-face?

Jessica Elgot of The Guardian tweeted:

One MP leaves declaring "outbreak of unity... not a single dissenting voice" at the 1922. Is she safe? "Well, you look over the cliff, consider the alternative, and then think, hmmmm, perhaps not."[45]

The reports in the press sound like the meeting ended with a very happy bunch of MPs with new-found confidence in the Prime Minister. Tory MP for Torridge and West

Devon, Geoffrey Cox, claimed the Prime Minister's speech was 'very good'[46].

Sky News reported Alan McGuinness tweeted[47]:

> *"Very happy. All good" smiles one MP as*
> *they stride out of the committee room.*

McGuinness also claimed[48] that former Home Secretary Amber Rudd even stated that the Prime Minister is in a "stronger position" than before the meeting, and that she "spoke emotionally and personally". MPs in turn reassured her that they will condemn any further violent language about her.

So, not only can we not trust Remain Tories, but we can no longer trust Brexit Tories. Brexit MPs got so close to ousting May, and backed out last minute.

The great Brexit betrayal is no exaggeration. It's happening right in front of you.

26th October
France Confirms the Calais 'Go-Slow' is Another Fearmongering Lie

How many times have we been told that a No Deal Brexit would result in a 'go-slow' policy at the port of Calais, which would force companies to use alternate ports and cause huge delays in transport? It has been repeated over and over again by the national press, but just like with the lie about planes being turned around from France, we've learned that the French government actually intends to put measures in place to ensure the 'fluidity' of trade.

Time after time we're told of the great threat that No Deal poses, as if it wasn't in the interest of France and other

European nations to work with the UK on sensible trade and travel agreements.

UK Brexit Secretary Dominic Raab warned earlier in the week that there would be major disruption in a 'worst case scenario', forcing British companies to use different ports. However, the President of the Hauts-de-France region, Xavier Bertrand, has said that in fact, ensuring the 'fluidity' of trade between the UK and France was essential.

The BBC reports[49] that another official said that closing the Calais port would be an 'economic suicide mission' – meaning, therefore, that France has no intention of stopping or hindering trade in the event of a No Deal Brexit.

When will our politicians learn that European leaders are going to talk tough because they want the best deal for them, and many of them even want to hurt the UK? Of course, big claims are going to be made, but if our leaders scratched the surface of these negotiations they'd see that there are plenty of officials without a political agenda who simply want to maintain easy trade and travel.

I also don't understand why Raab is adding to the fears. If Bertrand is talking about maintaining trade fluidity, why did Raab tell the House of Commons that France might choose to create additional delays? He said in Parliament:

> *"We also need to prepare for the worst-case scenario where the authorities at Calais are deliberately directing a go-slow approach by supporting a diversion of the flow of more amenable ports in other countries".*

Bertrand responded on Twitter[50] that it was 'not envisaged'.

So stop worrying, people. Our politicians are either completely useless or trying to scare us again – and after so-called 'rebel' MPs decided to support Theresa May at the recent 1922 Committee, I wouldn't put anything past so-called 'Brexiteer' Tories any more.

31st October
Raab Says We'll Have a Deal by 21st November

Could it really be true? Brexit Secretary Dominic Raab says that we could have a deal[53] with the European Union by the 21st November. Raab told a Brexit select committee that he would be happy to appear before them to provide evidence once the deal is finished, and that would currently be expected to be the 21st November.

So you might remember from my earlier reports that this was initially meant to be completed in October. Then it was moved to early November. Now, it looks to be late November...and who knows what will happen in the next three weeks?

Raab's department has confirmed that there is 'no set date for the negotiations to conclude', which means the date set for the 21st could in fact be completely meaningless. Ireland's foreign minister has said that it is now down to the UK to intensify the talks, suggesting that we're still stuck in the same old stalemate.

In the same letter to the Brexit select committee's chairman, Hilary Benn MP, Raab did say that the end of these negotiations was 'firmly in sight', and that the only remaining obstacles were something he felt the government was willing to navigate around.

He said:

"An agreement on the details of that backstop should be possible…We have resolved most of the issue and we are building up together what the future relationship should look like and making real progress".

I guess we'll see. Half of me wants this to be over and done with. We've waited years already. But I also know that as soon as we end up with a 'deal' from the EU, Brexit will have been betrayed.

References

[1] The Guardian, "Brussels rejects Theresa May's plea to break Brexit deadlock", Jennifer Rankin and Daniel Boffey, 1st October 2018,
https://www.theguardian.com/politics/2018/oct/01/eu-brussels-rejects-plea-from-theresa-may-to-break-brexit-deadlock

[2] The Guardian, "May appeals to 'decent patriots' in effort to halt Johnson leadership bid", Dan Sabbagh and Pippa Crerar, 2nd October 2018,
https://www.theguardian.com/politics/2018/oct/02/conservative-conference-boris-johnson-slams-chequers-outrage-in-direct-pitch-to-tory-members

[3] BBC News, "Theresa May on why Boris Johnson speech made her cross", BBC News, 2nd October 2018,
https://www.bbc.co.uk/news/uk-politics-45722675[1] BBC News, "Theresa May on why Boris Johnson speech made her cross", BBC News, 2nd October 2018,
https://www.bbc.co.uk/news/uk-politics-45722675

[4] The Guardian, "Boris Johnson appears to mock PM with 'field of wheat' run", Pippa Carerar, 1st October 2018,
https://www.theguardian.com/politics/2018/oct/01/boris-johnson-appears-to-mock-pm-with-field-of-wheat-run

[5] The Guardian, "Brexit: DUP threatens to pull plug on Theresa May's government", Lisa O'Carroll and Daniel Boffey, 2nd October 2018,
https://www.theguardian.com/politics/2018/oct/02/brexit-eu-hits-out-irresponsible-uk-northern-ireland

[6] Twitter, "So far @theresa_may's speech sounds like the relaunch of the SDP. Politically correct beyond belief.", Nigel Farage, 3rd October 2018,
https://twitter.com/Nigel_Farage/status/1047447345951068161

[7] BBC News, "Theresa May: Tories must be a party for everyone", BBC News, 3rd October 2018,
https://www.bbc.co.uk/news/uk-politics-45725615

[8] The Guardian, "Boris Johnson breaks ranks with Brexit 'vassal state' warning", Heather Stewart, 17th December 2018,
https://www.theguardian.com/politics/2017/dec/17/boris-johnson-breaks-ranks-with-brexit-vassal-state-warning

[9] The New European, "'He's better at burning bridges than building bridges' – Negotiator mocks Boris' bridge plan", Jonathan Read, 2nd October 2018,
https://www.theneweuropean.co.uk/top-stories/guy-verhofstadt-criticises-boris-johnson-jacob-rees-mogg-and-jeremy-hunt-1-5719029

[10] Independent, "We won't compromise our principles to rescue the Tory party from Brexit, Guy Verhofstadt warns Theresa May", Jon Stone, 2nd October 2018,
https://www.independent.co.uk/news/uk/politics/brexit-latest-theresa-may-guy-verhofstadt-tory-conference-european-parliament-eu-a8564401.html

[11] Sputnik International, "WATCH EU's Juncker Ape Theresa May's 'Dancing Queen' Moves Prior to EC Speech",
https://sputniknews.com/europe/201810091068716868-juncher-dance-May-mocking/

[12] Politico, "Juncker was not mocking Theresa May's dance moves, says Commission", Paul Dallison, 10th October 2018,
https://www.politico.eu/article/jean-claude-juncker-was-not-mocking-theresa-may-dance-moves-says-european-commission/

Chapter Five: October 2018

[13] BBC News, "DUP 'could vote against the Budget' over Brexit deal", BBC News, 10th October 2018,
https://www.bbc.co.uk/news/uk-politics-45806063

[14] BBC News, "Esther McVey won't say if she backs PM's EU trade plan", BBC News, 11th October 2018,
https://www.bbc.co.uk/news/uk-politics-45818777

[15] Business Insider, "Theresa May given until Monday to change her Brexit plan or suffer Cabinet walkouts", Adam Payne, 12th October 2018,
http://uk.businessinsider.com/theresa-may-weekend-to-change-her-brexit-backstop-plan-and-avoid-cabinet-resignations-2018-10

[16] The Guardian, "Brexit: No 10 says it will not agree to indefinite Customs Union with EU", Heather Stewart, 12th October 2018,
https://www.theguardian.com/politics/2018/oct/12/brexit-theresa-may-no-10-indefinite-customs-union-eu-ireland-backstop

[17] BBC News, "Theresa May says Brexit deal still 'achievable' despite differences", BBC News, 15th October 2018,
https://www.bbc.co.uk/news/uk-politics-45868503

[18] BBC News, "Brexit talks hit 'real problem' over Northern Ireland border", BBC News, 15th October 2018,
https://www.bbc.co.uk/news/uk-politics-45859282

[19] Express, "Theresa May ready to DUMP DUP to force Brexit plans through Parliament", Ciaran Macgrath, 13th October 2018,
https://www.express.co.uk/news/politics/1031035/brexit-news-theresa-may-dup-parliament-arlene-foster-backstop

[20] The Telegraph, "Brexit deal is 'achievable', Theresa May tells MPs as she is challenged in the Commons by Boris Johnson", Christopher Hope, 15th October 2018,
https://www.telegraph.co.uk/politics/2018/10/15/brexit-talks-hold-eu-wants-second-backstop-number-10-says/?fbclid=IwAR0tCUYDMRs7hREXW6cKcC2mdUp6yPyzBrTd_dd6XcbViiELakTdlfdjyCs

[21] BBC News, "Theresa May: Brexit deal possible with intensive work", 17th October 2018,
https://www.bbc.co.uk/news/uk-politics-45882360

[22] The Guardian, "Theresa May plays down idea of extending Brexit transition after fierce Tory backlash - as it happened", Andrew Sparrow, 18th October 2018,
https://www.theguardian.com/politics/blog/live/2018/oct/18/brexit-may-faces-angry-backlash-from-mps-over-proposals-for-transition-and-meaningful-vote-politics-live

[23] BBC News, "Brexit: EU ready to extend transition period", 18th October 2018,
https://www.bbc.co.uk/news/uk-politics-45897253

[24] Twitter, "Why would the PM appear to commit near political suicide by flaunting a transition extension?", Tom Newton Dunn, 18th October 2918,
https://twitter.com/tnewtondunn/status/1052883515954540544

[25] The Guardian, "EU leaders ready to help May sell Brexit deal to parliament", Daniel Boffey, Heather Stewart and Jennifer Rankin, 18th October 2018,
https://www.theguardian.com/politics/2018/oct/18/juncker-extension-brexit-transition-period-probably-will-happen

[26] The Telegraph, "Boris Johnson and David Davis tell Theresa May the British people 'will not forgive us' for Brexit surrender", Steven Swinford, 18th October 2018,
https://www.telegraph.co.uk/politics/2018/10/17/boris-johnson-david-davis-tell-theresa-may-british-people-will/

Chapter Five: October 2018

[27] Express, "BREXIT REVOLT: David Davis to oust May as Tories rebel over 'DEAD' plan?", Joe Duggan, 19th October 2018, https://www.express.co.uk/news/politics/1033767/brexit-latest-theresa-may-david-davis-lord-bridges

[28] The Times, "Cabinet mutiny threatens to kill Theresa May's Brexit", Tim Shipman and Caroline Wheeler, 14th October 2018, https://www.thetimes.co.uk/edition/news/cabinet-mutiny-threatens-to-kill-theresa-mays-brexit-gq895gjjj?utm_source=POLITICO.EU&utm_campaign=ed97518b10-EMAIL_CAMPAIGN_2018_10_14_02_03&utm_medium=email&utm_term=0_10959edeb5-ed97518b10-189777729

[29] Facebook, "There is an operation in progress by Tory Brexiters to persuade fellow backbenchers to write to Graham Brady, chair of the 1922 backbench ...", Robert Person posted on Facebook, 22nd October 2018, https://www.facebook.com/1498276767163730/posts/2192212034436863/

[30] Mail Online, "Theresa May slams 'dehumanising and derogatory' language that has 'no place in our politics' after anonymous Tories make violent claims she will be 'assassinated' over Brexit", Tim Sculthorpe, 22nd October 2018, https://www.dailymail.co.uk/news/article-6302565/Have-learned-Jo-Cox-Backlash-violent-claims-PM-killing-zone.html

[31] The Guardian, "Calls to remove Tory whip after 'disgraceful' remarks about May", Jessica Elgot and Peter Walker, 22nd October 2018, https://www.theguardian.com/politics/2018/oct/22/tories-identify-mps-vile-language-theresa-may-yvette-cooper

[32] Mail Online, "UKIP voters are racists, says Clarke: Minister in 'clowns' jibe as Tories declare war on Farage's party", Tim Shipman, 28th April 2018, https://www.dailymail.co.uk/news/article-2316033/UKIP-voters-racists-Ken-Clarke-clowns-jibe-Tories-declare-war-Nigel-Farages-party.html

[33] Express, "Brexiteers meet Barnier in Brussels TODAY as they SHAMELESSLY go behind May's back", Joe Barnes, 22nd October 2018, https://www.express.co.uk/news/uk/1034719/Brexit-news-ERG-MPs-Theresa-May-Michel-Barnier-Chequers-Ireland-UK-EU-latest

[34] Daily Star, "Theresa May could be SACKED in 48 hours – and THIS is who could replace her", Sophie Jones, 22nd October 2018, https://www.dailystar.co.uk/news/latest-news/737842/theresa-may-vote-of-no-confidence-david-davis-replacement

[35] Financial Times, "Theresa May offers 4-point plan to unblock Brexit talks", https://www.ft.com/content/de915670-d60d-11e8-a854-33d6f82e62f8

[36] The Guardian, "May's four tests before she will sign off on Irish border backstop deal", Lisa O'Carroll, 22nd October 2018, https://www.theguardian.com/politics/2018/oct/22/mays-four-tests-before-she-will-sign-off-on-irish-border-backstop-deal

[37] The Sun, "Theresa May vows to press ahead with her soft Brexit plan even if she loses her job", Tom Newton Dunn, 22nd October 2018, https://www.thesun.co.uk/news/7549106/theresa-may-to-continue-brexit-plan/

[38] The Sun, "Theresa May vows to press ahead with her soft Brexit plan even if she loses her job", Tom Newton Dunn, 22nd October 2018, https://www.thesun.co.uk/news/7549106/theresa-may-to-continue-brexit-plan/

[39] Evening Standard, "No10 planted decoy letters demanding PM confidence vote, Tories claim", Joe Murphy, 23rd October 2018,

Chapter Five: October 2018

https://www.standard.co.uk/news/politics/no10-planted-decoy-letters-demanding-pm-confidence-vote-tories-claim-a3969371.html

[40] *Evening Standard, "Brexit news latest: Theresa May to face critics at showdown 1922 committee meeting with Tory MPs", Ella Wills, 24th October 2018, https://www.standard.co.uk/news/politics/theresa-may-to-face-brexit-critics-at-showdown-meeting-with-tory-rebels-a3969921.html*

[41] *Twitter, "One MP leaves declaring "outbreak of unity... not a single dissenting voice" at the 1922. Is she safe?", Jessica Elgot, 24th October 2018, https://twitter.com/jessicaelgot/status/1055152021391765505?ref_src=twsrc%5Etfw*

[42] *Twitter, ""Very happy. All good" smiles one MP as they stride out of the committee room.", Allan McGuinness, 24th October 2018, https://twitter.com/Alan_McGuinness/status/1055150886341787653*

[43] *Twitter, "Former Home Secretary Amber Rudd says Theresa May is in a "stronger position" than before the meeting.", 24th October 2018, https://twitter.com/Alan_McGuinness/status/1055151887647936512*

[44] *Evening Standard, "Brits fear Theresa May's Brexit will make them worse off, damning poll reveals", Joe Murphy, 24th October 2018, https://www.standard.co.uk/news/politics/theresa-mays-brexit-will-make-people-worse-off-damning-poll-reveals-a3970186.html?fbclid=IwAR1yvQ-fOBrVTngKJ7b0lJCD6QMzuyFFabQHQfZGsQQwN9Jz3JdaUVYrMgE*

[45] *Twitter, "One MP leaves declaring "outbreak of unity... not a single dissenting voice" at the 1922. Is she safe?" , Jessica Elgot, 24th October 2018, https://twitter.com/jessicaelgot/status/1055152021391765505?ref_src=twsrc%5Etfw*

[46] *Twitter, "It was very good @Geoffrey_Cox says of @theresa_may 1922 speech", Nicholas Watt, 24th October 2018, https://twitter.com/nicholaswatt/status/1055150133199945728?ref_src=twsrc%5Etfw*

[47] *Twitter, ""Very happy. All good" smiles one MP as they stride out of the committee room.", Alan McGuinness, 24th October 2018, https://twitter.com/Alan_McGuinness/status/1055150886341787653*

[48] *Twitter, "Former Home Secretary Amber Rudd says Theresa May is in a "stronger position" than before the meeting.", Alan McGuinness, 24th October 2018, https://twitter.com/Alan_McGuinness/status/1055151887647936512*

[49] *BBC News, "Brexit: French officials dismiss UK fears of Calais 'go-slow'", BBC News, 26th October 2018, https://www.bbc.co.uk/news/uk-politics-45990243*

[50] *Twitter, @xavierbertrand, Xavier Bertrand, https://twitter.com/xavierbertrand?lang=en*

[51] *BBC News, ""Brexit: French officials dismiss UK fears of Calais 'go-slow'", BBC News, 26th October 2018, https://www.bbc.co.uk/news/uk-politics-45990243*

[52] *Twitter, @xavierbertrand, Xavier Bertrand, https://twitter.com/xavierbertrand?lang=en*

[53] *BBC News, "Brexit: Dominic Raab 'expects deal by 21 November'", BBC News, 31st October 2018, https://www.bbc.co.uk/news/uk-politics-46042886*

Chapter Six
November 2018

2nd November
The DUP Doubles Down

The Democratic Unionist Party is doubling down in its demands that Ireland isn't betrayed in a Brexit deal. DUP leader Arlene Foster has reiterated her red lines on Brexit with Brexit Secretary Dominic Raab today, and discussed in detail her party's concerns with the details of the proposal as it stands.

Speaking to the press following the meeting, Foster said[1]:

> *"Goodness, we have been here on a number of occasions and I hope we are close to a deal that will work for Northern Ireland. That is what we want".*

Foster also explained that she and her party had told Raab that, from constitutional and economic standpoints, it's essential for Northern Ireland to not have any customs barriers or regulatory barriers. That of course means Northern Ireland needs the same deal with the EU as the rest of the UK. The problem there, however, is that the backstop solution that keeps the entirety of the UK in the EU would be a betrayal of Brexit.

Foster wants no checks on the Irish sea and wants to maintain a close relationship with the rest of the UK – and the government says it agrees. The problem? Regulatory barriers seem like they're inevitable at this point. Michel Barnier has already said that regulatory checks would be necessary, and the EU isn't backing down on that. Even the UK government has previously agreed[2] with Brussels on this, with Theresa May accepting regulatory checks between Great Britain and Northern Ireland.

Back in September[3], it was revealed that Mrs May was to accept checks between Northern Ireland and Great Britain as a compromise with the EU. It was a tactic to break the deadlock, and it's unlikely the EU is going to back down on it. They want regulatory barriers between the UK and the EU post-Brexit.

In early October, Foster said that Mrs May couldn't 'in good conscience' recommend any deal on Brexit that put a trade barrier on businesses moving goods from one part of the UK to another – so how the government intends to please the DUP, I don't know. I'm just glad we can say that we have Arlene Foster on our side. She reminds me a lot of my grandmother. My dear old nan once took down a company that was trading illegally and made a pig's ear of a conservatory she paid them thousands for. She didn't stop until she got her money back and took the company down completely, God bless her. Foster's the same. She's a dog with a bone who won't give up until Ireland gets the deal they deserve, and which doesn't separate their country from the rest of the UK. She's a true unionist who won't back down, and I can't help but respect her for it.

It seems to me that Arlene Foster might actually be the woman who stops us from getting any deal at all, forcing the UK to leave without a deal. In which case, I hope she sticks to it. Come on Arlene, you can do this!

5th November
May's Secret Brexit Deal Keeps Us in the Customs Union

Did Theresa May strike a secret deal with the European Union over the weekend? It looks just like she might have done. The Sunday Times reported[4] that the

Prime Minister has made a secret Brexit deal with the EU that would keep the whole of the UK inside the Customs Union, which avoids a hard border in Ireland.

On the one hand, this does mean that an Irish backstop – the issue that's been stalling negotiations for months – wouldn't be necessary at all. There may be no more discussion about separating Northern Ireland from the rest of the UK, or creating a hard border between NI and the Republic of Ireland. But on the other hand, it means that the Prime Minister has simply cancelled Brexit.

The plan will no doubt be presented as a great compromise – delivering the results of the Brexit referendum, but ensuring Britain doesn't suffer the economic consequences that Remain establishment has been threatening for years. It's also a plan that the Prime Minister might be able to get Remain Labour and Tory MPs on board with.

In the plan, the Times says, there would be an 'exit clause' whereby the UK could eventually move towards a Canada-style free trade deal with the EU in the future. Given that the Prime Minister has had this option for a while, however, I wonder whether this is simply a carrot she plans on dangling in front of Tory Brexiteers in an attempt to get their votes when putting the deal through Parliament.

If she can win over Remain MPs by delivering a deal that keeps us in the Customs Union and, in effect, the EU – and she win over the Brexiteers by promising that there might be the deal they've been calling for all along at some point in the future – then the deal can be pushed through and Britain can *technically* leave the EU in March 2019.

It's also reported that May will warn Brexiteers that if they don't accept the deal, then *they'll* be to blame for a No Deal scenario. I doubt that will work with the likes of Mogg and Johnson, who would probably rather see that happen.

What I do know, though, is that this is next level deceitful, sneaky, and conniving. It wasn't all that long ago when I was willing to give Mrs May a chance to do this right, but it seems like she had no intention of delivering the result of the referendum from the start. For her to stand in front of the nation and say 'Brexit Means Brexit' – looking us in the eyes – and to turn around and fail to deliver Brexit in any meaningful sense means she will certainly go down as one of our worst Prime Ministers ever. If you can't trust her to deliver the results of the largest electoral mandate in British history, than what *can* we trust her to do?

Boris Johnson rightly fought back, too – leading what I'm sure he hopes will be a Brexiteer rebellion in the Tory party that won't sit back and accept May's deal. Johnson once again referred to May's plan as making Britain into an 'EU colony', and has urged the cabinet to reject her 'appalling' Brexit deal.

Writing in The Sun newspaper[5], Johnson said:

> *"Even after we leave, according to this so-called deal, we will remain in a nonsensical 'implementation period' in which we will be effectively non-voting members of the EU. For the first time in a thousand years we will have to accept foreign made laws, with no power to change or make those laws. We will be a vassal state, a colony, for at least 18 months and probably more".*

And he's right, isn't he? If we find ourselves within the Customs Union and accepting the rules and regulations of the EU without actually being voting members, then we have no power at all. We'll be under the control of EU powers and we won't even, at least, have the illusion of democracy.

This was always going to be difficult. Nobody said it would be easy to leave the EU. What we did say, however, is that it would be worth it. If we can solve the Irish border issue using technology, like Rees-Mogg and the ERG propose, then we can leave the EU in any which way we please. Mrs May doesn't seem to believe in her own country enough to do that. She's just handed our future over on a plate to greedy dictators in Brussels.

6th November
Labour Won't Vote for May's Brexit Deal

The Brexit deal that the Prime Minister was claimed to have made in secret with the EU won't be supported by Labour, it turns out. The deal that Downing Street has called 'speculation' appeared to be an attempt by the Prime Minister to bring together Remainers and Brexiteers alike, essentially encouraging MPs to vote for a deal that keeps the UK temporarily inside the Customs Union, to avoid a border between Northern Ireland and Great Britain.

Of course, the deal doesn't actually solve anything. It just kicks the can down the road and means we can *technically* leave the EU in March, while buying some extra time to work out those pesky…details. But Labour isn't on board, potentially throwing May's plans into the air.

Shadow chancellor and overall mental case, John McDonnell, told Newsnight last night that the Labour Party would reject any customs arrangement[6] with the EU…unless it was permanent. Amazing, isn't it? Labour have been so vague on their position on Brexit, but this really sets it in stone for us. They *want* Britain to be a vassal state and a colony of the EU. They want us to be bound to Customs Union rules and regulations without having any say on the matter. It's the worst case of political masochism I've ever seen.

If this is true, though, it means that Parliament is significantly more likely to reject her deal with the European Union when the crunch day comes. There isn't much time left, either! An agreement with the European Union needs to be made no later than the last week of November, and then it needs to go to Parliament. The news that Labour isn't on board with her policy will no doubt be troubling to Mrs May – as will the news that Brexiteers in the Tories are unlikely to agree to the proposal either.

Boris Johnson is clearly leading a revolt in the Tories against the proposal, and even moderate Brexiteer columnists and activists are speaking out against the deal. Iain Martin, columnist for The Times, wrote on Twitter[7]:

> *"Still necessary to repeat this, it seems. No country, certainly not the UK, would sign up to have its territory divided by a foreign power, or to be locked in someone else's Customs Union in perpetuity with no rights to leave".*

Well I'm sorry to say, but it seems like the Prime Minister is willing to do exactly that. But today, the Cabinet ministers will meet[8] to hear about the deal that Downing Street called 'speculation'. Ministers will need to discuss how to stop any new checks being made on goods arriving at the Irish border, and May will need to get her cabinet united behind her deal with the EU. There really isn't much time left – if the negotiations go beyond November, there simply won't be enough time for the UK and EU Parliaments to ratify the deal.

7th November
The Leaked Plot to Sell May's Brexit Deal to the Public

A PR plan for the Prime Minister to sell her Brexit deal has been leaked. The government, however, claims that the document doesn't reflect their thinking – but that's clearly a lie.

A document seen by The Guardian and BBC is said to lay out a timetable for the rest of the month – starting with a cabinet meeting on Tuesday and moving on to a House of Commons vote on the final Brexit deal that is said to be taking place on the 27th November. That's the crunch day – the day we find out whether the Prime Minister's Brexit deal will really happen, which is why this leaked PR strategy gives us a valuable insight into the government's thinking and plan to sell the idea to Parliamentarians.

The Guardian reports[9] that the days in between the two dates are packed full of media events, and a number of supportive statements from cabinet members, including an announcement by Dominic Raab that the government has agreed a deal with the European Union. The note reads:

> *"The narrative is going to be measured success, that this is good for everyone, but won't be all champagne corks popping".*

Other events lined up for the rest of the month include a speech by the Prime Minister to the Confederation of British Industry, on the same day that the agreement would be put before a vote in Parliament. Junior ministers, the note says, will do regional media throughout the rest of the day. It even explains:

"Government lining up 25 top business voices including (CBI director general) Carolyn Fairbairn and lots of world leaders eg Japanese PM to tweet support for the deal".

The plan would also focus on immigration, the NHS, and Northern Ireland, with 'themed days' in the Commons that will essentially form a sales pitch to the country. There is even talk of Theresa May gracing Northern Ireland with her presence, in an effort to win over Irish PM Leo Varadkar. And to top it all off, it looks like the Prime Minister will be doing an interview with legendary political journalist and TV host, David Dimbleby.

Make no mistake, this is a well-thought-out plan to make the Brexit deal appear like a positive step for Britain – the kind of plan required for a deal that isn't in fact good for Britain.

8th November
Cabinet Reviews May's EU Deal, Davis Says it Won't Pass Through Commons

Cabinet ministers were invited[10] to read the draft deal with the EU yesterday. The deal is believed to include controversial new measures that would keep the UK within the Customs Union for a period of time, which helps resolve some of the problems surrounding Ireland.

Michael Gove, after seeing the incomplete agreement, told Sky News that it was a 'great document'. Though, he would, wouldn't he?

May seems to be really upping the ante, preparing for a deal in a few weeks' time. She's reportedly also reaching out to Angela Merkel[11], who believes that avoiding No Deal is in the interest of Germany, to try and finalise the nearly-complete deal. The Prime Minister spoke with the German chancellor on Tuesday night, in an effort to complete the deal before next Monday when a summit to finalise the deal will hopefully be called.

The deal all rests on whether Parliament will even vote for the deal, though. Jacob Rees-Mogg told Robert Peston[12] that if the Brexit deal involves any extension to the Customs Union, then he will vote against it. You can bet that the membership of the European Research Group – as many as 80 Tory MPs – will also vote against it.

Former Brexit Secretary David Davis also believes that opposition to the deal will be so great that MPs will probably vote against it. He told BBC Radio Four[13] that he believed a defeat in the Commons would mean the UK and EU would agree a better deal, and that the UK already has 'hundreds' of plans ready in case the UK leaves the EU without a deal. There might be 'some hiccups', he said, but the UK is a big country and 'we can look after ourselves'. Which is certainly nice to hear.

I just can't help but wonder why the government, if it's true they have hundreds of plans in place, haven't been considering the benefits of leaving without a deal this whole time.

Some other updates:

- Brexiteer MPs are warning that the deal being proposed would be staying in the Single Market 'by the backdoor'. Chris Grayling, Transport Secretary, is said to have warned the Prime Minister during the Cabinet meeting yesterday that restrictions imposed on the UK by staying in the

Single Market would stop the UK from gaining any kind of trade advantage that comes with being outside of the bloc.

- In a speech in Paris, Foreign Secretary Jeremy Hunt has said that a Brexit deal probably won't be expected within the next seven days.

- Shortly after his speech, Government sources have told the national press that they don't expect a Cabinet meeting, **which will discuss the final deal, will happen before next week.**

12th November
Brexit Negotiators Up Until Early Hours, Scrambling for a Deal

Number 10 insists that UK and EU negotiators were up until 2.45am last night[14], and insists that progress is being made on the final deal. This reminds me of when I was in college. I'd have weeks to finish an assignment but I'd always somehow find myself up the night before, drinking energy drinks and pounding my keyboard, hoping what I was writing was making some kind of sense. This is literally what's happening right now.

The Tories dragged their heels triggering Article 50, and have spent two years umming and ahhing about which direction they're going to take. Now we are a matter of weeks and days away from the emergency, and they're up until silly o'clock in the morning trying to hash out a deal.

We're told that progress is being made, but we've been told that for a while now.

The pressure is on, too. Penny Mordaunt, Secretary of State for International Development, has warned Theresa May[15] that the Cabinet will be checking her deal to ensure that it delivers on the referendum results. She told Sky News there will be two checks on the Deal – Cabinet, and Parliament. If it doesn't pass Cabinet, then it won't even arrive at Parliament.

What are the chances of Cabinet voting it down, though? We had high hopes of Brexiteers in the Tories kicking out Theresa May with a vote of confidence when she was faced with the 1922 Committee, and they bottled that. What reason is there to believe the Brexiteers won't bottle it again?

The progress that was promised, by the way, doesn't seem to be being made. During a meeting in Brussels[16], Michel Barnier told European affairs ministers in the remaining 27 EU member states that negotiators had so far failed to make the kind of progress on the key issue – the Irish border – that is necessary to move forward in discussions. An agreement, he says, has yet to be reached. And time is ticking.

Meanwhile, in the opposition camp, the Shadow Secretary of State for Brexit, Sir Keir Starmer, has broken ranks and said that Brexit can be stopped. He's taking a different line to Jeremy Corbyn who is sticking to his Brexiteer credentials and saying he accepts the will of the people, while tentatively toeing the line of the rest of his Remain party. But Starmer doesn't seem to care about subtleties, telling the Today programme[17] that 'Brexit can be stopped'.

Just another day of Brexit negotiations, then.

13th November
We Won't Need Visas to Visit Europe, Post-Brexit

Throughout this entire Brexit negotiation process, I couldn't tell you how many times I've heard people complaining about having to apply for visas to visit Europe. Remainers have bemoaned the process of applying for a visa online before flying to driving to European countries, as if it was a great inconvenience – but it's turned out this was just another tactic of Project Fear, anyway.

The European Commission has today announced[18] that British travellers will not ned to apply for visas to visit the European Union for short trips, even if we are faced with a No Deal Brexit. How's that?

So we've debunked the myth that planes will be stopped from flying into Europe, and now we know we can easily and effortlessly travel through EU countries. Nice one.

The EU Commission issued the following travel advice:

> *"The European Commission has proposed to EU legislator to exempt UK nationals from visa requirements for short-term stays".*

So will this put an end to the fearmongering? Probably not. The next step is likely for the Remain camp to complain that the UK will have to take part in a new system being implemented by the EU, whereby every traveller (whether visa exempt or not) must apply for electronic travel authorisation in advance of their trip.

This works in the same way as the US Esta system. You simply go online, enter your details, pay a small fee, and you're granted access to the country you're visiting. It's a simple security measure that is easy for anyone to apply for. For the Remainers, though, I suspect it's the last thing they can cling to.

So be glad – the rumours were untrue, and even if we "crash out" of the EU without a deal, your holiday to Paris won't be interrupted. That is, if you're mad enough to want to go to Paris.

14th November
Theresa May's Brexit Deal is Leaked

Last night Theresa May met her Cabinet members one by one. The last person to do that was Margaret Thatcher, the night before she resigned as Prime Minister. Unfortunately, it doesn't seem like history is repeating itself, as she was still in office and fighting out her Brexit deal during PMQs this morning. She's sticking around for a little while longer, after presenting to her Cabinet her final Brexit deal.

She did say in PMQs this morning that the motion on the deal will be 'amendable' – so I suspect there are changes yet to be made – but the deal itself has been reportedly given to Irish media. The details of the deal have reached the British press, too. It seems near impossible for a commoner like me to get a hold of this document, but the national press is now reporting on the details of this final Withdrawal Agreement that is set to be put to the Commons.

It's a 400-odd-page document that has been provisionally agreed by the UK and EU, which sets out a transition period, obligations, and terms of leaving the European Union.

Here's what you need to know:

Dispute Resolutions

So the way in which this Withdrawal Treaty is being overseen is not simple. It's reported that the model of governing and overseeing the treaty is built on the EUs association agreement with Ukraine. It combines dispute resolution techniques with new, custom provisions that makes sure that the European Court of Justice has the final say on the bloc's laws.

We've talked about this before – the ECJ is set to have control over the interpretation of the Withdrawal Agreement. This system technically means that neither the UK or the EU will be bound by the other one's courts when it comes to interpreting what the agreement means. So independent arbitration will be required if there are any disputes over the treaty.

A pessimist might say that this is simply a get-out clause for the EU to keep changing parameters and changing their mind. An optimist might say that fact that matters relating to EU law being required to be referred to the ECJ could put Britain at a disadvantage.

The Customs Union

This is where the betrayal becomes most visible. Theresa May has been working to try and ensure that there is no hard border between NI and the Republic of Ireland, and that there is no separation between NI and GB. The European Research Group presented her with solutions to that, which involve a simple free trade deal – but instead, Theresa May is planning a UK-EU Customs Union deal that avoids the needs for any customs checks down the Irish Sea.

This means that Northern Ireland will apply the current and full union customs code. This allows Northern Ireland to have access to total free movement of goods within the

European Union. The UK, however, would apply a less extensive Customs Union model. It won't be full access to the Customs Union, but we'll technically apply some of its basic requirements so that there are no customs checks down the Irish sea, and no need for tariffs or quotas.

It solves the problem, that's for sure – but it means that the UK will technically remain, at least to some extent, within the Customs Union. This deal is *worse* than simply staying in the European Union. Now, we'll be bound by Customs Union regulations without even having a say in the European Parliament.

To stay within this Customs Union, the UK will need to follow all EU regulations on competition **and** promise to maintain some of the EU's existing laws surrounding taxation, environment, and labour. This literally means – as Boris Johnson has said multiple times[19] over the last few days – that the UK for the first time in one thousand years will not have a say over the laws that govern this country.

Oh, and by the way, The New European tried to use this comment[20] by Boris to suggest that he knew all along that Britain made its own laws while in the EU. They're being disingenuous, though. Boris never suggested that while in the European Union we had total control of our laws – what he said was, we at least technically had a *say* in those laws. It wasn't much of a say. The MEPs are really only there to rubber stamp bad legislation. But at least we technically had a say.

Under Theresa's deal, we have no say at all.

Northern Ireland gets an even worse deal than Great Britain, too. NI will be bound by **all** of the EU's customs code and Single Market rules. They simply can't escape those rules, and until a new deal is reached at a later date – if ever – they will be treated differently than the mainland UK. This is the backstop agreement we've been hearing a lot about for so long. Mrs May has repeatedly insisted that NI will not be treated any differently than Great Britain. It seems she lied. I can't imagine Arlene Foster is all too pleased about this.

Our fishing waters, by the way, aren't included in this customs deal. They are being excluded until the UK and EU can reach a deal on reciprocal access to each other's waters, which is a giant insult to our fishermen who voted leave to regain access to our OWN waters.

This is all a backstop deal – so it's technically temporary. But who knows? A joint committee will need to decide whether a deal agreed upon in the future will allow us to terminate this membership of the Customs Union. We have no idea of a timescale, so this could go on indefinitely. This simply isn't Brexit.

The Transition Period

The transition period for us leaving the European Union will go on until the end of 2020. That means four and a half years since voting to leave the European Union, we'll still be transitioning out of this tyranny. This is amendable, too – the deal allows for the transition date to be extended for a one-off period, for an unspecified amount of time. All it requires is both sides to agree on it.

During the transition period, Britain would technically leave all of the EU's institutions and we would have absolutely zero say in any decisions on EU law. Despite that, we will be bound by ALL EU law in full until we leave.

It is, therefore, no exaggeration to say that the UK will be a vassal state. This great nation, which once ruled a quarter of the land on earth, will be subject to foreign rules that we'll have absolutely no say over.

What makes this even worse is, we'll still have to abide by the EU's free movement rules. So we'll have many more years to come of total open border access to the rest of the EU. All the while, we'll be paying for the pleasure of suffering at the hands of this bureaucratic tyranny.

This is the deal that the Prime Minister is telling us is in the 'national interest'[21], and in a Cabinet meeting happening right now, she's saying the same thing for her government ministers.

UPDATE: 8PM

It's 8pm, and Theresa May just appeared on the steps of 10 Downing Street to discuss her intense 5-hour-long Cabinet meeting.

It's been a tough day for her so far. Not only did Mrs May face hostility from Jeremy Corbyn, the backlash from her own party was visible and audible. Peter Bone MP stood up and told her that she is not delivering the Brexit people voted for, and that by the end of the day, she would lose the support of many of her own MPs. A Tory MP standing up and saying that to the Prime Minister in front of the entirety of Parliament is serious. Mrs May knows her job is on the line, and so is her deal.

Jacob Rees-Mogg has been more vocal about his opposition to Mrs May, too. I remember in the early days whenever he was on national news, or even on *Have I Got News For You*, and he would repeat the line that he trusted the Prime Minister to get the right deal for Britain. I suppose back then he was hoping his European Research Group would exert rather more power than it has been able to.

The ERG also told Sky News today that the group's previous position was a desire to change policy on Brexit, and not leadership – but that now, they are calling for a change in leadership if the Prime Minister pushes forward with her deal.

And it looks like they'll be pushing for a change in leadership, because Mrs May's announcement wasn't exactly what they wanted to hear.

She said[22]:

> *"The Cabinet has just had a long, detailed and impassioned debate on the draft Withdrawal Agreement and the Outline Political Declaration on our future relationship with the European Union.*
> *These documents were the result of thousands of hours of hard negotiation by UK officials, and many, many meetings, which I and other ministers held with our EU counterparts.*
> *I firmly believe that the draft Withdrawal Agreement was the best that could be negotiated, and it was for the Cabinet to decide whether to move on in the talks.*
> *The choices before us were difficult, particularly in relation to the Northern Ireland backstop.*
> *But the collective decision of Cabinet was that the Government should agree the draft Withdrawal Agreement and the Outline Political Declaration – this is a decisive step which enables us to move on and finalise the deal in the days ahead.*
> *These decisions were not taken lightly - but I believe it is a decision that is firmly in the national interest.*
> *When you strip away the detail, the choice before us is clear. This deal which delivers on the vote of the referendum,*

which brings back control of our money, laws and borders; ends free movement; protects jobs, security and our union; or leave with no deal; or no Brexit at all.

I know that there will be difficult days ahead. This is a decision which will come under intense scrutiny and that is entirely as it should be and entirely understandable.

But the choice was this deal, which enables us to take back control and to build a brighter future for our country, or going back to square one with more division, more uncertainty and a failure to deliver on the referendum.

It is my job as Prime Minister to explain the decisions that the Government has taken and I stand ready to do that beginning tomorrow with a statement in Parliament.

If I may end by just saying this. I believe that what I owe to this country is to take decisions that are in the national interest, and I firmly believe with my head and my heart that this is a decision which is in the best interests of our entire United Kingdom".

Honestly, I thought she was about to resign. The minute she said "I firmly believe that the draft Withdrawal Agreement **was** the best that could be negotiated" I thought she was about to tell us that Cabinet didn't agree, that it was all over, and she was throwing in the towel. Once again, though, I've had to learn the hard way that we should never underestimate the staying power of Theresa May.

The meeting took so long because the Prime Minister took the time to address the concerns of each individual Cabinet member, as opposed to the usual practice of listening to each minister and summarising at the end. She really went as far as she could to unite her Cabinet, though she definitely benefitted from the fact that most of them are completely spineless.

Now, the press is reporting that May is advising Tory MPs that it's either this deal, or no Brexit at all, given how dedicated the other side is to achieving a second referendum. Even Tony Blair and Gordon Brown are out doing the circuit again, calling for a second referendum. Combine that very real threat with the fact that most MPs have no real desire to implement Brexit anyway, and she might just get away with this.

Jacob Rees-Mogg is really stepping up to the challenge, though. Following's May's statement, Rees-Mogg released the following statement:

Chapter Six: November 2018

Dear Colleagues,

Like you I supported the Prime Minister in her early approach to the Brexit negotiations. I agreed with her Lancaster house speech that this should be built around the ability of the UK to take back control of our laws, borders and money while safeguarding our precious Union.

Unfortunately the proposals for a UK/EU agreement released today do not match up to those early expectations. For four key reasons.

1. The proposed agreement will see the UK hand over £39 billion to the EU for little or nothing in return. The prospect of an agreed free trade agreement is as far away today as it always has been. The 15 page political declaration is neither binding nor clear in its intentions. If it aims to put in place the Chequers proposal it is neither workable nor respectful of the referendum result. In the absence of a trade agreement we should spend our money on our own priorities, for instance £39 billion could pay for 26,000 nurses for 40 years.

2. The proposed agreement would treat Northern Ireland differently than the rest of the UK. This is unacceptable to Unionists particularly in Northern Ireland, and Scotland where the SNP will seek to demand similar internal UK borders to weaken the Union.

3. This agreement will lock us into an EU customs union and EU laws. This will prevent us pursuing a UK trade policy based around our priorities and economy, Without the ability to regulate our own economy and form our own trade agreements we will lose out on the opportunities that Brexit affords us.

4. Agreeing to be subject to the rules of an EU Customs Union, in contravention of the 2017 Conservative manifesto, without any votes or influence is profoundly undemocratic. This is compounded by the lack of any ability for the UK to unilaterally escape, making the UK a permanent rule taker.

For these reasons I can not support the proposed agreement in Parliament and would hope that Conservative MPs would do likewise.

Yours

Jacob Rees-Mogg MP

So while Rees-Mogg is technically only calling on his fellow MPs to reject the deal in a vote in the Commons, I wonder whether really he wants more. There has already been discussion from members of the ERG that they now want to see a change in leadership. Rees-Mogg is a polite and courteous man – this is perhaps as far as he's willing to go, even at this point.

If the ERG is calling for a vote of no confidence, they should do so carefully. If May wins that vote, they won't be able to call for another vote of confidence for 12 months. This is a very careful game they must play, but it's one that the national media suggests the ERG might just be willing to play.

Tomorrow will be interesting. We're bound to hear more leaks about what really happened in that Cabinet meeting. So far, all we know is that Cabinet minister Esther McVey (Minister for Work and Pensions) was 'in tears' after being shouted at[23] during the five-hour meeting. Sources claim that McVey was aggressive towards the PM, arguing against the deal and calling for Cabinet to have a vote on the matter. She also warned May that she believed the deal would be voted down when it goes to a Meaningful Vote in Parliament and suggested that the opinion of everybody in Cabinet be put on record. I reckon McVey has ambitions beyond this government and wants to make sure the people know she was against this deal from the start.

Cabinet has been called to heel very successfully indeed, by a Prime Minister who seems pretty tough behind the scenes. At least she isn't throwing printers around the office like Gordon Brown, though.

Chapter Six: November 2018

16th November
The Letters Go In to the 1922 Committee

This morning started with another letter being sent to the 1922 Committee, this time by former culture secretary John Whittingdale, and more harsh words from former Brexit secretary David Davis. He claimed that Theresa May's proposal is 'dreadful' on BBC Radio 4 and accused the EU of deliberately delaying the negotiations.

The Chief Political Correspondent and Assistant Editor of The Daily Telegraph, Christopher Hope, reported around 10am that his sources were claiming that 48 letters of no confidence have now been submitted to the 1922 Committee, meaning a vote of confidence is inevitable, and could happen as soon as Tuesday. But, if Theresa May's speech from last night is anything to go by, it's unlikely she'll be resigning to avoid it. She's going to stick this through and hope she wins.

David Lidington, the chap responsible for holding quiet talks with Labour and Lib Dem MPs stated shortly after noon that he believes May would win the vote 'handsomely', and I agree with him. Who else would replace her? There seems little hope that a Brexiteer could even end up on the ballot to replace her, so what Remainer would be mad enough to A) want the job, and B) think they could unite Parliament any better? Nicky Morgan echoed this same sentiment, telling BBC Radio 5 Live she thinks May will survive the vote. That vote, by the way, is expected on Tuesday.

The Prime Minister, in a plot no doubt to win over the public, even appeared on a live LBC phone-in session this morning. One brave caller compared her to Neville Chamberlain, appeasing Europe all over again. She laughed, shrugged it off, and reminded us that this is the best deal 'in the national interest'. I don't know about you, but I don't believe May's slogans. She bleated on about creating a 'strong and stable' government throughout the 2017 general election. I suspect that even if she'd have been able to command a majority in Parliament afterwards, even that wouldn't have been strong or stable.

Soon after her appearance on LBC, MPs started choosing sides. Liam Fox, a Brexiteer, amazingly said that he stands behind the Prime Minister and that it is in the 'national interest' to provide certainty and go with May's deal. In fact, today, he even suggested that a deal is better than no deal[24]. That's quite the U-Turn, given that he and May were saying literally the exact opposite just a few weeks ago.

I cannot understate the sheer chaos in our national politics right now. It's getting difficult for me to fit everything into these daily posts, so I'm going to break up today's antics into a few sections.

Amber Rudd Returns, and a New Brexit Secretary Appointed

It was only in April that Amber Rudd had to resign as Home Secretary, but now she's back. The Prime Minister has appointed Rudd the new Work and Pensions Secretary, replacing Esther McVey. I suppose loyalty pays off. I didn't think Rudd would ever make it back to Cabinet after being slaughtered over the Windrush scandal, but here she is. May really doesn't have many people to choose from at this point.

Labour are up in arms about it, of course. David Lammy says the DWP role is a poisoned chalice and that the government is unlikely to survive until Christmas[25]. The Labour Whips twitter account tweeted that Rudd's appointment as a 'burning injustice'[26].

As for Brexit Secretary, May has gone for Steve Barclay. He's a former health minister, and head of anti-money laundering at Barclay's Bank. He's known as a true loyalist. He's technically a Brexiteer, but he has never rebelled in the Commons once, so May knows she's got someone she can control. He's no David Davis.

Though, as Rees-Mogg said during a press conference just a few days ago, there really isn't much point of a Brexit Secretary when the decisions are being made from No 10 anyway.

As for the other empty posts, May has brought in Stephen Hammond MP as Minister for Health and Social Care, John Penrose MP as Minister for Northern Ireland, and Kwasi Kwarteng as PPS for the Department for Exiting the European Union.

Can May Pass the Withdrawal Act Through Parliament?

Theresa May's goal, should she survive the impending vote of confidence, is to pass her deal through Parliament. Looking at the pure vitriol displayed by her own Tory MPs during PMQs, it's hard to imagine that she could pass any legislation right now – and BBC Research backs this up.

The Democratic Unionist Party has 10 votes, which we know won't be lent to the Prime Minister this time. Despite their Confidence and Supply Deal, the DUP aren't happy with the fact the Northern Ireland will be treated differently to the rest of the UK. So she's immediately 10 votes down.

The ERG claims to have between 80 and 100 members. BBC Research suggests roughly 58 hardcore Brexiteers, but the ERG knows who the secret hard Brexiteers are.

There are at least 14 Tory Remainers who don't want a deal, but who do want a second referendum.

The Prime Minister can command between 244 and 250 loyalists, and potentially 15 labour rebels. There are also rumours of two Lib Dems voting for the deal.

That means May could realistically command perhaps 259 Members, and that could be a generous number. She needs 329 votes to pass, and there is no chance in hell that the ERG Brexiteers are going to give it to her.

This is why, all that time ago, David Lidington was quietly meeting with Labour and Lib Dem MPs to discuss the future of the deal. Theresa May knew from the start that her own MPs wouldn't support Brexit – and the fact she has to turn to Labour to help her says a lot.

So what, then, do we do? George Galloway has suggested that in the event the deal is not passed in Parliament, the Queen should get involved and dissolve Parliament. This would mean a general election.

Conservative Party chairman Brandon Lewis has suggested that one way to avoid this would not to have a free vote. If he's suggesting that the party whips get involved, I think they'll have one hell of a tough time trying to force Tory MPs to vote for this Withdrawal Agreement. Just because Cabinet has (sort of) agreed, doesn't mean the rest of the party will.

The Irish Prime Minister Leo Varadker thinks MPs will support the deal, once it's clear that May's deal is the only option and better than no deal at all[27].

Playing Fast and Loose with the Economy

What the politicians are doing during this negotiation process is criminal in my books. It's quite easy for

Remainers to claim that Brexit has thrown the country into chaos. They might blame Brexit for the Pound seeing its biggest one-day drop in two years. But in reality, it's the lack of decisive action, the confusion, and the attempts to delay the implementation of this historic decision that is causing the trouble.

Brexit hasn't happened yet. What is happening right now is a betrayal, and it's **that** which is making the Pound unstable, and scaring (some) businesses.

Thankfully, the Pound is recovering after being hit on Thursday. The Pound is now 0.5% higher, reaching $1.283.

I could be a bog standard Brexit pundit and give you the usual spiel about how amazingly well the economy has done since Brexit, and that unemployment is lower than ever – but I want to be honest about this. First of all, Brexit hasn't happened yet, so we can't claim great successes here.

Secondly, unemployment is nowhere near as low as the government likes to claim. May's government has praised low unemployment rates for some time now. It has risen a little over the summer, reaching 4.1%[28] - but the reality is much different. The real story here is underemployment.

Poverty is an enormous problem in the UK. The United Nations has even gotten involved, warning that UK politicians are in denial, while child poverty remains at 'staggering' levels[29]. And it's true. The UK's unemployment figures count those working on zero-hour contracts as employed – and while zero-hour contracts are essential for a versatile economy, they don't suit everybody. People who aren't getting enough hours at work to even pay their bills are being considered employed, and the government seems to be ignoring it.

So as Brexiteers, we mustn't claim success here. Brexit **can** deliver, by stopping the importation of low-wage workers, raising wages for the average British worker, and opening up more opportunities to British workers. But right now, things aren't good. The working class are still suffering, and it's because the politicians are playing fast and loose with the economy, and with people's lives. Poor families are watering down baby formula, for God's sake[30].

I don't just take issue with the fact that Theresa May is refusing to implement the decision we made in 2016. I take issue with the fact that she and her government appear to be ignoring poverty, and trading away the future of millions of British people for the sake of politics.

19th November
Theresa May Survives Another Weekend

The Prime Minister survived the weekend, somehow. It's been turbulent, but it looks like the required 48 letters haven't been submitted so far. Nothing much else has changed, though – the DUP still aren't best pleased, and the Confidence and Supply agreement is under threat, and the Parliamentary arithmetic is against her. She still doesn't have the votes she needs to pass her bill, but she's still going ahead with her handful of allies and pushing for her idea of Brexit.

Oh, and remember how I talked about the leaked plans for the government to engage in a sophisticated PR campaign to push May's deal through, and convince the public it was the right deal? Well, it looks like they've started already.

Today, Theresa May gave a speech to the Confederation of British Industry, where she informed business leaders that the withdrawal deal had been 'agreed in full'.

She explained[31]:

> *Last week the Cabinet agreed the terms of the UK's withdrawal from the European Union.*
> *We also agreed a draft outline of the political declaration on the future relationship between the UK and the EU.*
> *Both documents were the result of many hours of negotiation between the United Kingdom and the European Union.*
> *Together they represent a decisive breakthrough – but they are not the final deal.*
> *We now have an intense week of negotiations ahead of us in the run-up to the special European Council on Sunday. During that time I expect us to hammer out the full and final details of the framework that will underpin our future relationship and I am confident that we can strike a deal at the council that I can take back to the House of Commons.*
> *The core elements of that deal are already in place.*
> *The Withdrawal Agreement has been agreed in full, subject of course to final agreement being reached on the future framework.*

So, make no mistake. She isn't budging on her deal, but simply intends to hammer out the finer details of the framework that will allow her to make this deal – completely ignoring what seems to be impending doom when the deal actually reaches a vote in the Commons.

What really surprised me, though, is that she did much more than just talk about the perceived 'benefits' of her deal, though. In a surprising twist, she attempted to appeal to the patriotic, anti-mass-immigration voters by claiming that her draft Brexit Withdrawal Agreement would stop migrants from the EU 'jumping the queue'.

May knows that the voters want immigration to be reduced. She has previously deployed tactics like suggesting her government will 'control' immigration, without suggesting that she would reduce the numbers. Now, she's claiming that her Brexit deal will stop EU nationals jumping the queue, ahead of engineers from Sydney or software developers from Delhi.

But here's what she gets wrong. People don't take issue with European migrants because they're European, or because they're jumping the queue. Instead, people take issue with immigration generally. The system is completely broken, and many people want to see a reduction in even QUALIFIED immigrants coming to this country. It's not about race, it's about jobs, homes, resources, and space. So I doubt very much that her attempt to spin this as a great patriotic victory will work with the public – especially when her current deal maintains freedom of movement until an indeterminate period of time passes, and the EU agrees to exit the backstop and move forward with a new deal. Great going, Theresa.

Has the Rees-Mogg Revolution Ended Already?

Well, that was less exciting than I thought. Last week there were rumours that the European Research Group had managed to encourage 48 MPs to send in no confidence letters to Sir Graham. Turns out only 26 MPs have publicly submitted letters of no confidence, with Tory MP Steve Baker admitting that some MPs have simply lied about supporting the coup.[32]

Here's who we know have submitted letters so far:

1. Philip Hollobone MP for Kettering
2. Sir Bill Cash, MP for Stone
3. David Joes, MP for Clwyd West
4. John Whittingdale, MP for Maldon
5. Ben Bradley, MP for Mansfield
6. Chris Green, MP for Bolton West and Atherton
7. Marcus Fysh, MP for Yeovil
8. Zac Goldsmith, MP for Richmond Park and North Kingston (this surprised me!)
9. Mark Francois, MP for Rayleigh and Wickford
10. Adam Holloway, MP for Gravesend
11. Peter Bone, MP for Wellingborough (Duh – if he hadn't, I'd have been shocked)
12. Martin Vickers, MP for Cleethorpes
13. Lee Rowley, MP for North East Derbyshire
14. Sheryll Murray, MP for South East Cornwall
15. Maria Caulfield, MP for Lewes
16. Henry Smith, MP for Crawley
17. Steve Baker, MP for Wycombe
18. Andrea Jenkyns, MP for Morley and Outwood
19. Andrew Bridgen, MP for North West Leicestershire
20. Philip Davies, MP for Shipley
21. James Duddridge, MP for Rochford and Southend East
22. Anne Marie Morris, MP for Newton Abbott
23. Simon Clarke, MP for Middlesborough South and East Cleveland
24. Nadine Dorries, MP for Mid Bedfordshire
25. Jacob Rees-Mogg, MP for North East Somerset
26. Laurence Robertson, MP for Tewkesbury

The media is suggesting as many as 40 have submitted, but we don't know who the others are.

The DUP Fires Warning Shots

The DUP really could be on the verge of backing out of their Confidence and Supply deal with the Conservative Party. Arlene Foster has repeatedly stressed that the deal was made with the Conservative Party and not Theresa May, and that they would continue the deal (whereby they provide 10 votes in Parliament to give May a majority) if there was a change in leadership. Following the news that a leadership challenge isn't necessarily going to happen any time soon, however, the DUP has fired warning shots to the government and abstained from voting during key budget votes this evening[33].

The move violates the terms of their agreement, and shows May that the party won't be accepting her deal as it stands. Assuming that the agreement comes to an end, the governing Tories will have 316 votes in Parliament, and her opposition will have 323 (I'm not counting Sinn Fein and speakers, who don't vote). That puts her firmly back in the minority government territory and doesn't necessarily mean Labour can form a government of their own – but it does mean she'll need to win over four MPs from the other side every time she wants to pass legislation. She'll also have to get heavy on the whip and ensure no member in her party votes against her.

Did May Insist on Customs Union Membership?

What Theresa May has done during these Brexit negotiations is nothing short of a betrayal of the British people. It's as simple as that. She might think she's doing the right thing (in fact, I don't doubt for a second that she thinks what she is doing is right) but she is betraying the people. Today's claims by Michel Barnier, however, show just how far she's willing to go to implement what she sees as the better alternative to Brexit.

Chapter Six: November 2018

Barnier told the press today that it was, in fact, Theresa May who asked for the future relationship between the UK and EU to be based on a stripped-back Customs Union.

Speaking to reporters in Brussels, Barnier said that it was the Prime Minister who in fact turned away from their free trade proposals and instead insisted on a single customs territory becoming a basis for the future relationship. He told the press:

> *"If you compare the guidance issued by the European Council and the white paper from Chequers, there's a free trade area...the minimum pint of departure if you like".*

He then went on to explain how the European Union had in fact compromised by moving towards a single customs area at the rest of Mrs May, to prevent a hard border in Ireland.[34]

Commendable, but also terrible. Sure, she prevented a hard Irish border – but in the process, constructed a deal that keeps the UK bound to EU regulations up until the EU decides they're happy for us to leave. I don't like to call this a conspiracy – I don't think Theresa May had this plot from the beginning to ensure that Britain would be controlled by the EU and unable to make its own decisions – but I do think she has plotted, schemed and planned for a deal that she thinks is good and the rest of the country recognizes as terrible. This makes her less of a coordinated schemer, and more of a terrible politician with horrible judgement.

For now, May remains. She's fighting harder than ever, determined to see her deal go through. I can only assume she has something up her sleeve. Surely she couldn't be mad enough to find this hard for a deal she knows has no hope of ever passing in Parliament.

21st November
May Heads to Brussels, without Her Brexit Secretary

Jeremy Corbyn asked Theresa May today whether the role of Brexit Secretary had become ceremonial at this point – and I see his point. The Prime Minister went to Brussels today to continue talks with Michel Barnier and EU officials.

The Prime Minister met for two hours in Brussels, where she discussed the future of EU-UK relations. This included discussions over Gibraltar, the UK territory at the southernmost part of Spain. Spanish leaders want more control over the region, which will be withdrawing from the European Union with the UK.

The Brexit deal not only has to be passed in the Houses of Parliament here in the UK, but EU member states will vote on it, too. Spain has said they will not agree to the Brexit deal unless we make concessions over the wording surrounding Gibraltar, but No 10 sources claim they expect a solution to arrive – no doubt something that sells off a little bit of control from Gibraltar – to be arrived at by this weekend[35].

May also agreed, today, to head back to Brussels on Saturday where she will continue negotiations and, hopefully, finalise the Brexit deal just a day before the final Brexit summit on Sunday.

That's right! The summit we've all been wondering about is happening this Sunday. The negotiations should of course all be out of the way by now, but Angela Merkel apparently threatened to pull the plug on the summit even happening, citing a lack of progress made on major issues.

May seems to have pulled it off, though, telling the press this evening:

"We have had a very good meeting this evening. We have made further progress and as a result, we have given sufficient direction to our negotiators. I hope for them to be able to resolve the remaining issued and that work will start immediately. I now plan to return for further meetings, including with President Juncker, on Saturday to discuss how we can bring to a conclusion this process and bring it to a conclusion in the interests of all our people".

Assuming it all goes well, the deal will be finalised at the summit on Sunday, and it will be put to a Meaningful Vote in Parliament in early December. We'll have to wait and see if Theresa May has a trick up her sleeve to pass the deal in December.

Not only does she have the DUP working against her, but Nicola Sturgeon – leader of the Scottish National Party – has confirmed that her SNP MPs will all vote against the Brexit deal, too[36]. That is, unless, May has offered the SNP some kind of special deal for Scotland behind the scenes. Sturgeon met with May in London yesterday, where they discussed the deal. If May manages to sweeten Sturgeon's SNP with some kind of special Brexit deal for Scotland, she might just get the extra votes she needs to pass the deal in Parliament.

Amber Rudd Lets the Con Slip

Amber Rudd has only been back in the Cabinet a matter of days, and she's already reminding us why we didn't like her. The new Work and Pensions Secretary undermined the Prime Minister May, suggesting that Parliament wouldn't allow a No Deal Brexit to happen, and that a second referendum could in fact be on the cards.

Since revealing her plan, the Prime Minister has been warning ministers and MPs that it's her deal or no deal, but Rudd suggested today that as there isn't a majority in the House of Commons in favour of No Deal, then it simply wouldn't happen.

Speaking to BBC Radio 4'S Today programme about the vote on Mrs May's deal, expected to take place next month, she said[37]:

> "If it doesn't get through, anything could happen. The Brexiteers may lose their Brexit".

This is a real fear for Brexiteers. It seems that Mrs May is positioning this option as the only way we'll ever get Brexit – and if we reject it, well, it's just our own fault. We had our chance to support a Brexit deal, she'll say. We ruined it, she'll say.

Liz Truss, Chief Secretary to the Treasury, echoed Rudd's statements, too. She suggested that this is a 'historic opportunity to leave the EU' and that it might be put at risk. On BBC Radio 5 Live, she said:

> "If my colleagues don't vote for this in parliament, we are in serious danger of not leaving at all".

So there we have it. We were wondering all along just how they would get away with conning us out of Brexit, and it's not through a second referendum. It's through the *threat* of a second referendum. And that threat is real. Even Jeremy Corbyn during PMQs today, quipped that it's good that other people are 'considering all options' (second referendum) while May makes such a mess out of the Brexit negotiations.

Amber Rudd let slip today. She showed us how the Brexit con is going to work.

22nd November
Theresa May Secures Political Declaration Agreement with the EU

Theresa May has today confirmed that negotiators in Brussels have reached an agreement on the text of the document that outlines our future relationship with the EU. This isn't the Withdrawal Agreement, but the political declaration that sets out the framework for the future relationship between the UK and the EU.

Here's the difference.

Withdrawal Agreement

The Withdrawal Agreement sets out the parameters within which the United Kingdom will withdraw from the European Union. The draft agreement, as it stands, is 585 pages long[38], and it explains everything from time frames and territories, to the handling of customs matters, the backstop, and rights.

This agreement will be put to a vote in the European Parliament on Sunday, and later to a Meaningful Vote in the House of Commons in early December. Spain has signalled its intent to vote against the deal, citing issues disagreements over control of Gibraltar, but the vote will take place on a qualified majority basis and is likely to pass.

This is **not** a Brexit deal, per se. This is a deal that facilitates our withdrawal. It does not explain how Britain will trade and cooperate with the EU when the transition period ends.

Political Declaration

This document's full title is 'Political Declaration Setting Out the Framework for the Future Relationship Between the European Union and the United Kingdom'.

It acts as a basis for how the UK will trade and cooperate with the European Union after the transition period has come to an end (whenever the UK and the EU decides that will happen). This will require further Brexit negotiations that are likely going to continue for a period of years – at least until 2020. As I've mentioned before, though, this can be extended once for an unspecified period of time, according to agreements made between the UK and the EU. This is all assuming the 'deal' passes in the Commons, of course.

This declaration document was just seven pages long originally, though after continued negotiation with the EU just days before the final November summit, it has been expanded to 26 pages and now sets out a more detailed basis for our future relationship.

May Announces the Final Political Declaration

This afternoon, the Prime Minister appeared outside No 10 and delivered a statement of intent over Brexit, saying that she is determined to agree a deal in full by this Sunday. She said:

> *"I have one goal in mind – to honour the vote of the British people, and to deliver a good Brexit deal. Last week we achieved a decisive breakthrough, when we agreed with the European Commission the terms for our smooth and orderly exit from the EU. Alongside that Withdrawal Agreement, we published an outline*

Political Declaration, setting out the framework for our future relationship.

Last night in Brussels I had a good, detailed discussion with President Juncker, in which I set out what was needed in that Political Declaration to deliver for the United Kingdom. We tasked our negotiating teams to continue working overnight, and as a result the text of that declaration has been agreed between the European Union and the United Kingdom.

I have just updated the Cabinet on progress, and I'll be making a statement to the House of Commons later this afternoon".

Before going back inside 10 Downing Street, May insisted that this was the right deal for the UK, and that it delivers on the results of the referendum…but does it?

The document, which has already been leaked to the press, reveals more betrayals that shows just how long she intends to continue this disastrous negotiation process. Make no mistake, Sunday isn't the end of May's terrible negotiating. Should she remain as leader of the Conservative Party, she'll be continuing this process of scrambling for some kind of deal with the EU for at least another two years during the transition period.

What's Inside the Political Declaration?

The Political Declaration has already been leaked, and it contains plenty of new insights that should give Brexiteers even more cause for concern.

This is not a legally binding document, but instead a declaration that provides the parameters for a deal on our future relationship. The negotiations for this deal will take place following our exit from the European Union in March, and during our 'transition period' where we will be subject to EU rules without having any say on them.

Let's take a look at what the declaration reveals.

1. Objectives and Principles, Paragraph 19

The Parties recall their determination to replace the backstop solution on Northern Ireland by a subsequent agreement that establishes alternative arrangements for ensuring the absence of a hard border on the island of Ireland on a permanent footing.

This is a new addition to the draft, which shows the Prime Minister's commitment to avoiding a hard border in Ireland, and securing new ways to avoid a Northern Ireland backstop. With the DUP abstaining from important budget votes over the last few days, the Prime Minister is clearly keen to ensure that they remain happy. I don't suspect this will be enough.

2. Tariffs, Paragraph 23

The economic partnership should ensure no tariffs, fees, charges of quantitative restrictions across all sectors, with ambitious customs agreements that, in line with the Parties' objectives and principles above, build and improve on the single customs territory provided for in the Withdrawal Agreement which obviates the need for checks on rules of origin.

This is easy to miss, but it essentially outlines how the future agreement will work. There appears to be no intention to create some kind of free trade deal with the European Union, but to instead build on the 'Single Customs Territory' that Theresa May has negotiated for use during the transition period.

In short? The Single Customs Territory is the building blocks for a future agreement, and Theresa May appears to be intending to negotiate some kind of Customs Union deal with the European Union on a permanent basis.

3. Dispute Settlement, Paragraph 134

Should a dispute raise a question of interpretation of Union law, which may also be indicated by either Party, the arbitration panel should refer the question to the CJEU as the sole arbiter of Union law, for a binding ruling.

We have been promised by Theresa May that we would no longer be under the jurisdiction of the European Court of Justice, but this document suggests otherwise. There will be instances, clearly, where the European Court of Justice has sole say over matters relating to law that affects both the UK and the EU. This crosses a red line set out by the government.

There is another issue regarding fishing rights, where the Political Declaration sets out an agreement to negotiate rights over fishing waters, though it's hard to comment on that right now. The government insists that all the UK's red lines have been met, but we won't know until the negotiations begin.

25th November
EU Leaders Give the Withdrawal Deal Their Blessings

The European Union leaders so graciously approved the Brexit deal at a Brussels summit, this weekend. All 27 leaders, including Spain, approved the deal – which should be a sign to any level-headed person that this deal isn't really going to give Britain any kind of competitive edge in the global market.

Mrs May must be relieved to finally have this out of the way after 20 months of negotiating, but she isn't done yet. The deal will now be put to the House of Commons, and I can only assume the Prime Minister has some kind of trick up her sleeve. I'm not saying it's going to be an effective trick, but we should be prepared for lots of spin, propaganda, and marketing to not only make the deal look attractive to MPs, but to the general public. If May can win over the public, perhaps she can sway opposition MPs to give in and back the deal.

I suppose the talk of how we're going to run out of drinking water[39] under a No Deal Brexit is probably enough to sway a few of the less intellectually gifted MPs. No, I'm not about to make a joke about Diane Abbott...

Speaking in Brussels, the Prime Minister now urged Remain and Leave voters to unite behind her agreement and said that the British people 'do not want to spend any more time arguing about Brexit'.

I beg to differ.

The vote in the Commons in the UK will take place on the 12th September, but it isn't looking good for the Prime Minister. I've previously crunched the numbers in this book, but The Sun is predicting that she could lose the vote by as many as 200 votes[40]. They're predicting 221 for the deal –

210 from the Tories, 10 from Labour, and one from the Lib Dems – and 418 votes against the deal. I find it hard to disagree.

Not only will that be a great defeat for the Prime Minister, but it's also likely going to mean an end to her premiership. May has previously said that she has no intention of standing down, but I don't see how she couldn't.

Theresa's Letter to the Nation

The Prime Minister began her campaign to pitch her finalised deal to the public with a letter to the nation. It immediately reminded me of that cringeworthy 'contract' to the voters. Remember that? It was during the 2010 general election campaign, when he put his party's manifesto into a contract format, signed it, and told the voters that they should vote him out if he doesn't deliver what he promises in five years.

Well, he didn't deliver, and for some reason the British people voted for him *even harder* five years later. Work that one out.

DAVID CAMERON'S CONTRACT WITH YOU

If we don't deliver, kick us out

David Cameron promotes his 'contract' in a Tory election newspaper.

Unlike Cameron's contract however, May's letter to the nation was more sad than it was cringeworthy. In it, she explained[41]:

> "When I became your prime minister, the United Kingdom had just voted to leave the European Union.
> "From my first day in the job, I knew I had a clear mission before me - a duty to fulfil on your behalf: to honour the result of the referendum and secure a brighter future for our country by negotiating a good Brexit deal with the EU.
> "Throughout the long and complex negotiations that have taken place over the last year and a half, I have never lost sight of that duty.
> "Today, I am in Brussels with the firm intention of agreeing a Brexit deal with the leaders of the other 27 EU nations.
> "It will be a deal that is in our national interest - one that works for our whole country and all of our people, whether you voted 'Leave' or 'Remain'.
> "It will honour the result of the referendum".

Which is a lie, of course. She goes on to lie about taking back control of our borders (which isn't true – the Prime Minister is signing the UN Global Migration Compact next month), and she lies about taking back control of our laws (we will be bound by EU regulations for as long as we maintain a customs agreement). We all know by now, though, that the Prime Minister is perfectly comfortable lying to us.

Either that, or she's a well-intentioned fool.

The DUP Won't Back Down

There really is no going back for Theresa May, now. The DUP really isn't happy with her – so much so, that they invited Boris Johnson to their conference just days ago. Arlene Foster and the rest of her Members of Parliament welcomed Boris onto their stage and gave him a platform to blast the Prime Minister and the Brexit deal.

If that isn't a sign the DUP are willing to blow this deal up and threaten to remove the Conservative Party's power in the Commons, then I don't know what is. Mrs May *knows* this.

Deputy leader of the DUP Nigel Dodds has also called for a 'third way' between No Deal Brexit and Theresa May's Withdrawal Agreement, writing in the Belfast Telegraph[42]:

> *"Rather than waste any more time putting forward false choices, we need the Government to get on with securing a better deal.*
> *"Our party wants a good deal for the United Kingdom, a deal which delivers upon the referendum result and a deal which ensures that Northern Ireland leaves with the rest of the UK.*
> *"But it is not this deal. It is not a deal at any price."*

There really is not turning back, though. If Mrs May turned her back on the deal now, she'd lose the loyal support she *does* have, and risk struggling to regain the support of the Brexiteers she betrayed.

The Mail on Sunday even reports that Philip Hammond and a 'gang of five' within the Cabinet who are all supporting a soft Brexit, would lead a cabinet exodus if the Prime Minister opted for a hard Brexit option[43].

And to top all this chaos off?

May sold out on Gibraltar to gain the support of Spain, who wouldn't have been able to veto the deal in an EU vote anyway. The vote on the UK/EU Withdrawal Agreement was performed on a qualified majority basis, so Theresa May appeasing Spain by giving into their demands on Gibraltar was particularly spineless.

Spain now has a veto over Gibraltar benefitting from future trade agreements between the UK and Brussels, and the Prime Minister of Spain Pedro Sanchez says that Gibraltar's political, legal and geographic relationship with the EU in the future will all go through Spain[44].

27th November
Trump Trashes the Brexit Deal, and May Starts Her UK Tour

Yesterday, President Donald Trump took down the Brexit deal in that calm, I-don't-really-care attitude that he does so well. Speaking on the White House lawn, he said that the agreement that Theresa May has secured with the European Union 'sounds like a great deal for the EU'.

He said[45]:

> *"I think we have to take a look at, seriously, whether or not the UK is allowed to trade. Because, you know, right now, if you look at the deal, they may not be able to trade with us. And that wouldn't be a good thing.*
>
> *I don't think they mean that. I don't think that the Prime Minister meant that. And, hopefully, she'll be able to do something*

*about that. But right now, as the deal
stands, she may not, they may not, be
able to trade with the US and I don't think
they want that at all".*

He's right, of course. I've explained before how this
works. If we want to trade with the US, we must be able to
control our own regulations. If we cannot set our own rules
and regulations, we cannot accept all products from the
United States, which has different rules and regulations to
us.

Even Peter Mandelson, a key political figure under the
Blair and Brown governments, admitted it in a piece in The
Guardian today[46].

Theresa May has hit back, though. She has begun her
tour of the country promoting her Brexit deal before the vote
in the Commons on December 12th, defending her plan in
Wales and Northern Ireland and claiming that the political
declaration document means the UK will be able to
negotiate trade deals with countries around the rest of the
world.

The reality is quite different, however, as the political
document is merely a wish list. It is not a document that
outlines in any great detail what relationship the UK will
have with the EU. Instead, it explains what the UK wishes
to achieve. No promises, no details, no substance – just a
wish list of things that Theresa May hopes to negotiate in
the next couple of years.

Her language is purposely misleading, too. She didn't
mention the transition period, in which the UK will be locked
into a customs agreement with the EU. We'll have to abide
by EU laws for many more years to come (without having a
say on them), and no, we won't be able to trade with the
US.

Speaking at the Royal Welsh Winter Fair in Builth Wells, the Prime Minister said that she was 'working very well' on a new trade deal.

She said[47]:

> *"As regards to the US, we have already been talking to them about the sort of agreement that we could have in the future. We have a working group set up and that is working very well, has met several times and is continuing to work with the US on this".*

More wishful thinking, more vague promises, more detraction. What do facts matter these days, anyway? Theresa May wants to sell this deal to the public and pick up some support in the Commons in the meantime.

I'm expecting some new card to be played in the coming days, so I'll be on the lookout for it. There's no way she thinks that saying everything she's already said before, but at country fairs and in supermarkets, is going to change anything. The people aren't stupid.

28th November
The Bank of England Predicts No Deal Catastrophe

Almost as if by magic, the Bank of England came out with a report today that might just scare enough people into opting for Theresa May's Brexit deal.

Bank of England governor Mark Carney gave a press conference, offering some pretty dire predictions for the UK economy in the event of a No Deal Brexit. He told the press that the UK economy might shrink by 8% if we left without a deal, house prices could fall by almost a third, and that the pound could fall by a quarter.

The Bank of England even predicted the possibility of migration reversing from 150,000 per year, to falling by 100,000 per year – which doesn't sound so catastrophic if you ask me.

The thing is, though, it's all just possibilities. Carney said it himself in his press conference that these aren't forecasts, but 'scenarios'.

He said:

> *"These are scenarios, not forecasts. They illustrate what could happen not necessarily what is most likely to happen.*
>
> *Taken together the scenarios highlight that the impact of Brexit will depend on the direction, magnitude and speed of the effect of reduced openness of the UK economy".*

These predictions are based on the worst possibilities, and of course ignore the fact that President Trump offered Theresa May a free trade deal four months ago (which she rejected)[48], and the many possibilities for trading outside the European Union.

Jacob Rees-Mogg had some choice words for Mark Carney, too. He told the press today:

> *"Mark Carney is a second-tier Canadian politician who failed to get on in Canadian politics and then got a job in the UK. I don't think he's greatly respected, and he's been deeply politicised to the damage of the Bank of England's*

*reputation. The Bank of England is meant
to be impartial, set interest rates avoiding
politics, for the benefit of the economy –
and he's talking about racking interest
rates up to 5% because he's cross about
Brexit. I'm afraid his reputation has fallen
even faster than his economic forecasts
predict".*

Carney's predictions serve only to scare the public. It's almost too convenient.

I've been saying for a while that Theresa May must have a trick up her sleeve to scare people into voting for her terrible deal, and perhaps this was part of it. Even the carmakers in the UK have suddenly piped up warning about a No Deal Brexit, claiming it will be 'catastrophic'.

I'm not into conspiracy theories, but this has to be pre-planned. Theresa May has warned that it's her deal or no deal, and it likely is. We can't renegotiate the deal in time, it's unlikely we can extend Article 50 – so when March 29th comes along, if we aren't signed up to Theresa's deal then you can bet we're leaving the EU without a deal.

If I was in May's camp, I'd be praising her right now. She has all the right people on her side – the economic giants, the big companies, all saying that No Deal would be catastrophic. Meanwhile, May has delayed so long that there simply isn't an alternative to her deal. Vince Cable can stand up in the Commons all he likes and berate May for her deal, but when she responds by saying not backing her Brexit agreement would lead to 'chaos and uncertainty', it's hard for the Remainers to disagree.

Chapter Six: November 2018

29th November
Theresa May Accepts TV Debate with Jeremy Corbyn

Well this is a real turn of events – Theresa May has proposed a televised debate with Jeremy Corbyn over the Brexit deal, and Corbyn has accepted.

Theresa May famously rejected the option to have a televised debate during the last general election. Her logic, I'm sure, was that the debate would simply give Jeremy Corbyn extra attention she didn't want him to have. She was up in the polls (at least, at that point) and didn't see any need to fight him.

Things are different, now. The Labour Party regularly matches the Tories in the polls, and some days even outdoes them, so May has to take the ageing socialist seriously. Right now, there's a scramble for who gets to host it. Theresa May has accepted the BBC's offer to take part in a Brexit debate, but Corbyn has said he prefers ITV's bid.

Corbyn claims he'd rather take ITV's bid so that he and millions of others don't have to miss the final of ITV's 'I'm a Celebrity Get Me Out of Here' – but there's more to it than that. Both camps are trying to fix the debate so it works best for them.

No 10 believes that a Sunday night slot with the BBC, after the final of Strictly Come Dancing, will play to Theresa May's strength. The show will feature an expert panel, rather than a traditional debate audience. May obviously knows her deal inside out, so rather than answering to emotive questions from the public, she can get down to the nitty gritty and show up Corbyn in the same way she does every PMQs.

The Labour camp, however, would rather see Corbyn and May perform in front of a live studio audience, something he could probably do better than the Theresa May. She's called the MayBot for a reason.

What I don't understand, however, is how Corbyn thinks this could work in his favour. He has no plan for Brexit. Labour have never offered an alternative to Brexit. Corbyn has, however, recently said in PMQs that he believes it's good some people are considering 'all possibilities', alluding to a second referendum.

The only way Corbyn could really stand out here is by going radical and proposing a second referendum. Otherwise, he'll just be vaguely disagreeing with May's terrible plan, without offering any solution.

References

[1] Reuters, "Dublin, London, DUP talk up chances of Brexit deal", Amanda Ferguson and Padraic Halpin, 2nd November 2018,
https://www.reuters.com/article/uk-britain-eu-nireland/dublin-london-dup-talk-up-chances-of-brexit-deal-idUSKCN1N71UT

[2] Independent, "Theresa May to accept checks between Northern Ireland and Great Britain in major concession to avoid Brexit no-deal", Jon Stone, 19th September 2018,
https://www.independent.co.uk/news/uk/politics/brexit-latest-northern-ireland-irish-border-backstop-customs-regulatory-checks-theresa-may-salzburg-a8545701.html

[3] Independent, "Theresa May to accept checks between Northern Ireland and Great Britain in major concession to avoid Brexit no-deal", Jon Stone, 19th September 2018,
https://www.independent.co.uk/news/uk/politics/brexit-latest-northern-ireland-irish-border-backstop-customs-regulatory-checks-theresa-may-salzburg-a8545701.html

[4] The Times, "Revealed: Theresa May's secret Brexit deal", Tim Shipman, 4th November 2018,
https://www.thetimes.co.uk/article/revealed-theresa-mays-secret-brexit-deal-3vvn3c0sf

[5] The Sun, "£40billion Brexit divorce bill means we'll effectively become a non-voting EU colony", Boris Johnson, 4th November 2018,
https://www.thesun.co.uk/news/7658106/boris-johnson-eu-colony-brexit-divorce-deal/

[6] BBC News, "McDonnell: We'll vote against temporary Customs Union", Nicholas Watt, 5th November 2018,
https://www.bbc.co.uk/news/uk-politics-46101243

[7] Twitter, "Still necessary to repeat this, it seems. No country, certainly not the UK, would sign up to have its territory..", Iain Martin, 5th November 2018,
https://twitter.com/iainmartin1/status/1059387499376721926

[8] BBC News, "Brexit: Cabinet aims for deal by end of November", BBC News, 6th November 2018,
https://www.bbc.co.uk/news/uk-politics-46103051

[9] The Guardian, "Leaked plan to sell Brexit deal: 'Measured success is the narrative'", Peter Walker and Dan Sabbagh, 6th November 2018,
https://www.theguardian.com/politics/2018/nov/06/leaked-plan-to-sell-brexit-deal-measured-success-is-the-narrative

[10] BBC News, "Brexit: Ministers invited to read draft EU deal", 7th November 2018,
https://www.bbc.co.uk/news/uk-politics-46130338

[11] The Times, "Brexit: Theresa May appeals to Angela Merkel in final push for divorce deal", Francis Elliott and Sam Coates, 7th November 2018,
https://www.thetimes.co.uk/article/may-appeals-to-merkel-in-final-push-for-divorce-deal-nwxcjgc59

[12] Twitter, "If the Brexit deal involves an extension to the Customs Union then I will vote against it.", Jacob Rees-Mogg, 8th November 2018,
https://twitter.com/Jacob_Rees_Mogg/status/1060464074251821059

[13] BBC News, "David Davis: MPs will 'probably' vote against Brexit deal", BBC News, 8th November 2018,
https://www.bbc.co.uk/news/uk-politics-46137594

Chapter Six: November 2018

[14] *The Guardian, "Labour to use humble address vote to try to force government to release Brexit legal advice - as it happened", Andrew Sparrow, 12th November 2018, https://www.theguardian.com/politics/blog/live/2018/nov/12/brexit-may-cabinet-labour-starmer-contradicts-corbyn-and-says-brexit-can-be-stopped-politics-live?page=with:block-5be96514e4b016737f1f30b3#block-5be96514e4b016737f1f30b3*

[15] *The Telegraph, "Downing Street says reports of a Brexit deal should be 'taken with a bucket of salt'", James Rothwell and Asa Bennett, 12th November 2018, https://www.telegraph.co.uk/politics/2018/11/12/brexit-latest-senior-cabinet-members-brand-pms-plan-worrying/*

[16] *The Guardian, "UK all but gives up on November Brexit summit", Dan Sabbagh, Daniel Boffey and Jennifer Rankin, 12th November 2018, https://www.theguardian.com/politics/2018/nov/12/may-has-little-room-for-manoeuvre-brexit-german-minister-warns*

[17] *The Spectator, "Labour U-turn: 'Brexit can be stopped'", Steerpike, 12th November 2018, https://blogs.spectator.co.uk/2018/11/labour-u-turn-brexit-can-be-stopped/*

[18] *Independent, "Brexit: EU says British citizens will not need visas to visit member states in event of no deal", Jon Stone, 13th November 2018, https://www.independent.co.uk/news/uk/politics/eu-brexit-visas-no-deal-british-citizens-latest-a8631671.html*

[19] *The New European, "Boris Johnson finally admits we could make our own laws before Brexit", Jonathon Read, 13th November 2018, https://www.theneweuropean.co.uk/top-stories/boris-johnson-on-brexit-and-making-our-own-laws-on-bbc-news-1-5778244*

[20] *The New European, "Boris Johnson finally admits we could make our own laws before Brexit", Jonathon Read, 13th November 2018, https://www.theneweuropean.co.uk/top-stories/boris-johnson-on-brexit-and-making-our-own-laws-on-bbc-news-1-5778244*

[21] *The Sun, "Theresa May pleaded with Cabinet ministers to act in the 'national interest' and back her draft Brexit deal agreed with EU", Tom Newton Dunn, Harry Cole, Steve Hawkes and Lynn Davidson, 14th November 2018, https://www.thesun.co.uk/news/brexit/7733661/theresa-may-cabinet-ministers-brexit-plead/amp/?fbclid=IwAR0_PUGYFMirUjlfn0P3QgvEDX6u_MaRvF14ew1U6UDdFHmlOs4yISVtq-k*

[22] *Mirror, "Theresa May Brexit speech in full: Prime Minister gives address on crucial draft deal", Bradley Jolly, 14th November 2018, https://www.mirror.co.uk/news/politics/theresa-brexit-speech-live-prime-13590343*

[23] *Mirror, "Cabinet Minister Esther McVey 'in tears' after being 'shouted' at during crunch Brexit meeting", Elaine McCahill, 15th November 2018, https://www.mirror.co.uk/news/politics/cabinet-minister-esther-mcvey-in-13591899*

[24] *Independent, "Brexit: Liam Fox admits 'a deal is better than no deal' as he backs Theresa May's plan", Joe Watts, 16th November 2018, https://www.independent.co.uk/news/uk/politics/brexit-deal-liam-fox-theresa-may-draft-agreement-eu-withdrawal-cabinet-a8637086.html*

[25] *Twitter, "Rudd made inexcusable errors over Windrush. It is wrong that she has been given a new job before any victims have had compensation. ", David Lammy, 16th November 2018,*

Chapter Six: November 2018

*https://twitter.com/DavidLammy/status/1063469854429188096?ref_src=twsrc%5Etfw%7Ctw
camp%5Etweetembed%7Ctwterm%5E1063469854429188096&ref_url=https%3A%2F%2F
www.bbc.co.uk%2Fnews%2Flive%2Fuk-politics-46200010*

[26] *Twitter, "Extraordinary that Theresa May has managed to bring Amber Rudd back into
Cabinet faster than the Home..", Labour Whips, 16th November 2018,
https://twitter.com/labourwhips/status/1063469362630283265*

[27] *The Sun, "Taoiseach Leo Varadkar says Brexit terms can't be negotiated again – and
believes more MPs will support May 'once reality sinks in'", Kieran dineen, 16th November
2018,
https://www.thesun.ie/news/3400603/varadkar-brexit-terms-support-may/*

[28] *Evening Standard, "UK unemployment rate rose by 21,000 in summer, official figures
show", Ella Wills, 13th November 2018,
https://www.standard.co.uk/news/uk/uk-unemployment-rose-by-21000-in-summer-official-
figures-show-a3988416.html*

[29] *BBC News, "Poverty causing 'misery' in UK, and ministers are in denial, says UN official",
BBC News, 16th November 2018,
https://www.bbc.co.uk/news/uk-46236642*

[30] *Inews, "Poor families are watering down baby formula. Some parents are getting pay day
loans to buy it", Alison Thewliss, 16th November 2018,
https://inews.co.uk/opinion/comment/families-are-watering-down-baby-formula-and-parents-
are-skipping-meals-to-pay-for-it/*

[31] *Gov.uk, "PM speech to CBI: 19 November 2018", Prime Minister's Office, 10 Downing
Street and The Rt Hon Theresa May MP, 19th November 2018,
https://www.gov.uk/government/speeches/pm-speech-to-cbi-19-november-2018*

[32] *Mail Daily, "Coup plot to oust Theresa May would unleash 'appalling chaos' warns Foreign
Secretary as Lemming rebels admit they still don't yet have the 48 letters needed to spark a
leadership vote", James Tapsfield and Tim Sculthorpe, 19th November 2018,
https://www.dailymail.co.uk/news/article-6405099/Tory-Eurosceptics-claim-force-no-
confidence-vote-two-days.html*

[33] *Independent, "DUP abstains on crucial votes in warning over May's Brexit agreement",
Benjamin Kentish and Shehab Khan, 18th November 2018,
https://www.independent.co.uk/news/uk/politics/dup-brexit-budget-vote-theresa-may-
government-confidence-and-supply-agreement-terms-a8642131.html*

[34] *Express, "Furious Barnier reveals MAY asked for Customs Union as EU gets blamed for
constraining UK", Joe Barnes, 19th November 2018,
https://www.express.co.uk/news/uk/1047224/Brexit-news-Michel-Barnier-UK-EU-withdrawal-
agreement-deal-Theresa-May-latest*

[35] *BBC News, "Brexit: May to return to Brussels for talks ahead of crunch summit", BBC
News, 22nd November 2018,
https://www.bbc.co.uk/news/uk-politics-46297725*

[36] *BBC News, "Nicola Sturgeon confirms SNP MPs will vote against Brexit deal", 18th
November 2018,
https://www.bbc.co.uk/news/uk-scotland-scotland-politics-46253055*

[37] *Independent, "Amber Rudd admits new Brexit referendum on table if Theresa May's deal
rejected by parliament: 'Anything could happen'", Rob Merrick, 21st November 2018,*

Chapter Six: November 2018

https://www.independent.co.uk/news/uk/politics/amber-rudd-brexit-final-say-referendum-theresa-may-latest-a8644141.html

[38] *Draft Agreement on the withdrawal of the United Kingdom of Great Britain and Northern Ireland from the European Union and the European Atomic Energy Community, as agreed at negotiators' level on 14 November 2018, 14 November 2018,*
https://ec.europa.eu/commission/sites/beta-political/files/draft_withdrawal_agreement_0.pdf

[39] *Evening Standard, "No-deal Brexit could lead to clean drinking water shortage", Hatty Collier, 25th November 2018,*
https://www.standard.co.uk/news/politics/nodeal-brexit-could-lead-to-clean-drinking-water-shortage-a3999491.html

[40] *The Sun, "Theresa May could suffer a 200-vote defeat when the Commons decides on her Brexit deal — dealing a fatal blow to her Premiership", Tom Newton Dunn, Matt Dathan and Steve Hawkes, 28th November 2018,*
https://www.thesun.co.uk/news/brexit/7843364/theresa-may-commons-200-vote-defeat-brexit-deal/

[41] *BBC News, "Brexit: Theresa May's 'letter to the nation' in full", BBC News, 25th November 2018,*
https://www.bbc.co.uk/news/uk-politics-46333338

[42] *Belfast Telegraph, "DUP claims there is a third way on Brexit", David Young, 26th November 2018,*
https://www.belfasttelegraph.co.uk/news/brexit/dup-claims-there-is-a-third-way-on-brexit-37564364.html

[43] *Politics Home. "Philip Hammond 'to lead Cabinet exodus' if Theresa May goes for no-deal Brexit", Kevin Schofield, 25th November 2018,*
https://www.politicshome.com/news/uk/foreign-affairs/brexit/news/100113/philip-hammond-lead-cabinet-exodus-if-theresa-may-goes-no

[44] *The Guardian, "Brexit: May gives way over Gibraltar after Spain's 'veto' threat", Daniel Boffey and Sam Jones, 24th November 2018,*
https://www.theguardian.com/politics/2018/nov/24/brexit-may-gives-way-over-gibraltar-after-spains-veto-threat

[45] *CNN Politics, "May defends Brexit deal as Trump casts doubt on UK ability to trade with US", Euan McKirdy and Hilary McGann, 27th November 2018,*
https://edition.cnn.com/2018/11/27/politics/trump-brexit-deal-claims-gbr-intl/index.html

[46] *The Guardian, "Yes, Donald Trump is talking perfect sense on May's Brexit deal, Peter Mandelson", Opinion Brexit, 27th November 2018,*
https://www.theguardian.com/commentisfree/2018/nov/27/donald-trump-theresa-may-brexit-deal-peter-mandelson

[47] *Sky News, "Theresa May hits back at Donald Trump as she begins bid to sell Brexit deal", Greg Heffer, 27th November 2018,*
https://news.sky.com/story/theresa-may-hits-back-at-donald-trump-as-she-begins-bid-to-sell-brexit-deal-11565344

[48] *The Telegraph, "Donald Trump offered Theresa May trade deal four months ago, but she rejected him, former minister claims", Camilla Tominey, 27th November 2018,*
https://www.telegraph.co.uk/politics/2018/11/27/donald-trump-offered-theresa-may-trade-deal-four-months-ago/

Chapter Seven
December 2018

1st December
Mrs May's Roadshow Continues

Theresa May is still on the road trying to sell her Brexit deal, but support for her deal doesn't appear to be growing one bit. Laura Kuennsberg, political editor for the BBC, noted that the Prime Minister failed to even mention the latest minister from her cabinet[1]. Science and Universities minister Sam Gyimah – who was hailed recently on Question Time as a future leader of the Conservative Party, though I found him quite tedious – stepped down from his position in the cabinet over a row involving the EU Galileo satellite-navigation project[2].

Gyimah is the 10th minister to resign over Brexit, and there seem to be few signs that Members in the Commons are changing their minds. If they're going to change their minds and decide to support Brexit last minute, then it'll be a private decision made in the heat of the moment during a last-minute panic.

Meanwhile, hardcore Remainers are still on the march for a second referendum. 17 Members of Parliament from both sides of the Commons have come together to say that they believe the British people deserve a new referendum. Conservative arch-Remainer Anna Soubry has been joined by Labour's Chuka Umunna, Chris Leslie, Angela Smith and Ian Murray, as well as a host of other Labourites, the Lib Dems' Norman Lamb, and other Tory rebels in a new campaign for a second referendum[3].

As spineless as I think Mrs May has been this whole time, I don't suspect their campaign will come to anything. Our Prime Minister is too focused on getting her deal passed than betraying the British people. When she says there will be no second referendum on her watch, it's the only time I believe her.

Stuck in the Backstop Indefinitely?

Leaked legal advice given to Theresa May by the Attorney General Geoffrey Cox suggests that Britain could end up stuck in the Customs Union indefinitely. The documents have only been seen by the cabinet and have been withheld from Members of Parliament, despite Parliament demanding they be published in full multiple times before.

AG Geoffrey Cox, however, outlined his concerns in a letter that was seen by The Sunday Times that the UK would end up stuck in the backstop indefinitely. The government has refused to release the full details of this legal advice provided by Cox, and the rest of Parliament continues to push to see it.

In fact, Labour is threatening the government with Contempt of Parliament action over the legal advice issue. The official opposition want to see the legal advice on May's Withdrawal Agreement, provided to the government by AG Geoffrey Cox, or they will vote to find the government in Contempt of Parliament.

Traditionally, legal advice isn't published – though there are provisions that allow for parliament to see the advice in extreme circumstances. Labour is arguing that this is an extreme circumstance, and that the government would be guilty of obstructing the legislature to carry out its functions if they do not release it. In British history, no government has been found in Contempt of Parliament.

While Labour and the Tories battle that out, Liam Fox has been out campaigning for May's deal. It's quite the U-turn for Fox, a Brexiteer, who is now calling for people to accept Theresa May's imperfect deal so that Brexit happens[4]. What he means, of course, is that Members of Parliament should accept the deal so at least some *kind* of Brexit happens. He knows very well that it's looking like the Brexit vote will be betrayed in the near future.

2nd December
Labour Prepares for May's Meaningful Vote Failure

It remains clear that Theresa May is lacking any kind of majority in Parliament, and that her deal is not going to pass. I could be wrong, but right now, the Parliamentary arithmetic simply doesn't support it.

For that reason, the Labour Party is preparing for what happens after the Withdrawal Agreement is voted down. It's reported today that the official opposition will seek to topple Theresa May and her government and force a general election[5]. This is of course what Jeremy Corbyn has been wanting all along, knowing very well that he could tap into the disaffection with the Tories. Amazingly, I think people are so unhappy with May's lack of leadership that they'd be willing to vote for a party with a wishy-washy Brexit policy. That's how bored people are, and Corbyn knows it.

Shadow Brexit Secretary Keir Starmer said to Sky News today[6]:

> *"It seems to me that if the Prime Minister has lost a vote of that sort of significance, then there has to be a question of confidence in her government".*

I don't agree that a general election is necessary, but I do think it's highly likely at this point. We're facing a few options – there will either be a general election if May's deal doesn't pass, or there could be another referendum. That would, of course, require us to extend Article 50 – which might even mean we hold European elections in May along with the rest of the EU. If the second referendum doesn't anger voters enough, the European election certainly would.

Another possibility is that the Brexit vote is scrapped or delayed. The vote is still planned to go ahead next week and Mrs May still seems determined to get to the vote, but there are reports that Tory whips are urging the Prime Minister to go back to the European Union and renegotiate her deal[7]. In the meantime, the vote would be delayed or even scrapped so that Mrs May can come back with another deal from the EU and not face a crushing defeat of up to 200 votes next week.

That won't happen, though. There is absolutely no way Mrs May is going to give in. She's already told us that she can't get a better deal, and we've already seen how stubborn she is. Mark my words, she will not delay this vote.

What About the TV Debate?

We haven't heard much about the TV debate between Corbyn and May. We've been waiting for years to see this happen, and we seem to have reached a bottleneck. Neither leader can agree on the format of the debates, and Downing Street claims that Corbyn is simply 'running scared'[8].

The debate is meant to go ahead on the 9th December, but Corbyn is being picky. He's said he'll take the BBC offer if the format is the same as the ITV debate he preferred – that means, he refuses to take questions from the expert panel being proposed for the BBC debate. May knows she would do better taking questions from experts, given she was the architect of this entire deal. She knows the betrayals inside-out.

3rd December
Bercow Allows Motion to Find Government in Contempt of Parliament

The legal advice debate is heating up, with Speaker of the House John Bercow allowing Labour, the Democratic Unionist Party, and four other opposition parties to file a motion to be voted on on Tuesday. Bercow allowed the motion just before five days of debate begin on May's Withdrawal Agreement, explaining there was an "arguable case that a contempt has been committed".

The motion is simple: the opposition parties claim that the government should be found in Contempt of Parliament for not publishing the full legal advice from the Attorney General. Now, Conservative Members of Parliament have been put on a three-line whip to prepare to defend the government[9]. A three-line whip means that Tory MPs are being demanded by the party whip, in a written notice underlined three times, urging them to vote in support of the party.

So the whips are out in force, pressuring MPs as best they can, to vote and defend their government – but will it work? Theresa May has nearly been on the chopping block multiple times already, so I'm not sure how effective a three-line whip will be.

The fact that the DUP has taken part in this contempt motion is significant. The DUP are propping up the government, and without their votes, they're left unprotected against the opposition. 10 votes form the DUP could make all the difference that Theresa May needs, so I don't expect her to win this vote. How can she? Half her party is against her, and is she really likely to receive supportive votes from Labour? I don't think so.

We must ask ourselves not whether she will survive the vote, but what happens when she loses the vote. What happens when May's government is found in Contempt of Parliament?

4th December
May Makes History: Government Found in Contempt of Parliament

Today was Theresa May's toughest day. Pressure is mounting with new challenges facing her every day. The House of Commons today began its five-day-long debate on the proposed Withdrawal Agreement, but before that began, May's government faced three votes – and she lost all three.

MPs debated an opposition motion that found the government in Contempt of Parliament for not releasing the full legal advice on Brexit. This is the first time any government has ever been found in contempt of Parliament, losing the vote by 311 to 293. That means members of May's party voted to find her and her ministers in contempt of Parliament, and some even sat on their hands and abstained.

Andrea Leadsom MP, leader of the House of Commons, was forced to act. She announced that the government would be releasing the full legal advice tomorrow, which could potentially damage their deal with the European Union. Legal advice is provided in many instances to the government and is not expected to release it, though a clause does recommend that in extreme circumstances these details can be released. Evidently, in this instance, the Parliamentarians thought it relevant for the advice to be released.

This would, however, give the European Union an advantage – they'll know the UK's strengths and weaknesses, and if this deal Theresa May has negotiated doesn't go through, they'll be in an even better negotiating position the second time round. Assuming, of course, there is a second time round.

The vote came after MPs from six different parties wrote a joint letter in which they urged John Bercow, Speaker of the House of Commons, to launch the contempt of Parliament proceedings. The primary face behind the push was Shadow Secretary of State for Exiting the European Union, Keir Starmer MP[10].

Interestingly, Jacob Rees Mogg said that the legal advice should be published, but that he thinks the motion to put the government in contempt was 'badly worded' – so he didn't vote for May's ministers to be found in contempt. I suspect he's playing a game here, knowing that this vote has hurt the Tories more than he'd like. He is, after all, a card-carrying Conservative and this was a big win for Labour.

May's job, after this decision, is to continue selling her Brexit deal to the country and to Members of Parliament. The five-day debate began immediately afterwards, with Theresa May speaking for over an hour in an attempt to sell her deal to Parliament. One thing she said really struck me, and I thought it summed up the problem with her deal perfectly.

Speaking about her deal, she explained:

> *"Yes, it is a compromise. It speaks to the hopes and desires of our fellow citizens who voted to leave, and those who voted to stay in, and we will not bring our country together if we seek a relationship that gives everything to one side of the argument and nothing to the other. We should not let the search for the perfect Brexit prevent a good Brexit that delivers for the British people."*

She then said:

> *"We should not contemplate a course that fails to respect the result of the referendum, because it would decimate the trust of millions of people in our politics for a generation."*

Here's the thing – by compromising on Brexit, she is decimating the trust of millions of people. Upon becoming Prime Minister, it became May's duty to deliver on Brexit in a way that reflects the results of the referendum. The Leave side won, and she should therefore deliver the desire of the winning side. That's how referenda work.

In a parallel world, where Remain won, would the David Cameron government have sought a new policy direction that offered Brexit supporters some kind of concession? Or would they have carried on as before, maintained their membership of the European Union, and brushed off the Brexiteers?

Theresa May has been coming at this problem from the wrong angle from the beginning, and it isn't going down well with the public, or with her own party.

Her speech to the Commons today insisted that as it stands, Parliament must choose between her deal or no deal. That is her main pitch, and it's the only way she could possibly get this atrocious plan through Parliament. But, we could also be watching the final days of Theresa May. When she ended her speech, colleagues beside her reached out and patted her on the shoulder, as if to say 'well done'. I couldn't help but think that those around her knew they were congratulating a woman who tried her best, but who was ultimately doomed to fail.

May's narrative isn't believed by everybody, though – and today, a top advisor to the European Court of Justice completely undermined her by saying that the UK could still stop Brexit without European Union approval[11]. Campos Sanchez-Bordona, senior legal adviser to the ECJ, has said that the UK could simply revoke Article 50 independently without permission from any EU member state. This, of course, has emboldened Remainers who may otherwise have been scared into voting for May's deal to avoid a No Deal scenario.

So I suppose Mark Carney offering more No Deal doom and gloom today hasn't had quite the effect I'm sure he wants. He told MPs today that, in the evet of a No Deal Brexit, food prices could rise between 5 and 10%[12].

What's Next?

Today, the Commons began five days of debate over the agreement. The motion for the debate is as follows:

> *SECTION 13(1)(B) OF THE EUROPEAN UNION (WITHDRAWAL) ACT 2018*
> *The Prime Minister*
> *That this House approves for the purposes of section 13(1)(b) of the European Union (Withdrawal) Act 2018, the negotiated Withdrawal Agreement laid before the House on Monday 26 November 2018 with the title 'Agreement on the withdrawal of the United Kingdom of Great Britain and Northern Ireland from the European Union and the European Atomic Energy Community' and the framework for the future relationship laid before the House on Monday 26 November 2018 with the title 'Political Declaration setting out the framework for the future relationship between the*

European Union and the United Kingdom'.

Tonight, the debate lasted long into the early hours of the morning, as every MP is expected to contribute until the five-day session is called to an end. Once the debates have come to an end, there will be a Meaningful Vote at the end of the day on Tuesday 11th December.

If Theresa May somehow wins this vote, then it's likely that her plan will go ahead and that will be the Brexit deal we get. But if Theresa May loses, then the Labour Party will kick it up a gear. They will pounce on the Prime Minister while she is vulnerable. The DUP are no longer supporting her (hence her loss on the Contempt vote earlier today), and the Labour Party will use this to their advantage and bring a vote of no confidence against the government. Keir Starmer confirmed today on Sky News that it's not a matter of if, but *when* the Labour Party decide to place this no confidence vote against the government.

It might hold some weight, too. If the DUP are sufficiently unhappy, then between the SNP, DUP, Labour, and the Lib Dems, they could bring the government down. Corbyn might try and make a play to form his own minority government, but it's much more likely we would see a call for a general election.

Assuming May loses and Labour call for this vote of no confidence, ministers would be given 21 days until New Year's Day to offer a statement about how they intend to proceed. Following this, they would have until the 15th of January when a vote in the Commons would be made, based on the statement provided by the government. Should that statement be rejected, then the UK would likely just leave the European Union without a deal.

Dominic Greave MP tabled a motion in Parliament today[13], which passed 321 votes to 299 and gives MPs a say over what happens if May's deal doesn't pass in Parliament. The system whereby ministers would be given 21 days to offer a statement about how they intend to proceed was introduced by Greave and conservative rebels (and former loyalists) Damian Green, Michael Fallon, and Jo Johnson. This was the third defeat for the government tonight, and the amendment is intended to ensure that any motion put forward by the government following a loss by May, could be amended by MPs.

This is all a game of chess and a game of chicken. Corbyn, the Labour Party, and Tory rebels are trying to prove they're willing to play the game of chess, but how far are they really willing to go?

5th December
Here's What the Legal Advice Reveals

As promised by Andrea Leadsom MP, the full legal advice from the Attorney General on Theresa May's Withdrawal Agreement was released today. And it's revealing.

In fact, it's proven to me that Labour and the DUP were right to push for it. This legal advice shows just how bad Theresa Mays' deal is and confirms all our fears. We're not conspiracy nuts and swivel-headed loons; we were right all along!

It certainly doesn't help our cause much, though. Parliamentary opposition will use this to their advantage as much as they can, and it won't work out well for the Prime Minister. Whether it's a general election, a second referendum or just an overturning of Brexit, we're all pretty screwed. I do wonder what is going through Jacob Rees-Mogg's head at this point. Is he happy that the Remainers are winning the argument? What exactly is he hoping for right now? I'm as staunch a Brexiteer as he is, and I certainly can't think of any scenario where we end up on top.

There are 33 points made in the six-page document[14] which offer advice on our legal status, the operation of the protocol, the EU's perspective of the deal, and the Article 19 review mechanism. The Article 19 review mechanism is a provision that allows for termination of the deal by mutual consent.

Within these 33 points, I see five that are particularly worrying.

> *Operation of the Protocol*
> *7. Pursuant to Article 6.1. the UK as a whole (ie GB and NI) will form a single customs territory with the EU. This is a fiscal arrangement only. The arrangements as a whole apply differently in GB and NI, albeit that those applicable to NI are dealt with in Article 6.2. (see below). NI remains in the EU's Customs Union, and will apply the whole of the EU's customs acquis, and the Commission and pass from NI to Ireland without any fiscal checks. GB in a separate Customs Union with the EU creating a single customs territory between the EU and the UK, meaning NI and GB are not in separate customs territories. GB is required to align with the EU's Common External Tariff for any goods coming into the country. GB goods will also be able to pass between the UK and EU tariff-free. Goods passing from GB to NI will be subject to a declaration process. Compliance with these requirements in GB will not be subject to*

the jurisdiction of the Commission or the CJEU.

In short, this means that Northern Ireland will stay in the existing customs arrangement and the UK will have an arrangement that's slightly different. Therefore, goods passing between GB and NI would still be subject to a declaration process, meaning a border down the Irish Sea. Theresa May told us that this is something no Prime Minister would ever sign up for.

> *The Indefinite Nature of the Protocol*
> *16. It is difficult to conclude otherwise than that the Protocol is intended to subsist even when negotiations have clearly broken down. The ordinary meaning of the provisions set out above and considered in their context allows no obvious room for the termination of the Protocol, save by the achievement of an agreement fulfilling the same objectives. Therefore, despite statements in the Protocol that it is not intended to be permanent, and the clear intention of the parties that it should be replaced by alternative, permanent arrangements, in international law the Protocol would endure indefinitely until a superseding agreement took its place, in whole or in part, as set out therein. Further, the Withdrawal Agreement cannot provide a legal means of compelling the EU to conclude such an agreement.*

Here, Cox notes that despite statements in the protocol that the backstop is not intended to be permanent, it could in fact endure indefinitely under international law until a superseding agreement takes its place. The Withdrawal Agreement cannot provide any legal means for compelling the EU to come to an agreement on a new superseding agreement, meaning the UK could be stuck within the backstop indefinitely. We'll be at the mercy of the EU for as long as they like.

> *The Article 19 Review Mechanism*
> *26. Article 19 does not expressly state that the review mechanism is intended to be arbitrable under the governance provisions of the Withdrawal Agreement, but I consider that the better view is that it is. Either party could invoke this review mechanism. Therefore, Article 19 provides also for the EU to argue that the Protocol is no longer necessary "in whole or in part": it would be open to the EU, under the pressure of the factors set out above, if it considered negotiations had clearly broken down, or were taking an unsatisfactorily long time, to argue that Article 50 TEU no longer provided a legal base for a UK wide Customs Union. They could, therefore, submit a formal notification to the Joint Committee arguing that the Protocol was no longer necessary in part and that the GB elements of the Customs Union should fall away, leaving only NI in the EU customs territory as the minimum necessary to achieve the objectives in Article 1.3. That contention would meet the strong objection that it would contradict the very clear intention of the parties that the single customs territory created by Article 6.1. was not to be treated as severable.*

When Cox explains that the deal provides for the EU to argue the protocol is no longer necessary in whole or in part, he's saying that that GB element of the Customs Union could simply fall away and leave NI as the bare minimum required to maintain the backstop. This is yet another red line crossed, with NI left in the Customs Union as decided by the EU.

> *The Article 19 Review Mechanism*
> *30. In conclusion, the current drafting of the Protocol, including Article 19, does not provide for a mechanism that is unlikely to enable the UK lawfully to exit the UK wide Customs Union without a subsequent agreement. This remains the case even if parties are still negotiating many years later and even if the parties believe that talks have clearly broken down and there is no prospect of a future relationship agreement. The resolution of such a stalemate would have to be political.*

In his Review Mechanism section, he concludes by saying that the Protocol doesn't provide for a mechanism that will enable the UK to leave the UK-wide Customs Union without a new agreement in place. That means we'll be stuck inside the backstop until the EU decides to make a deal, and even if we think talks have broken down and there is no prospect of a future relationship agreement we simply won't be able to leave without mutual consent. We can be held to ransom by the European Union.

Cox concludes:

> *"It is important to take into account the changing political context in which it is to operate and that the solution to any essentially political question is rarely wholly or even predominantly legal. In the absence of a right of termination, there is*

> *a legal risk that the United Kingdom might become subject to protracted the repeating bounds of negotiations. This risk must be weighed against the political and economic imperative on both sides to reach an agreement that constitutes a politically stable and permanent basis for their future relationship. This is a political decision for the government."*

This legal advice from Geoffrey Cox confirms what we've suspected all along and will make May's job even more difficult. I see no way Mrs May can continue to claim she has achieved a good deal with the UK. Any possible deals the Prime Minister was hoping to make with Members of Parliament will now be out the window, as every Member of Parliament who reads this will see that signing this deal will put our United Kingdom at severe risk. The European Union will be given power over the future of our union, and power to separate NI from GB. This is utterly unacceptable.

No matter how much doom and gloom Mark Carney and the Bank of England throw at us in an attempt to scare us into accepting a deal, giving away our future is simply not a good deal.

10th December
May Delays the Meaningful Vote

This morning, Downing Street told us that the Meaningful Vote would be going ahead tomorrow. In fact, Brexit Secretary Stephen Barclay told Andrew Marr that the vote would "100%" be happening on Tuesday – but the rumours started at around 11am that the Prime Minister was planning to delay the vote.

Quite a bold move, considering the Prime Minister has already spent £100,000 on Facebook advertising in an attempt to build up public support for her deal[15].

Theresa May made a statement to Parliament at 3:30pm that she would be delaying the Meaningful Vote. She thanked the honourable members for their input, and told the House that she had listened to their concerns. Up until now, I suspect she'd only merely *heard* them.

DUP leader Arlene Foster tweeted last night[16]:

> *"Just finished a call with the Prime Minister. My message was clear. The backstop must go. Too much time has been wasted. Need a better deal. Disappointed it has taken so long for Prime Minister to listen".*

For some reason, it made the Prime Minister listen. Just a day away from her deal being voted down by a huge majority in Parliament, she decided to delay the vote and try something different. I can't help but wonder whether a phone call from Arlene Foster was really enough to make her realise. I feel like something happened through the night or before midday today. Either Mrs May received a phone call from Brussels that something new was on offer, or she learned from a group within her Parliamentary Conservative Party what it would take to win them over. It had to have been something serious like this, or she wouldn't have delayed a vote that MPs have already spent four days debating.

Interestingly, though, a European Commission spokeswoman made it clear just before the postponement of the vote that the European Union would not be offering a new Brexit deal.

So what did Theresa May mean today when she stood up in front of the Commons and announced that she would be going back to the European Union to seek further 'reassurances' that the UK would not get stuck in the backstop?

Multiple Members of Parliament asked the Prime Minister exactly that. When asked whether she was seeking a change in the deal or simple 'reassurances', the Prime Minister fed us standard lines about seeking new assurances from the European Union that we won't be stuck in the backstop. If that's what she really thinks it will take to win over Parliament, then she's delusional. But, perhaps she knows something we don't. Perhaps there's something more cunning happening here.

I give May more credit than most. I think she's a tactical mover, and I'd be surprised if she was going into this on a wing and a prayer. I think she has a plan.

Labour MP Grabs Ceremonial Mace in Parliament

At the end of a long day in Parliament, following Theresa May's decision to delay the Meaningful Vote on her Withdrawal Agreement, a Labour Member of Parliament has caused a stir and broken Parliamentary protocol.

MP Lloyd Russel-Moyle picked up the ceremonial mace following the postponement of the vote and attempted to leave the House[17] with the important ornament.

The ceremonial mace is a symbol of Royal authority. It reminds Parliament and the Government that they are working for Her Majesty the Queen. It is a silver gilt ornamental club, and around five foot in length. It's a symbol of our great parliamentary tradition, and the mace itself dates back to the reign of Charles II, who became king in 1650.

On every day that the House of Commons is sitting, the mace is carried into the Chamber by the Serjeant at Arms and is placed on the table between both sides of the House. It is left untouched by Parliamentarians, and removed by the Serjeant at Arms at the end of sessions.

This Labour MP didn't randomly decide to do this. He knew what he was doing has some precedent, and of course, he wanted some attention. Russel-Moyle, in protest of Theresa May and her government's actions, picked up the mace just like Labour Party Member John Beckett did in 1930[18]. Beckett was suspended for attempting to leave the Chamber with the mace in protest against the suspension of another member of the House.

A Conservative Party Member of the House once removed the mace – Michael Heseltine – in protest against Labour MPs signing the socialist anthem 'The Red Flag' in Parliament. For the most part, though, this is a Labour tradition. Ron Brown MP did it in 1988, John McDonnell did it in 2009, and now Lloyd Russel-Moyle has done it.

Russel-Moyle is unlikely to face any disciplinary action other than being suspended for the day, but his actions have shown that Parliament is in total disarray. Theresa May surely cannot last much longer.

What on Earth Happens Now?

In 109 days, we leave the European Union. Today's postponement is pushing her government dangerously close to the deadline. Technically, we would be forced to leave the EU simply without a deal if we're unable to come to an agreement by then – but things have changed. Parliament simply wouldn't allow that to happen, following motions put forward by Dominic Greave. Furthermore, the European Court of Justice announced this morning that the UK would be able to simply cancel Brexit without the permission of the remaining 27 EU member states[19].

That means if Theresa May can't find a deal and doesn't want to continue fighting for her version of Brexit she could decide to cancel Brexit without any further discussion with the rest of the EU.

Right now, though, she is focused on going back to the European Union to secure new assurances. If she comes back with a new deal or new assurances, there will still need to be a vote in Parliament. If she fails, as she was expected to fail in the Meaningful Vote she delayed, then she'll be given 21 days to outline her new plan.

The cut-off date for amending any new plans would be January 21st, meaning we might have no answers for a further six weeks.

This could all be stopped, however, if the Labour Party successfully pushes for a vote of no confidence in the government. Vince Cable, leader of the Liberal Democrats, announced today that his party would be willing to support Labour in that endeavour, but the only way it would be possible is if Corbyn could win over the DUP.

As much as the DUP is angry, I can't see them siding with Corbyn any time soon.

11th December
Theresa May Meets EU Leaders to Secure New 'Reassurances' Over Backstop

Forgotten about the looming threat of a no confidence vote? So had I.

There are rumours that Sir Graham Brady has now received the 48 letters required to call for a vote of confidence in the Prime Minister, but that this won't be announced until Mrs May has returned to the UK after beginning new talks with European leaders. Tim Dawson of the Telegraph and Spectator announced on the news on Twitter[20].

It's not just the Tories who are calling for a vote of confidence, either. The cross-party People's Vote campaign has called on Labour leader Jeremy Corbyn to push a vote of no confidence in Theresa May[21]. Within that People's Vote campaign, you'll find Members from the SNP, Lib Dems, Green Party, Plaid Cymru, and even the Tories. In fact, arch-Remainer Anna Soubry is right at the forefront of the campaign calling for her own party's government to be brought down.

Meanwhile, the Prime Minister hopped across the Channel today to begin talks with European leaders to try and secure new concessions, or likely just new 'reassurances', in an attempt to rescue her Brexit deal. She met German Chancellor Angela Merkel and Dutch Prime Minister Mark Rutte today in order to secure assurances over the backstop issue. She needs to find a way to convince Parliamentarians that if the backstop comes into play, the UK will not be held indefinitely within it and Northern Ireland will not be treated different to the rest of the UK.

It's not looking good, though. Merkel said today that the Brexit deal could not be renegotiated[22], and so did Jean-Claude Juncker. Speaking to MEPs in Strasbourg, the Commission President Juncker said that he was willing to offer 'further clarification' over the backstop, but that there is 'no room whatsoever' to change the agreement at this stage[23].

That means Eurosceptics won't be won over by any reassurances May might get from her visit. If the ERG is to vote in favour of her deal, or even non-ERG Brexiteers in Parliament, she would need a change to the withdrawal text. Therefore, her mission is to fully reassure Remainers and loosely-pro-Brexit MPs that her deal will not leave us stuck in the backstop.

12th December
Theresa May Survives Confidence Vote

The rumours were true. This morning, Sir Graham Brady informed the Prime Minister that the required 48 letters had been submitted, and a confidence vote was being called. Unlike last time, those who submitted the letters didn't back out last minute. The vote happened, and Mrs May has spent the day wondering whether she could win it.

Downing Street is said to have believed that as few as 70 MPs would vote against her, but that didn't stop them restoring the whip of a Tory MP who was suspended during a sex text scandal. Andrew Griffiths MP had his whip restored after being suspended for six months after inappropriate text messages were unearthed and he responded in kind, voting in support of the Prime Minister[24].

Before the vote took place, Andrea Jenkins (a staunchly pro-Brexit MP) told Sky News that Members of Parliament who were expected to vote in favour of the Prime Minister had been telling her that, in the secret ballot, they may not support her after all. So of course, there was a great amount of talk about Mrs May losing the vote and being forced to resign as Prime Minister. But that's not how it worked out.

The results were as follows:

Confidence in the Prime Minister: 200
No Confidence in the Prime Minister: 117
Majority: 83

Chapter Seven: December 2018

Her win is being spun in many different ways. May loyalists claim that the result strengthens her position, as she gained one extra vote compared to the number of Tory MPs who initially voted for her during the leadership election. Jacob Rees-Mogg and the Brexiteers, however, see it quite differently. Speaking to the press shortly after the result was announced, Rees-Mogg explained that with 139 Tory MPs on the payroll, she really only got a further 61 MPs to back her. He said that she should behave like Thatcher and resign, rather than like Major and lead the Tory Party to defeat.

A very likely explanation for the Prime Minister's victory tonight is that she gave up her opportunity to fight another election. Before the vote, Mrs May announced that she would not be leading the party into the 2022 election[25] – potentially swaying some MPs who might have been concerned she would be unable to lead the party to victory in the next general election. The Prime Minister was, however, unclear during the 1922 Committee meeting whether she would fight an election held before 2022. With the threat of a vote of no confidence being made against the government – which is possible if the DUP decides to team up with Labour – then Mrs May would need to make a decision to step down, or fight. Given a snap election would happen quite quickly, she'd probably be forced to fight it.

As a result of her win, and according to the Conservative Party's own rules, May is safe as leader of the party for a further 12 months. No more votes of confidence can be made until those 12 months are up.

Mrs May now has a job to finish. She will go to a European Union summit where she will continue seeking further assurance over the backstop issue, and I'm beginning to think she might have something up her sleeve. She won't be able to change the Withdrawal Agreement, but if her legal reassurances are strong enough, she could win enough of her own party over. Not only will she use the threat of a Corbyn government or no Brexit at all, but some legal reassurances could be enough to sway some MPs who accept they lost the no confidence vote. Even Jacob Rees-Mogg told Sky News tonight that if she comes back with a change to the backstop issue, then even he will compromise and vote for it. Surely she knows that, and perhaps she can even do more than just gain reassurances. If she can convince the EU that this is important enough, she could make the changes she needs to win Brexiteers over with – and maybe she'll even get the DUP back on board.

Will it all be worth it, though? Upon taking the reigns as Prime Minister, May told us that she was intending to fight burning injustices. She now has to completely abandon her domestic agenda, deliver the Withdrawal Agreement, deliver a trade deal, and step down before 2022 comes along. She will, at least, be fighting harder than ever to cement her legacy as the successful Brexit Prime Minister.

17th December
No 10 Escalates 'No Deal' Planning

Theresa May has been back in Brussels after delaying the Meaningful Vote on her Brexit deal last week, but she has had little success. The European Union has reconfirmed that they are not willing to reopen negotiations for the Withdrawal Agreement, meaning Mrs May has nothing to offer Members of Parliament who would be willing to support the deal if the backstop provisions were scrapped.

Instead, Mrs May is planning on seeking reassurances, but we'll have to wait and see whether that's enough to sway Tory and Labour MPs. I doubt very much it will convince anyone from the DUP.

Chapter Seven: December 2018

The natural response to this, of course, is planning for a No Deal Brexit. We've been told by the government many times before that they've planned for No Deal, but I suspect nobody really thought it would happen. Still, I'm not convinced it either will, or even can happen. Would our Parliament really let it happen? We have a very small group of Brexiteers who would be willing to work with a No Deal exit from the EU, and a vast majority who would use whatever power they can pull together to stop it.

Parliament has the power to vote down Mrs May's deal, and I suspect they'll have the power to throw a spanner in the works and stop a No Deal exit, too.

Regardless, the government is getting ready for it. I know Theresa May has lied before, but I believe her when she says she doesn't want another referendum. She knows it would be betraying the trust of the British people and she wouldn't want to destroy her legacy in one fell swoop. Mrs May also wants to avoid a 'hard Brexit', and so I know she'll fight tooth and nail for her deal – but if it fails, I would expect her to push for No Deal.

Chancellor Philip Hammond has put together a plan to hand over £2 billion to transport, energy, law enforcement and healthcare in the event of a No Deal Brexit. Speaking to The Sun, a government source said[26]:

> *"The Chancellor knows what needs to be done and if action is necessary you will see decisions very soon".*

And I think we just might.

While the cabinet discusses a second referendum, and Mrs May continues to slam the idea[27], I think Hammond will make these plans in the background in case everything goes to hell.

May's Cabinet Considering a Second Referendum

Theresa May says she doesn't want a second referendum. In fact, it's the only thing I believe she's being honest about. I don't think she wants one, and I certainly don't think she'll want to tar what's left of her legacy with it.

She said today that a second referendum would break the trust of the British people, and she's right[28].

The government has ruled out a second referendum today too, but it's not that simple. Some members of the Cabinet support it, and so do many in Parliament.

In Theresa May's head, she thought that she could pass a deal that satisfied both Remain and Leave camps. She underestimated just how poisonous politics has become, though. I'm confident she thought that MPs would support her moderate betrayal, and I doubt she ever would have thought that just so many in Parliament would have wanted to *completely* overturn Brexit. A moderate betrayal was a given from the start, but a clear, visible, and honest betrayal? Surely not.

May's compromise deal isn't going through any time soon, and Parliament is whispering about all the other options on the table.

They don't want No Deal, so they hope that they've now sufficiently scared the public that we'd vote differently in a second referendum. That is exactly what is being discussed in May's cabinet right now.

Amber Rudd is one of the MPs leading the charge, too. She's the cabinet member who was booted over the Windrush scandal but welcomed back in when May started running out of cabinet ministers.

The Standard reported[29]:

Chapter Seven: December 2018

Amber Rudd said it is possible Theresa May will ultimately be unable to persuade enough of her own MPs to back her deal, suggesting it is time to "abandon outrage and accusations" and "try something different".

She also said we need a 'practical, sensible and healing approach' for MPs to come around to stop us crashing out of the EU. She's talking about a second referendum.

Five cabinet members in total are now reported to be considering a second referendum if Parliament can't agree on a deal when it's voted on next month.

They include David Lidington – who earlier this year was holding secret meetings with Labour and Lib Dem MPs in an attempt to get their support for a deal he knew his Tory MPs wouldn't back – as well as Amber Rudd, Philip Hammond, David Gauke, and Greg Clark.

Business Secretary Greg Clark has admitted that a second referendum could be triggered as cabinet ministers are split[30] – and Mrs May has essentially run out of people to put in her cabinet.

And with pressure from the Labour side – even from ex-PM Tony Blair – I don't see any reason why this wouldn't happen.

Parliament could easily vote for a second referendum, and the betrayal would be complete. If they pull it off, you shouldn't expect a referendum choice between deal or no deal. You should expect a choice between Remain, Deal, or No Deal. And that's how they'll betray us.

18th December
Cabinet Clarifies Preparations for No Deal

May's Cabinet might be divided, with at least five members calling for a second referendum, but that hasn't stopped them preparing for a No Deal Brexit. Today the cabinet has decided to 'ramp up' those preparations, explaining how they are splitting up the £2 billion being set aside to assist public services in the event of a clean exit from the European Union.

140,000 British companies will be receiving letters from the government explaining what they should do if this happens, and 3,500 troops will be put on standby to assist government departments. Remainers use this as some kind of evidence that the country is going to collapse into chaos, but the reality is that these troops are likely just there to assist in more administrative and logistical endeavours. Defence Secretary Gavin Williamson told MPs today that the military personnel will include logisticians and engineers alongside infantry units, and will be ready to be deployed only if necessary[31].

Out of the £2 billion being set aside, the Treasury has said that £480 million will go directly to the Home Office, to employ more Border Force officers and boost our national security resources. DEFRA (Department for Environment, Food and Rural Affairs) will also receive £410 million to focus on fish, food and chemical trade. The Department for Business will get £190 million, Department for International Trade £128 million, and £375 million will be given to HMRC to hire over 3,000 members of staff to handle increased customs activities.

I'm the first to admit that a No Deal Brexit won't be the easiest thing to pull off, but it'll be worth it. The investment now will pay off in the long run, and I'm happy to see that the government is at least preparing.

This could, of course, also be a measure to try and force Brussels to re-open negotiations. If Mrs May shows she's serious about her preparations for No Deal, then Brussels will have to listen. They do, after all, have much more to lose than the UK. Not only would they not receive the £39 billion pay-out Theresa May agreed, but the EU's agricultural exporters could be cut off from the UK overnight. They'll have no access to our markets unless we agreed on some new kind of deal. EU capital costs would be raised and the smaller economies within the EU would struggle – so why exactly we've been so terrified of a No Deal situation this entire time, I don't know. Well, I do know, but you see what I'm saying.

The EU are scared of No Deal, and perhaps that's why Mrs May has ramped up the preparations.

A New Plan to Pass Her Deal?

Mrs May had something up her sleeve all along, and now we know what it is.

For some time now, the Prime Minister has been pushing ahead with her 'deal or no deal' option in Parliament. MPs would have the option to vote for her deal, or risk leaving the European Union without a deal. The threat doesn't seem to have worked, however, as many MPs are pushing for a second referendum and trying to bring her deal down to achieve it.

Now, according to the BBC's sources[32], Mrs May wants the Meaningful Vote to go ahead in the third week of January and she wants it to be a 'moment of reckoning' for Brexit. In an attempt to force MPs to support her deal, she'll give them an illusion of choice.

By allowing votes to be made on amendments to the motion on her Brexit deal, knowing very well that no faction within the Commons has enough support for individual amendments to be passed, the Prime Minister will push her deal through Parliament through a process of elimination. That will leave only a No Deal Brexit as the alternative to her deal.

And it might just work.

19th December
EU Unveils Their No Deal Plans

In what is either a sign of what's to come, or a great double bluff from Brussels, the European Commission has announced they have begun implementing their preparations for a No Deal Brexit. Just like the UK is setting aside £2 billion to fund government departments, the Commission is aiming to reduce disruption as much as possible in finance and transport sectors.

In a statement, the Commission explained[33]:

> *Given the continued uncertainty in the UK surrounding the ratification of the Withdrawal Agreement, as agreed between the EU and the UK on 25 November 2018 – and last week's call by the European Council (Article 50) to intensify preparedness work at all levels and for all outcomes – the European Commission has today started implementing its "no deal" Contingency Action Plan. This delivers on the Commission's commitment to adopt all necessary "no deal" proposals by the end of the year, as outlined in its second preparedness Communication of 13 November 2018.*
> *Today's package includes 14 measures in a limited number of areas where a "no-*

deal" scenario would create major disruption for citizens and businesses in the EU27. These areas include financial services, air transport, customs, and climate policy, amongst others.

The Commission considers it essential and urgent to adopt these measures today to ensure that the necessary contingency measures can enter into application on 30 March 2019 in order to limit the most significant damage caused by a "no-deal" scenario in these areas.

They need to do this, of course. If the UK is stepping up preparations then it's wise for the European Union to do the same – but I feel like they'd much rather renegotiate that really implement these measures. It'll cost them money they don't want to spend. So could this really just be one big double bluff? I mean, if I've figured out that Mrs May is bluffing to re-open negotiations, then they surely have too.

Regardless, though, the Commission is putting in place 14 measures to ensure the most seamless transition possible, focusing on transport, finance, climate policy, animals and plants, data protection, and customs matters. Their measures will mean that freight carried by road into the European Union could continue for nine months without permits, and UK financial services regulations will be considered equivalent to EU regulations to up to two years.

It will also continue to allow British airlines to operate flights in and out of the EU, but not *within* the EU. Not ideal, but certainly something that could be negotiated further down the line. We know this is really just a matter of the EU throwing their toys out of their pram. Once they've had a stern talking to, I'm sure they'll straighten up and fly right.

The European Commission urged the remaining member states to also take a 'generous' approach to protecting the rights of UK citizens who live in their countries. Theresa May certainly won't be repatriating anyone, so I'd be surprised if any EU nation decided to start shipping ex-pats back to Britain.

Interestingly, though, the statement explains how these new arrangements will be time-limited, and that they'll be able to end this period without consulting the UK. That's considerably different to what they've offered in our Withdrawal Agreement, whereby the UK can only leave backstop conditions if agreed by both sides.

Funny how they can be inconsistent like that.

UK Sets Out New Migration Rules

Home Secretary Sajid Javid has today revealed new migration plans for the UK, post-Brexit. Unsurprisingly, they don't include a target for reducing numbers into the UK. Despite promising to reduce migration to the 'tens of thousands' for the last eight years, the Tories have not made any significant progress whatsoever. Why would they start now?

Their intention, they claim, is to bring net migration to 'sustainable levels' – another get-out clause. It wasn't long ago that Theresa May would repeatedly refer to 'controlling' immigration as opposed to 'reducing' immigration. To some voters, it sounded like she wanted to get tough. To those who know how she works, it was clear she was just buying time and making it look like she planned to do something. She didn't.

Javid was actually asked about this during BBC Radio 4's Today programme. When asked whether the Tories were sticking to their pledge to reduce immigration to the tens of thousands, he simply replied 'the objective is to bring net migration down to more sustainable levels'. So again, no answer.

The White Paper released today suggests scrapping the current cap on the number of skilled workers coming from the EU and elsewhere, and a consultation on a minimum salary requirement of £30,000 for those skilled migrants looking to obtain five-year visas. It also sets out plans to phase in the new immigration system from 2021.

We'll have to wait and find out what eventual deal we have with the European Union until we know, in full, how our immigration system is going to work. Mrs May has told us she intends to end free movement, though I suspect we'll see a new system with tweaked rules that still allows for easy movement of people. There's no way this woman will ever clamp down on immigration in any meaningful way.

20th December
Amber Rudd Says Second Referendum 'Plausible'

Amber Rudd let the con slip, again. She said in an interview with ITV's Robert Peston that while she doesn't want a 'People's Vote' (yeah, sure), she thinks there would be a plausible argument to hold a referendum if Parliament fails to agree a deal[34]. She is of course ignoring the fact that it was Parliament's duty to begin with to implement the decision made by the British people.

It's funny how politicians can take something simple and make it infinitely more complicated, isn't it?

Rudd's comments haven't gone down well with everybody, though. Andrea Leadsom, the Brexiteer MP who stood for leadership against Theresa May and who is now inexplicably supporting May's deal, has suggested her own rival plan if Parliament fails to vote for May's deal. She told the press today that a second referendum would be 'unacceptable' and that our Plan B should be a 'managed no deal'[35]. That is, a No Deal Brexit that still maintains some kind of transition period and means the UK isn't immediately hit with operating on WTO rules. I suppose this is designed to be more palatable than a real, clean exit.

The official spokesman for the Prime Minister, however, has shot down both suggestions – suggesting that a second referendum was not plausible in the event of a gridlocked Parliament, and that Leadsom's idea is 'not something that is available'. The spokesman reiterated that the EU has been clear, and that there is no Withdrawal Agreement without a backstop, meaning a managed No Deal would almost certainly be off the cards.

By the sounds of it, Downing Street is preparing for only one eventuality – Parliament voting for Theresa May's deal. Parliament certainly isn't going to let No Deal happen without a fight. Today, Tory and Labour MPs joined together to stop the UK leaving the European Union without a deal. Or, as the 'Independent' calls it, 'crashing out'[36].

MPs are planning a showdown vote in early 2019, and have tabled an amendment to the finance bill, which would stop any new taxes earmarked for No Deal preparations from being put in place without the consent of the Commons. Once again, Parliamentarians will use their power to stop the Prime Minister's plans to at least deliver some kind of Brexit. More amendments are expected in the new ear, too, which will focus on fisheries, health, and trade. Make no mistake, these MPs – which include Labour's Yvette Cooper, Hilary Benn, Rachel Reeves and Harriet Harmen, as well as Tories Nick Boles and Oliver Letwin – will do everything in their power to stop the government implementing the will of the people.

Silly us! We should have realised when David Cameron told us the government will implement what we decide, what he really meant was the government would offer us a wishy-washy deal and Parliament will stop even that going through.

The UK Triple Bluffs

After the European Union ramped up its own preparations for No Deal, the UK is doubling down and triple bluffing. Faisal Islam of Sky News noticed that within the last 24 hours, the government quietly edited all No Deal technical notices to remove the word 'unlikely' from relevant sentences. What once said 'in the unlikely event of no deal', the government now says 'in the event of no deal'[37].

The Department for Exiting the European Union released a statement, explaining:

> *The language on gov.uk has been updated to reflect Tuesday's cabinet decision to enact the remaining elements of our no deal preparations. We fully expect to get a deal and believe that is the most likely outcome - that is what we are focused on delivering.*

The department knew this would be spotted, and I'm convinced it's another bluff. They don't want this to happen, but they want the EU to know they're seriously preparing for it.

Your move, Brussels.

21st December
Varadkar Shuts Down Hard Border Fears Over 'No Deal'

Republic of Ireland Prime Minister Leo Varadkar has shut down concerns over a hard border being implemented in Ireland, in the event of No Deal.

At a media briefing after the publication of a 131-page document which outlines Ireland's contingency plans for No Deal, Varadkar said his government has made "no preparations whatsoever" for a hard border in Ireland[38]. He stated that it would become a "self-fulfilling prophecy" if his government started making the plans.

He also said:

> *"The answer I've been giving people all along is the honest truth…We're not making plans for a hard border between Northern Ireland and Ireland. Our focus is entirely on getting an agreement that ensures that doesn't happen".*

The Republic of Ireland has published its own contingency plans for No Deal, including plans for border inspections to be implemented at Rosslare and Dublin ports, and Dublin airport. And, by not revealing any plans for a hard border, he's essentially doing the same as the UK government. We have no plans, they have no plans…it's almost as if they both know that a hard border won't be necessary!

In fact, today, Jacob Rees-Mogg succinctly explained how there won't even be a need for an Irish backstop within the Withdrawal Agreement if Ireland has no plans of implementing a hard border. Varadkar surely thinks that not unveiling a plan means No Deal, won't happen, but it could well backfire.

In a tweet, Rees-Mogg said[39]:

> *"No deal means no hard border so no need for the backstop".*

Which is true, isn't it? The whole purpose of the backstop is to avoid a hard border in Northern Ireland – but nobody is even planning one in the first place! Could it be (shock horror!) that the government is totally incompetent and unwilling to negotiate a deal that actually makes sense?

One thing we can take from all this is that, no matter what happens, there will not be a hard border in Northern Ireland. This whole issue has been manufactured from the start by the architects of betrayal in Theresa May's ever-rotating cabinet to implement a terrible 'compromise' Brexit deal.

22nd December
Corbyn Pledges Brexit Support Under Labour Government

A day into the Christmas Parliamentary recess, Jeremy Corbyn has said that his party would support Brexit if they were to win a snap general election amidst pressure for him to support a new referendum[40]. Corbyn said that, as Prime Minister, he would offer Brussels softer exit terms but didn't expand on whether it would involve delaying Brexit past 29th March 2019.

Not everyone is behind him, though. In fact, Labour's Chuka Umunna said that Corbyn's comments were 'deeply depressing' and 'disappointing', claiming that the decision would actually be one for the party to make. Umunna is just one of many Remain-supporting and 'People's Vote'-

backing MPs in the Labour Party who would unquestionably seek to undermine Corbyn over the issue of Brexit.

Wes Streeting MP also criticised Corbyn, asking 'Why peddle this myth that Labour would be able to renegotiate a Brexit deal at this 11th hour? How would Labour's Brexit be any better than remaining in the EU?"[41].

Good question.

28th December
Corbyn Wants Christmas Recess to End Early

Corbyn has called for the House of Commons to be recalled early following the Christmas recess, in order to give MPs the chance to vote on May's deal. Of course he does – the Prime Minister hasn't had the time she was looking for to seek new assurances over the backstop issue.

Parliament will reconvene on January 7th, meaning news is slow and very little will happen for another week or more.

In an interview with the i newspaper, Corbyn said about the Prime Minister:

> *"Well, it is in her hands to recall Parliament. I want us to have a vote as soon as possible, that's what I've been saying for the past two weeks, and if that means recalling Parliament to have the vote let's have it"[42].*

He also accused Mrs May of running down the clock and offering MPs 'the choice of the devil or the deep blue sea'. Which is exactly what she is doing.

The Prime Minister knows that her deal will only pass if she leaves it as late as possible and sufficiently scares MPs into thinking that the only option if her deal fails is No Deal. And No Deal is the bogey man underneath every MPs bed. They're terrified of it.

References

[1] BBC News, "Brexit: Support for Theresa May's deal seems to be shrinking", Laura Kuenssberg, 1st December 2018,
https://www.bbc.co.uk/news/uk-politics-46415574

[2] BBC News, "Brexit: Sam Gyimah resigns over Theresa May's 'naive' deal", BBC News, 1st December 2018,
https://www.bbc.co.uk/news/uk-46407249

[3] The Guardian, "Letters: 17 MPs call for a second Brexit referendum", 1st December 2018,
https://www.theguardian.com/politics/2018/dec/01/letters-17-mps-call-for-a-second-brexit-referendum

[4] The Telegraph, "Accept this imperfect deal or Brexit may never happen", Liam Fox, 2nd December 2018,
https://www.telegraph.co.uk/politics/2018/12/02/accept-imperfect-deal-brexit-may-never-happen/

[5] CNN, "UK's Labour will seek no confidence vote in May if Brexit bill fails", James Griffiths, 3rd December 2018,
https://edition.cnn.com/2018/12/02/uk/brexit-no-confidence-referendum-gbr-intl/index.html

[6] Sky News, "Sophy Ridge on Sunday - highlights", 2nd December 2018,
https://news.sky.com/video/sophy-ridge-on-sunday-highlights-11569862

[7] Mail Online, "Could next week's Brexit vote be SCRAPPED? Tory whips 'discuss plan to send Theresa May back to Brussels in bid to win new concessions rather than face Commons defeat'", Connor Boyd, 3rd December 2018,
https://www.dailymail.co.uk/news/article-6453301/Could-weeks-Brexit-vote-SCRAPPED-Tory-whips-discuss-plan-send-Brussels.html

[8] Sky News, "Jeremy Corbyn 'running scared' of Brexit TV debate, Downing Street claims", 3rd December 2018,
https://news.sky.com/story/jeremy-corbyn-running-scared-of-brexit-tv-debate-downing-street-claims-11570363

[9] The Guardian, "Brexit: senior minister could be suspended over legal advice", Dan Sabbagh and Jessica Elgot, 4th December 2018,
https://www.theguardian.com/politics/2018/dec/03/cabinet-minister-suspension-brexit-legal-advice-deal

[10] Twitter, "The Government has failed to publish the Attorney General's full and final legal advice on the Brexit deal, as was ordered by Parliament. ", Keir Starmer, 3rd December 2018,
https://twitter.com/Keir_Starmer/status/1069652504542105601

[11] The Guardian, "Remainers welcome ECJ expert's view that UK can abandon Brexit", Severin Carrell and Peter Walker, 4th December 2018,
https://www.theguardian.com/politics/2018/dec/04/uk-can-stop-article-50-without-eu-approval-top-ecj-adviser-says

[12] BBC News, "Brexit: Food prices could rise 10%, says Mark Carney", BBC News, 4th December 2018,
https://www.bbc.co.uk/news/business-46439969

[13] The Guardian, "MPs win right to Meaningful Vote on Brexit plan B", Heather Stewart, 4th December 2018,
https://www.theguardian.com/politics/2018/dec/04/mps-seek-power-to-amend-plan-b-brexit-motion-if-may-loses-vote

Chapter Seven: December 2018

[14] *Attorney General Rt Hon Geoffrey Cox QC MP, Letter to Rt Hon Theresa May MP, "Legal Effect of the Protocol on Ireland/Northern Ireland", 13th November 2018, https://assets.publishing.service.gov.uk/government/uploads/system/uploads/attachment_da ta/file/761852/05_December-*
_EU_Exit_Attorney_General_s_legal_advice_to_Cabinet_on_the_Withdrawal_Agreement_a nd_the_Protocol_on_Ireland-Northern_Ireland.pdf

[15] *Express, "WHAT A WASTE! May spent £100K on Facebook advertising before Brexit vote SCRAPPED", Carly Read, 10th December 2018, https://www.express.co.uk/news/politics/1056863/brexit-news-theresa-may-house-of-commons-vote-cancelled-Facebook-adverts-instagram?fbclid=IwAR09MGWqbqLA4iaJNkq8jLeE6Z4HBl-HyLj7nszO4oDw6D934Sw_kzR1lg*

[16] *Twitter, "Just finished a call with the Prime Minister. My message was clear. The backstop must go. Too much time has been wasted.", Arlene Foster, 10th December 2018, https://twitter.com/dupleader/status/1072142368973963264?s=21*

[17] 251 *BBC News, "Commons stir: Labour MP Lloyd Russell-Moyle picks up mace", 10th December 2018,*
 https://www.bbc.co.uk/news/av/uk-politics-46514458/commons-stir-as-labour-mp-picks-up-mace

[18] *Trove, "EXCITEMENT IN COMMONS.", 17th July 1930, https://trove.nla.gov.au/newspaper/article/33340967*

[19] *BBC News, "Brexit ruling: UK can cancel decision, EU court says", 10th December 2018, https://www.bbc.co.uk/news/uk-scotland-scotland-politics-46481643*

[20] *Twitter, "Breaking: apparently the 48 letters have been reached but Sir Graham Brady will not announce until Mrs May is back in the country.", Tim Dawson, 11th December 2018, https://twitter.com/Tim_R_Dawson/status/1072524488024223745*

[21] *BBC News, "Brexit: People's Vote campaign urges Corbyn to call no-confidence vote", 11th December 2018, https://www.bbc.co.uk/news/uk-politics-46524696*

[22] *BBC News, "Brexit: Theresa May says EU leaders 'determined' to solve Irish border issue", 11th December 2018, https://www.bbc.co.uk/news/uk-politics-46515743*

[23] *Financial Times, "Juncker rules out renegotiation of Theresa May's Brexit deal", https://www.ft.com/content/32849728-fd1a-11e8-aebf-99e208d3e521*

[24] *The National, "Sex text Tory's suspension lifted – and he immediately backs May", National Newsdesk, 12th December 2018, https://www.thenational.scot/news/17293967.sex-text-torys-suspension-lifted-and-he-immediately-backs-may/?fbclid=IwAR1pQwy4TvmYJWus8kAwzgYrm690APp_B_7dtWxToXHZTF2vSaKb6h2u csQ*

[25] *The Guardian, "May signals she will step down before 2022 election", Heather Stewart and Peter Walker, 12th December 2018, https://www.theguardian.com/politics/2018/dec/12/theresa-may-signals-she-will-step-down-before-2022-election*

[26] *Express, "UK getting READY for no deal Brexit - £2BILLION pumped into preparations for EU withdrawal", Brian McGleenon, 16th December 2018, https://www.express.co.uk/news/politics/1059650/brexit-news-philip-hammond-no-deal-money-preparations-theresa-may-eu*

[27] CNN, "Theresa May accused of leading the UK into a 'national crisis' as she sets date for vote on her Brexit plan" Bianca Britton and James Griffiths, 17th December 2018, https://edition.cnn.com/2018/12/17/uk/brexit-second-referendum-may-intl/index.html

[28] CNN, "Theresa May accused of leading the UK into a 'national crisis' as she sets date for vote on her Brexit plan" Bianca Britton and James Griffiths, 17th December 2018, https://edition.cnn.com/2018/12/17/uk/brexit-second-referendum-may-intl/index.html

[29] Evening Standard, "Brexit news latest: Amber Rudd urges MPs across parties to 'forge a consensus' to avoid no-deal.... as five Cabinet ministers 'consider second referendum'", Ella Wills, 15th December 2018, https://www.standard.co.uk/news/politics/brexit-news-latest-amber-rudd-urges-mps-to-forge-a-consensus-to-avoid-crashing-out-of-eu-with-nodeal-a4018246.html

[30] Express, "Brexit BREAKTHROUGH? Cabinet ministers PILE PRESSURE on May to hold second referendum", Oli Smith, 17th December 2018, https://www.express.co.uk/news/uk/1060049/Brexit-News-Theresa-May-Greg-Clark-second-referendum

[31] BBC News, "Brexit: Cabinet 'ramps up' no-deal planning", 18th December 2018, https://www.bbc.co.uk/news/uk-politics-46600850

[32] BBC News, "Brexit: Theresa May to hold a series of MPs' votes on options", 18th December 2018, https://www.bbc.co.uk/news/uk-politics-46608952

[33] European Commission, "Brexit: European Commission implements "no-deal" Contingency Action Plan in specific sectors", 19th December 2018, http://europa.eu/rapid/press-release_IP-18-6851_en.htm

[34] BBC News, "Brexit referendum 'plausible' if MPs can't decide - Amber Rudd", 20th December 2018, https://www.bbc.co.uk/news/uk-politics-46626967

[35] BBC News, "Andrea Leadsom and Amber Rudd suggest rival Brexit 'Plan Bs'", 20th December 2018, https://www.bbc.co.uk/news/uk-politics-46631581

[36] Independent, "Conservative and Labour MPs join forces to stop Theresa May pursuing no-deal Brexit", Rob Merrick, 20th December 2018, https://www.independent.co.uk/news/uk/politics/no-deal-brexit-conservative-labour-mp-theresa-may-eu-leave-remain-second-referendum-a8693181.html

[37] Twitter, "No Deal no longer "unlikely" - Government", Faisal Islam, 20th December 2018, https://twitter.com/faisalislam/status/1075724156631703552?ref_src=twsrc%5Etfw%7Ctwca mp%5Etweetembed%7Ctwterm%5E1075724156631703552&ref_url=https%3A%2F%2Fww w.theguardian.com%2Fpolitics%2Flive%2F2018%2Fdec%2F20%2Fbrexit-latest-theresa-may-andrea-leadsom-makes-case-for-managed-no-deal-politics-live%3Fpage%3Dwith%253Ablock-5c1b86d9e4b02fb91ff06832

[38] The Guardian, "Ireland has no plans for hard border after Brexit, says Varadkar", Lisa O'Carroll, 21st December 2018, https://www.theguardian.com/world/2018/dec/21/ireland-has-no-plans-in-place-for-hard-border-after-brexit-varadkar

Chapter Seven: December 2018

[39] Twitter, "No deal means no hard border so no need for the backstop.", Jacob Rees-Mogg, 20th December 2018,
https://twitter.com/jacob_rees_mogg/status/1075822302862942208

[40] Independent, "Brexit will go ahead if Labour wins snap election, Jeremy Corbyn says", Rob Merrick, 22nd December 2018,
https://www.independent.co.uk/news/uk/politics/brexit-jeremy-corbyn-labour-second-referendum-peoples-vote-remain-general-election-final-say-a8695941.html

[41] BBC News, "Brexit: Remainers criticise Corbyn's pledge to pursue leaving the EU", 22nd December 2018,
https://www.bbc.co.uk/news/uk-politics-46658335

[42] The Guardian, "Recall MPs from holiday to vote on May's Brexit deal, says Corbyn", Heather Stewart, 28th December 2018,
https://www.theguardian.com/politics/2018/dec/28/recall-mps-from-holiday-to-vote-on-mays-brexit-deal-says-corbyn

Chapter Eight
January 2019

2nd January
New Year, New May? PM Hopes MPs Come Together for Her Brexit Deal

Theresa May has urged Members of Parliament to back her deal, no doubt hoping that they'll be coming back to Parliament feeling merrier and more festive. I must say, after a little time away from Brexit over the Christmas period, the whole situation does feel a little different. I'm not sure whether it's simply the fact the issue has been less prevalent or whether the looming threat of a No Deal Brexit has finally struck the politicians who were planning to vote May's deal down.

In her New Year message, the Prime Minister has asked MPs to support her deal so that the UK can 'turn a corner' and put this period of turmoil and disruption behind us[1]. She acknowledged that the 2016 referendum was 'divisive' but that 2019 could be the year where we put our differences aside and move forward together.

And it seems like Corbyn was listening, because today the Labour leader said that Theresa May should return to Brussels and get a new deal with a full Customs Union that his party could support[2]. Now of course, we know Mrs May can't get a new deal. We also know that the British people would be betrayed if May opted for a full Customs Union option with the EU – but it shows that Corbyn is worried about the possibility of not leaving the EU in at least some form.

A life-long Brexiteer, Corbyn will want to see at least some action taken on Europe, and I suspect he knows that unless he is able to support some kind of deal then his party will turn their back on Brexit entirely. He'd be right to fear that, too, as almost 90% of his party's members would opt to remain in the European Union through a second referendum, according to a new survey[3]. In a study from the Party Members Project at Queen Mary University of London, which looks at the attitudes of British political parties, it was found some 88% would opt for remain in a second referendum. It also found that 72% of party members think Corbyn should support that referendum.

Corbyn may have watered down his views on Brexit, but he'll at least want some kind of separation – and if he wants to achieve it then he'll have to back May's deal. It's as simple as that.

So could 2019 really be the year that the parties put their differences aside and move together with May's deal? Well, I suppose it depends on what kind of reassurances Mrs May comes back from Brussels with. If any. We have just three weeks until her deal is put to the vote in the Commons, and if she can't provide any new assurances, Corbyn is going to have to find some new excuse to support her in the Commons vote. Either that, or he'll have to become a fully-fledged Remainer and reject the will of the people completely.

3rd January
EU Rules Out New Irish Backstop Talks

Looks like the EU Brexit negotiating team hasn't come back from the Christmas break feeling more festive and charitable. Today, a spokeswoman for the European Union has said that there will be no further meetings on the Brexit deal – a huge blow to Theresa May who still needs to find a way to convince British MPs to vote for her deal.

Chapter Eight: January 2019

Spokeswoman Mina Andreeva said at a press conference in Brussels this morning:

> *"We have said many times the deal that is on the table is the best and only deal possible. And the EU27 leaders confirmed on December 13 in their conclusions that it will not be renegotiated... We are not renegotiating what is on the table, our solutions are on the table, we are ready to listen but at this stage there are no further meetings and the EU 27 leaders have been very clear that it will not be renegotiated, what is on the table."*

An EU source also said that nothing has happened regarding Brexit over the last ten days[4], despite May speaking with Donald Tusk on Wednesday and Angela Merkel twice over Christmas. That means Mrs May has made essentially no progress on renegotiating her deal. The only thing that has changed with her Withdrawal Agreement is that even more time has passed by. MPs are truly being put to the test – will they risk the No Deal Brexit they're terrified of, or will they vote in favour of May's unchanged, botched deal?

The EU is playing a risky game by flat out refusing to renegotiate, though. At this point, they must be betting on MPs being too afraid of No Deal. If they can get May's deal passed without any changed, the EU won't lose out on the £39 billion we've promised and they won't be hit with trade problems that would unquestionably be more complicated for them than us.

In fact, former Brexit Secretary David Davis has today urged Theresa May to delay her Meaningful Vote even further, in order to put more pressure on the European Union and Members of Parliament. The vote is expected to take place in the week beginning 14th January, with a deadline of the 21st January – but Davis said in The Daily Telegraph[5] that it could be further delayed if the parliamentary arithmetic still doesn't add up for the Prime Minister's deal. He even suggested that the EU would get back to the negotiation table and offer a better deal if it looked like the UK was on the verge of 'crashing out' without a deal.

This is a giant game of chicken, and No Deal is a real possibility at this point.

6th January
May Teases New Assurances in Coming Days

Mrs May has turned her focus back to Britain, telling MPs that the UK will face 'uncharted territory' if Parliament rejects her Brexit deal. The Prime Minister also confirmed that the Meaningful Vote on her deal would 'definitely' go ahead next week, too, as she promises now assurances for the Northern Ireland backstop issue. But the question remains – what assurances has she exactly achieved, and have the DUP agreed to anything yet?

During an interview with the BBC's Andrew Marr[6], the Prime Minister said that she will redouble her efforts to win over MPs and that she believes the UK will face unchartered territory if her agreement doesn't pass in the British parliament. Marr challenged her on what changes she had managed to make since last month, and Mrs May told him that she had simply continued to talk to European leader and offer 'confidence' to support her deal. While she didn't offer any detail, she did say that in the coming days we'll be given more information regarding her new measures for Northern Ireland.

She also said that she'll unveil a bigger role for Parliament in the negotiations for the next stage of discussions with the EU, as well as new assurances from the EU that will address concerns about the Irish backstop.

Let's see.

7th January
Date Unveiled for Theresa May's Meaningful Vote

The can can't be kicked down the road much longer. Government sources have revealed that Theresa May is planning for the Meaningful Vote on her Brexit deal to go ahead on Tuesday 15th January, just six days before the deadline[7]. This week, we'll also be offered new assurances that Mrs May must have achieved during her multiple nagging phone calls to Angela Merkel and others over the Christmas period.

May's primary tactic for winning MPs over is to scare them into thinking No Deal is on the cards, but if today's news is anything to go by it looks like it won't work for a large proportion of parliament. 200 MPs have signed a letter to the government urging them to take No Deal off the table. The politicians come from essentially all opposition parties – Labour, SNP, Lib Dem, Plaid Cymru – as well as the government's own party.

In their letter, MPs wrote[8]:

> *"As a cross-party group of MPs, business leaders and representatives, we are united in our determination that the UK must not crash out of the EU without a deal".*

Nothing new, of course – it's just a reassertion of where these 200 MPs stand. But, they're technically still a minority. All it takes is for Mrs May to win over the DUP and defectors in her party and she can pass this deal. She probably believes she can.

There's more to this than just a letter, though. Another cross-party group will take direct action in parliament, with Labour's Yvette Cooper and Tory Nicky Morgan planning on proposing an amendment to the Finance Bill which would stop the Treasury from implemented measures designed to facilitate No Deal. That means Parliament could effectively shut down the government in a similar way to the shut down in the United States right now. If No Deal happens, politicians might make it impossible for the country to function.

It's funny that the same politicians who warn a No Deal Brexit would result in catastrophe are actually the ones who would facilitate that catastrophe. I've been saying this for some time now – these people are the architects of this entire problem. Brexit isn't the problem, the people doing the negotiations and standing in the way of progress are.

No Deal Lorry Tests Begin in Kent

The post-apocalyptic car park of doom prediction is being put to the test today[9], as a lorry rehearsal takes place in Kent. A live rehearsal of a new emergency traffic system took place with 89 lorries, in an attempt to see how traffic will flow in the event of a No Deal Brexit. The trial was organised by the Department for Transport and took place at a disused airport, but only 89 lorries took part.

Starting at their journey at the airport, lorries queued, drove to second holding areas, and continued their journey – but the Road Haulage Association branded the exercise 'too little too late'. While only 89 took part in the trials today, the disused Manston airport will potentially be used as a parking facility for as many as 6,000 lorries under No Deal contingency plans.

It's good to see the government taking No Deal seriously. If this is really just a way of bluffing the EU into thinking the UK is willing to leave without a deal, then I take my hat off to Mrs May. I think this is the real deal, though.

9th January
A Crafty General Election Could Force 'No Deal'

I'm not expecting a second referendum – at least, under Theresa May's leadership. It's the only thing I stil believe her on. I don't think she wants to deliver a real Brexit, but I do believe she wants to deliver a compromise Brexit without a second referendum. That's why the news of a general election in a few months makes more sense to me.

Today it was reported that the Prime Minister is being urged by senior ministers to face down the rebels in her party who are threatening to bring down the government to stop us leaving the European Union without a deal[10]. If May's deal isn't passed in Parliament on the 15th, and it doesn't look like it will, then she will be faced with having to leave the EU without a deal or even extending Article 50. But, the threat of the Finance Bill being amended to stop funds being allocated for No Deal Measures means that No Deal is pretty much off the cards.

The way round it? A general election whereby new Tory candidates can be chosen and the voters given an option to vote for a Tory government that would implement a No Deal Brexit. The catch? It would be held in April, just days after we are due to leave the EU.

It's pretty plausible that this could really happen. More than a dozen Tory MPs have said that they will back a no-confidence vote in the government and force a general election if Theresa May tries to leave without an agreement. This is where it gets interesting, though – Brexiteers are also calling for a general election in an attempt at forcing No Deal. It's a really interesting tactic.

It works like this: Brexiteers would force a general election and allow the Prime Minister to use her discretion and set the date for a general election on April 4th. That means that Parliament would have to shut down for the entire month of March for the campaign, meaning we'll leave the European Union without any Parliamentary involvement at all. There would be no sitting MPs on March 29th, meaning there would be no way that the politicians could stop us leaving without a deal.

Assuming Mrs May fought the election, she could either gain massively or lose marginally. If she were to fight the election as a Brexiteer supporting no deal, she could pick up working class Labour voters who voted to leave and are unhappy with Labour politicians trying to disrupt the process. Mrs May could win even more support if her party deselected Remain Tory MPs and replaced them with new, pro-Brexit candidates.

This would be her lasting legacy. She would be the woman who wobbled with the EU, but who stopped the politicians getting in the way of what the British voted for and who stood up for the little guy. "Her deal didn't work out, but hey, she was the one who shut down parliament and risked her own position as Prime Minister just to ensure the politicians couldn't stop Brexit".

But, time will tell.

10th January
May Suffers Second Commons Defeat in 24 Hours

Theresa May has suffered another Commons defeat, following a vote that decided the government will no longer be given 21 days to come up with a 'plan B' if May's deal is voted down on Tuesday. May lost the vote by 11, meaning she will now only have three working Parliamentary days to come up with an alternative with a deadline of Monday 21st January.

17 members of her own party voted against her – including former ministers Sam Gyimah, Jo Johnson, and Justine Greening.

This was the second humiliating defeat in the Commons, after MPs yesterday voted to limit ministers' ability to increase taxes in the event of a No Deal Brexit. Of course, it was Nicky Morgan (backbench Conservative MP) and co behind the disruption – the Tory rebels keen to see Brexit thwarted at any cost.

These two Commons defeats mean things aren't boding well for her Meaningful Vote on Tuesday. If she has anything new to show ministers, she better get a move on. So far, 17 of her own MPs are voting against her. I struggle to see how anything can change in just five more days.

Speaking of which, the five-day-long debate on the Meaningful Vote has begun once again. Speaker John Bercow was thrust into controversy yesterday, too, following his decision to allow a rebel amendment in the Commons which gave MPs greater control over Brexit policy direction. Bercow claimed that while a decision like this had never been made before, he didn't believe it was reason not to allow it. Convention, he said, simply stops Parliament progressing.

Meanwhile, Jeremy Corbyn is ramping up for a general election – though he might be forced to change direction. Believe it or not, Labour's manifesto pledge is to see Brexit through. At least, that's what they **say**. What they mean is that they would go to the EU, ask for a better deal, not get a better deal, but just take it anyway and claim victory. That could all change though, if Corbyn's party have their own way.

Corbyn's spokesman has today admitted that all manifesto commitments for the Labour Party, in the event of a fresh election, would be decided by the usual 'internal party democracy'. That spells bad news to secret Remainer Corbyn, whose party is as rabidly pro-EU as the Liberal Democrats. Unfortunately for him, the working class, traditional Labour voters are not. I suspect a pro-EU stance could mean Corbyn's fall from grace – and an opportunity for Theresa May to position herself as the Brexit Prime Minister.

She'd have to get on board with a World Trade Brexit, though.

11th January
CBI Warns Thousands of Jobs at Risk Over Brexit

The Confederation of British Industry warns today that a No Deal Brexit will have severe economic consequences[11]. This isn't the first time the CBI has warned us about Brexit, and it won't be the first time they're wrong. This notoriously anti-Brexit organisation warns today that failure to back Theresa May's deal will result in GDP shrinking by as much as 8% (!!) and thousands of jobs being lost.

Mrs May will no doubt be delighted to hear the news, however. The CBI is urging MPs to back her deal, suggesting it is a 'solution' that businesses will be able to work with as it offers a transition period between the status quo and whatever new deal we agree with the EU after March 29th. Director general Carolyn Fairbairn, in a speech, today called on MPs to 'safeguard the security and prosperity of our country' – and put jobs before of politics when they vote on Tuesday.

Fairbairn has been very vocal about this already, so it remains to be seen just how much impact her new speech will have. Yesterday, Fairbairn wrote on Twitter[12]:

> *"Business Secretary @GregClarkMP reflects the voice of business. 1000's of firms in despair at prospect of no deal. Rising costs & border disruption will cost jobs for years to come. Business will work with PM's deal. If politicians can't, they must find a way to stop no deal".*

We have a lot to be sceptical about, here. The CBI hardly has a great history of accurately predicting the effects of Brexit. In fact, time and time again, the CBI has been proven to be an anti-Brexit mouthpiece that tries to influence policy direction in a way that favours the EU. In July, Jacob Rees-Mogg urged the government to simply ignore the CBI[13]. He said that they have "got everything wrong in the whole of their history" – and that their "vested interests" were colouring the views of major firms in the UK.

Rees-Mogg isn't exaggerating. The CBI really has gotten everything wrong on Brexit...and they're funded by the EU. Vote Leave revealed in 2015[14] that the CBI received almost £1 million from the European Commission between 2009 and 2015. So excuse me if I brush off this new doomsday prediction as the nonsense it is.

14th January
Theresa May Announces Her Backstop Assurances, Ahead of Critical Meaningful Vote

The Meaningful Vote on the withdrawal deal is tomorrow. It's finally crunch time, and Mrs May doesn't have time to delay it again. It's happening tomorrow, no matter what, and her statement in the House of Commons today was intended to bring together Parliament and get them back on board with her deal.

But, she may have failed.

May's primary goal was to assure the House – and in particular, the Democratic Unionist Party (on which her Parliamentary majority hangs) – that the UK-wide backstop would be a temporary solution only. Throughout the Christmas period, the Prime Minister spoke with EU leaders in an attempt to gain new assurances, after being told changes to the Withdrawal Agreement weren't possible. The question all along has been whether these assurances could be strong enough to sway Remain and Leave MPs that the deal is a good one, and that the backstop would not remain indefinitely.

In a speech to the Commons today, Mrs May finally outlined the assurances she has been given. She referred to letters between the UK government and Presidents Juncker and Rusk, which were published today[15]. Her statement explained how the letters showed that the EU would 'use its best endeavours' to ensure that the backstop would only remain in place for as long as necessary. She says that the EU doesn't like the backstop either – as it would mean Britain 'benefitting' from the EU without having to accept freedom of movement and other requirements.

While it may have convinced some, it didn't seem to impress the DUP. The party today rejected her assurances and branded them 'meaningless'[16], meaning the Prime Minister can almost certainly count on 10 fewer votes when the time comes. Commons DUP leader Nigel Dodds said that his party was simply not reassured by the communication from Tusk and Juncker, explaining:

> *"Despite a letter of supposed reassurance from the European Union, there are 'no legally binding assurances' as the Prime Minister talked about in December...In fact, there is nothing new. Nothing has changed".*

He's not wrong. Today's announcement was a total nothing burger, to borrow a phrase from the Americans, and appears to be little more than a political manoeuvre designed to win people over last minute. Hopefully, she thinks, some MPs will come around and change their mind last minute when they consider just how badly this might go if we leave without a deal. That's why the Prime Minister left this announcement to the last minute – and, it's likely why she has begun warning Leave supporters that the politicians in Westminster are more likely to cancel Brexit than they are to allow it to go ahead without a deal[17].

Mrs May is crossing her fingers and her toes tonight that Brexiteers in the Commons will come around and support her deal to ensure some kind of Brexit goes ahead. She knows the Remainers won't budge.

15th January
May's Brexit Day of Destiny Arrives

Today truly is the Brexit day of destiny. It's the day that Theresa May's withdrawal deal with the European Union is put to the test, and MPs have an opportunity to vote for or against it[18].

The final day of debates began earlier in the day, beginning with attorney general Geoffrey Cox who gave an impassioned speech for around an hour. Cox was interrupted many a time, initially refusing to take interventions but soon being forced to break his flow and answer questions from MPs on the other side. I've never seen a speech in Parliament quite like it. Theresa May sat with her watchful eye, just over his shoulder, as he poetically described the benefits of the Prime Minister's deal and how MPs would be judged in the history books if they fail to support this Brexit deal.

His narrative echoed that of the Prime Minister, explaining that Brexit was less likely to happen at all, than for a No Deal scenario to occur. It was quite obvious what he was doing – the Attorney General was attempting to win over Brexiteers in the Conservative Party in the hope that they'd change their minds last minute and stop May's crushing defeat in the afternoon.

One Tory MP has done exactly that, in fact. Sir Edward Leigh, a Brexiteer, explained on Sky News this morning why he's decided to support Theresa May's deal after all. He told the cameras that he didn't want to vote alongside the Labour Party and the SNP, and that Remainers have now taken control of Parliament. In his mind, it's better to support May's deal to ensure that some kind of Brexit at least happens. While I see the logic there, I just can't bring myself to support such a terrible deal that gives so much away. Mrs May and her party are very aware that not delivering Brexit would be a huge betrayal – she has said it plenty of times already – and so I struggle to believe that no Brexit is more likely than no deal.

Opposition MPs noticed the scheme in the Commons this morning, too. One MP stood up and asked why the

Attorney General had spent so much time addressing the concerns of his party, rather than addressing the concerns of the House. The obvious answer, of course, is that the concerns of the House are less important for Mrs May. She wants to win over only those who can realistically be won over.

Now, we wait – not so much to see the results of the vote, but to see the magnitude of her defeat.

16th January
May's Deal Voted Down in Parliament – What Now?

Theresa May's deal went down in flames last night. In what must have been a totally expected result for May, the Withdrawal Agreement was voted down by a massive 432 votes to 202 – the biggest defeat suffered by a government in Parliamentary history[19]. Mrs May certainly doesn't do anything by halves.

Now, the future of Brexit is anybody's guess. We leave the European Union on the 29th March, and without a deal, we simply leave without a deal – but, if Nicky Morgan MP and others have their way, the amended finance bill won't allow us to leave without a deal. So where does that leave us?

Jeremy Corbyn has put forward his idea – he wants a new general election to decide the fate of Brexit. Immediately after the vote was lost last night, Corbyn tabled a vote of no confidence that is due to take place today. It doesn't seem like he has much of a chance of winning, though – if a vote of no confidence in the government will do anything, it's unite the Conservative Party. It's quite astonishing that Corbyn can better unite the Tories than their own leader can. So, I expect when this vote takes place around 19:00 tonight, the government will win.

That doesn't mean there aren't questions to ask, though. After such a gigantic loss by the Prime Minister, why doesn't she resign? The only reason she is likely to win the support of her party in the vote tonight is the fear of a Corbyn government – but that can't be the basis of a functioning and effective government. She'll win, she'll stay in office, but she'll struggle to pass any deal in parliament unless she starts negotiating with the other parties.

So, that's what I expect she's going to do. There's no way she can unite her own party around a Brexit deal, so she'll have to start reaching out to Labour again. Interestingly, this gigantic defeat might have even strengthened her hand with the European Union. While they've already told us that they're not willing to renegotiate the deal, the fact that Parliament overwhelmingly rejected it might just be the kick up the arse they need in order to start rethinking the deal. We know Brussels doesn't want No Deal.

Following the crushing defeat in the Commons, May has said that she will now reach out to 'senior parliamentarians' across party lines in order to find a Brexit consensus that will be popular on both sides of the house. Commons leader Andrea Leadsom also said that the Prime Minister is seeking more 'constructive' and 'positive' ideas that will allow her to get her deal through parliament[20]. It's interesting to see the government continuing to push her deal, as opposed to suggesting they'll draw up something completely new. I wonder just how much Theresa May can really achieve with a slightly tweaked deal.

May has until Monday to return to the Commons with her 'Plan B' alternative deal. That isn't much time at all – but if the European Union know what's good for them, they'll offer concessions. They should be willing to do it, too – after all, Theresa May wants Britain to remain as closely tied to the European Union as possible. Surely that's a better result for the EU than No Deal.

May might even get the DUP back on board. Arlene Foster tweeted earlier this afternoon[21] that she and her party will be willing to work with the government for a better deal, saying 'Toxic backstop is the problem'. If May can get rid of the backstop clause – somehow – then she can win over those essential 10 votes from the DUP and potentially enough of her own party in order to pass a deal that doesn't even need the support of Labour.

So we'll see soon enough whether her comments about working across party lines is merely lip service.

May Wins the Confidence Vote

She survived – though not by much. Mrs May's government saw off Corbyn's bid this evening to remove the government from power, by a vote of 325 to 306. That's close, and in any other situation with any other government, the prime minister would have resigned. But, we live in a topsy turvy Brexit world, and Mrs May has managed to hang on thanks to the support of her party and the DUP.

Jeremy Corbyn accused May of running a 'zombie administration' and said she'd lost the right to govern – but let's be honest, Corbyn hardly has greater right to govern. It's clear that in a fresh general election, we'd end up with yet another minority government...likely a minority Tory government with a slightly stronger Labour opposition. Corbyn has no path to a clear majority and the only way the Tories could gain a majority is replacing the leader with somebody competent. For now though, it looks like her party are willing to keep her on to at least see Brexit through. But how?

May responded to the result and said that she will "continue to work to deliver on the solemn promise to the people of this country to deliver on the result of the referendum and leave the European Union". But with her own personal intention to betray our decision in 2016 in a more subtle way, combined with her new plans to engage in cross-party talks, I have no hope that this promise will be delivered on. She said it herself during her Commons address, when she said "We must find solutions that are negotiable and command sufficient support in the House".

The next step? Well, Corbyn wants May to start by ruling out No Deal. May now has to engage with the opposition and she might be forced to begin by hurting our negotiating hand by ruling out the one thing the European Union doesn't want. It's amazing just how much Corbyn is able to betray his own beliefs.

Corbyn told MPs tonight:

> *"The government must remove clearly, once and for all, the prospect of the catastrophe of a no-deal exit from the EU and all the chaos that would come as a result of that".*

Mrs May also gave a statement outside Downing Street announcing her marginal win in the confidence vote, saying:

> *This evening, the government has won the confidence of Parliament. This now gives us all the opportunity to focus on finding a way forward on Brexit. I understand that to people getting on with their lives away from Westminster, the events of the past 24 hours would have been unsettling. Overwhelmingly, the British people want us to get on with delivering Brexit, and also address the other important issues they care about.*

Chapter Eight: January 2019

But, the deal which I have worked to agree with the European Union was rejected by MPs and by a large margin.

I believe it is my duty to deliver on the British people's instruction to leave the European Union, and I intend to do so. So now MPs have made clear what they don't want, we must all work constructively together to set out what Parliament does want. That's why I'm inviting MPs from all parties to come together to find a way forward – one that both delivers on the referendum and can command the support of Parliament. This is now the time to put self interest aside.

I have just held constructive meetings with the leader of the Liberal Democrats, and the Westminster leaders of the SNP and Plaid Cymru. From tomorrow, meetings will be taking place between senior government representatives, including myself, and groups of MPs who represent the widest possible range of views from across Parliament – including our confidence and supply partners, the Democratic Unionist Party. I am disappointed that the leader of the Labour Party has not so far chosen to take part, but our door remains open. It will not be an easy task, but MPs know they have a duty to act in the national interest, reach a consensus, and get this done. In a historic vote in 2016, the country decided to leave the EU. In 2017, 80% of people voted for parties that stood on manifestos promising to respect that result. Now, over two and a half years later, it's time for us to come together, put the national interest first, and deliver on the referendum.

The reason Corbyn isn't sitting down and talking to May? He doesn't want her to get any deal through Parliament. He knows in order to become Prime Minister, he needs to destroy her first. He also doesn't know what kind of deal he could even negotiate with May, as his party is so divided...and mostly against him.

It'll also be interesting to see what kind of deal May can get the SNP and others to get on board with. Most of Parliament are Remainers, so any deal that can command a majority in the House of Commons is going to undermine Brexit.

17th January
Corbyn Refuses to Negotiate New Deal with May

Jeremy Corbyn still hasn't come to the table to talk with Theresa May. This makes it clear that Corbyn isn't interested in a deal with the European Union. He'd rather take Theresa May down so that he can replace her, win a general election, and try and get his own deal with the EU – one that includes a brand-new Customs Union. He'd rather betray the people on his own terms, than team up with Theresa May.

Corbyn has asked all his Labour MPs not to participate in any of May's Brexit talks until she rules out no deal – an extremely damaging move for May that would give the upper hand to the EU and almost guarantee she obtained few new concessions. The full text of Corbyn's message to his MPs was obtained by Sky, and it reads[22]:

> *The Prime Minister has offered to open talks with Opposition Parties, however, I have been absolutely clear that any starting point for talks about breaking the Brexit deadlock must be on the provision that the threat of a disastrous 'no deal' outcome is rules out. This is a position that has now been adopted by the First Minister of Scotland, Nicola Sturgeon.*
>
> *I urge colleagues to respect the condition and refrain from engaging with the government until 'no deal' is taken off the table.*

It seems like the behaviour of a petulant child. For the last two years Corbyn has wanted to be a part of the negotiations, and now when he finally has the opportunity to do so, he'd rather cross his arms and refuse to have any involvement. I do wonder whether this is a sly move on his behalf, in an attempt at forcing the government to opt for No Deal. We know he's a secret Brexiteer, and it could be a smart move if he's thinking this far ahead. It's just as likely that he's hoping that standing in May's way will result in her leaving government and calling a general election. Given her stubbornness, I don't see that happening any time soon.

May, of course, is urging Corbyn to come to the table and negotiate[23]. She needs all parties to get involved, and importantly, she needs Labour on board. She's unlikely to make any significant progress with the SNP or Lib Dems – so it's Labour she needs to please.

In a letter to the Labour leader, May explained that ruling out no deal was an "impossible condition" as it wasn't in the government's power to actually do it – which is true, and not true. No Deal is the default position, but the government could negotiate with the EU to cancel Brexit. That, she won't do. That's the only way to stop No Deal.

The only alternative is a deal, which can't be achieved while Corbyn refuses to sit down and talk.

A new plan agreed by the Prime Minister and other parliamentary parties will be published on Monday, and a full debate on the plan will be scheduled for Tuesday 29th January. This will also be the date of a vote on the deal, giving the UK just two months to get the deal agreed with the EU and written up into legislation.

What's interesting about all of this is that, while I doubt very much that any new deal will deliver the Brexit we voted for, this situation has technically strengthened the Prime Minister's hand in negotiations with the EU. We'd previously been told by Barnier and Juncker that they were unwilling to renegotiate the deal. Now they know that Parliament won't approve it, they're being forced to sit down, renegotiate, and listen to what MPs are saying across the party divide. This strengthens the UK's hand, but it doesn't mean we'll get a better Brexit.

Former EU trade official Hosuk Lee-Makiyama – who now leads the European Centre for International Political Economy – said today that the sheer scale of May's defeat in the commons will serve as a reality check and force Brussels to reconsider their stance on Brexit. He said that negotiators had previously worked hard to secure favourable terms over the UK, but they now risk losing it because they cannot be ratified. The ball, he says, is in the EU's court[24].

But our MPs will simply use this strengthened hand to renegotiate a deal that keeps us tied to the EU. Brexit won't happen unless May is forced to leave without a deal, against her own will.

18th January
The Germans Are Worried About No Deal

Predictably, the Germans are getting worried about the prospects of a No Deal Brexit. A letter signed by the frontrunner to succeed Angela Merkel as the next German chancellor, along with leaders from German politics, industry and art, said: "From the bottom of our hearts, we want them to stay".

The sickly letter reflects on our quirks as Brits and tries to make us believe the Germans will really miss us – as if we're actually lifting an anchor and sailing off into the Atlantic. It reads[25]:

> *"Without your great nation, this continent would not be what it is today: a community defined by freedom and prosperity...After the horrors of the Second World War, Britain did not give up on us. It has welcomed Germany back as a sovereign nation and a European power. This we, as Germans, have not forgotten and we are grateful...Our door will always remain open: Europe is home...We would miss the legendary British black humour and going to the pub after work hours to drink an ale. We would miss tea with milk and driving on the left-hand side of the road. And we would miss seeing the panto at Christmas. But more than anything else, we would miss the British people – our friends across the Channel".*

Gross.

It's funny how they're acting like they're suddenly not going to have access to British comedy on Netflix, and milk in their tea is going to be outlawed by Frau Merkel before she steps down. This is a clear attempt at sweet talking us into backing another referendum, and it's pretty pathetic. They have reason to be concerned, though – it looks like No Deal is more popular than the politicians think.

Despite Project Fear continuing their campaign of terrifying the British people about the prospects of leaving the EU, a new poll by ComRes has found that a clear majority are in favour of respecting the result of the referendum[26]. 65% agreed that the result should be respected, while only 35% disagreed.

A Question Time audience also turned heads last night, when the people cheered (loudly!) at the prospect of a No Deal Brexit[27]. Journalist Isabel Oakeshott suggested that the only option left on the table for the Prime Minister was No Deal, which saw the audience erupt into applause. Twitter went mental – they seemed shocked to see evidence of the majority of British people wanting to leave the EU. It's almost as if we voted to leave already...

The Germans are afraid of No Deal, and they should be. If it happens, then the UK will become an infinitely more competitive economy, and we know they don't want that. That's why, I suspect, a No Deal Brexit won't happen. EU leaders are bound to come back round the negotiating table and agree to something that resembles continued membership of the EU.

Boris Johnson recognises it, too. The former Foreign Secretary says that the UK should be focusing on getting a better deal from the EU, now that the deal has been shot down. He says that the UK hasn't even tried to get rid of the backstop solution, and that now is the time for the UK to go back to Brussels and demand real change to the backstop[28]. He says the EU will be flexible – but the question is whether Theresa May will seek changes to the deal that will simply appease the Remainers in Parliament, or which would respect the results of the referendum, get the ERG Tories back on board, and get the deal passed in Parliament by the slightest margin. It's still possible for the Prime Minister to respect the wishes of the voters.

21st January
May Announces 'Plan B' – and Offers Nothing

Theresa May has had just three working days to turn around a new proposal to the House of Commons, after her Withdrawal Agreement was shot down in a historic defeat. That new proposal was announced today in the Commons, and it was underwhelming to say the lease. I listened intensely, and heard very little substance – just more promises and suggestions that she will talk to other parties, come up with a new solution, and then take it back to the EU and see if they'll go for it.

There have been multiple suggestions on the rolling news coverage this morning that Mrs May wasn't about to announce a Plan B, but instead, a Plan A version 2.0. That's what happened. She's even been mocked for dragging MPs into a 'Brexit Groundhog Day'[29] after her announcement sounded like more of the same. This is the same deal, and she's seeking new concessions just like she did last time.

The only solid proposal I heard in her statement today was that she was scrapping the £65 fee[30] that millions of EU citizens here in the UK were going to have to pay to secure the right to stay here. It is an attempt to win over some Remain-leaning MPs I'm sure, but I doubt it will make any real impact. What will change things, however, is if she follows through with her promise of further discussions with the DUP to discuss their concerns about the Northern Irish backstop.

There were rumours floating around yesterday that the Prime Minister might have considered amending the Belfast Agreement (The Good Friday Agreement, which agreed on a peace process on the island of Ireland). The Prime Minister shot down this claim today when she said in Parliament that she had never considered this option, and never would consider this option. Number 10 sources also indicated that the report was false[31], and that the Prime Minister was not considering revisiting the agreement that guarantees no hard border between Northern Ireland and the Republic of Ireland.

So what are we faced with here? Well, it look like Theresa May has taken note of Labour's refusal to cooperate, and will now work with the DUP to solve the backstop issue and secure support not just from her colleagues in Northern Ireland, but also her own rebel MPs. If she gets the DUP on board, she can get Rees-Mogg and many other rebels on board too. Interestingly, though, her 'Plan B' has already been rejected by European leaders[32].

Dublin today said no to Downing Street's request to ask for backstop concessions, and the Vice President of the European Parliament also rejected the idea of a new Anglo-Irish treaty to remove the backstop from the EU agreement.

Mrs May now has until the 29th January to come up with a new deal and put it before Parliament. Unless she scores real concessions this time, she'll be forced to either extend or revoke Article 50, propose a second referendum, or leave without a deal. Leaving without a deal doesn't appear to be on the cards, however. Mrs May is determined to betray the democratic will of the people – no matter how much she might claim otherwise – and I'd be greatly surprised if she found herself in that situation. That is, despite the fact that No Deal was today shown to be the most popular Brexit option according to an ICM poll[33].

23rd January
MPs CAN'T Stop No Deal Brexit

In a parallel universe, Jeremy Corbyn is leader of the opposition and he's slamming Theresa May for not opting for No Deal. Life-long Brexiteer Jeremy Corbyn, for some reason, now appears to be leading a Remain party and trying to force the government to rule out No Deal. Today, Corbyn claimed that the Prime Minister is 'clearly not listening' over his Brexit claims, and renewed his demand for No Deal to be taken off the table.

No Deal clearly cannot be taken off the table. I forgot who said it first, but No Deal *is* the table! Brexiteer MP Liam Fox confirmed it, too, during an interview in Davos[34]. The Secretary of State for International Trade also said that the Prime Minister is talking to a variety of MPs about coming to a new deal and that he believes there is an increasing will to achieve a compromise – but he didn't suggest which MPs.

It seems to me that May's tactic hasn't changed. She's going for the DUP vote, and attempting to win over her rebel MPs – and it looks like it might be possible. Jacob Rees-Mogg, staunch Brexiteer and one of the 118 Tory rebels who voted against the Prime Minister, now claims "things are going our way"[35]. Rees-Mogg said that he believes Theresa May's deal could be reformed and win over opponents, but that he wouldn't be supporting it unless the Northern Ireland backstop is removed.

Meanwhile, Michel Barnier isn't backing down. The chief Brexit negotiator for the EU warned today that Labour MP Yvette Cooper's plan to try and block the Prime Minister from delivering No Deal wouldn't work, unless a majority is found for a Withdrawal Agreement[36]. In a speech in Brussels, Barnier said that the default for the UK will still be leaving without a deal unless they come up with an agreement the EU can accept.

That means MPs in Westminster can do what they like to try and stop No Deal, but unless an agreement is made or Article 50 extended, Britain is leaving. Without a deal. And there's nothing they, or Jeremy Corbyn, can do about it.

What is Yvette Cooper's Amendment?

Yvette Cooper's amendment could be so effective that the Labour Party might just whip its MPs to support it. The amendment will go to the Commons on Tuesday 29th January, and it will seek to allow Parliament time to debate her private member's bill that would mandate government ministers to extended Article 50 if a deal could not be reached on Brexit. It's effectively an attempt at thwarting No Deal, which is why the Labour Party is considering demanding all its MPs to vote in favour of it. This is the culmination of Cooper's work with Labour and Tory former ministers and backbenchers.

What Does Europe Have to Say About It?

Europe has effectively shrugged off these plans, however. Barnier has reiterated that should Britain and the European Union be unable to negotiate a deal by March 29th, then we simply leave without a deal. That is the default position and there's very little the UK can do about it. MPs might simply be wasting their time trying to stop something that is inevitable if they refuse to work with the Prime Minister on a deal.

During a meeting with Le Monde in his Brussels office, Barnier discussed the possibility of postponing Brexit to avoid No Deal. He told reporters[37]:

> "...if this question were to be asked, the Heads of State and the governments would ask three questions. For what

reason? For how long? They would also have a third concern: that this possible prolongation might interfere with the democratic working of the European elections. We also have a democratic debate and European elections in the month of May."

His comments during this meeting have gone essentially unreported in English-speaking press. He didn't just talk about avoiding postponement of Brexit, he even suggested that the UK should have to pay the £39 billion divorce settlement in the event of a No Deal Brexit.

He said:

"Concerning the European Union budget, we have always put it very simply: the totality of the commitment of the United Kingdom, as long as the country is a member of the European Union, will be respected. It will be more difficult to have them respected in the case of a 'no deal' but we will continue to insist: these commitments are of a legal nature in international law and I do not imagine that the British will not respect their international commitments."

Given Theresa May has regularly committed to meeting our obligations under international law, or at least, the obligations that the EU says we have, this could be a very real issue. If Theresa May is forced to go down the route of a No Deal Brexit, which is possible but unlikely, then we could still end up paying the £39 billion divorce fee for the pleasure of doing so.

An alternative, that could be proposed by a Brexit Prime Minister, would be to leave, begin trading on WTO terms, and withhold the £39 billion. Though, some Brexiteers in Parliament have suggested on the rolling news coverage that they would be willing to offer the EU some of the divorce settlement to 'sweeten the deal' in the case of a new Withdrawal Agreement being negotiated that doesn't come with the Irish backstop uncertainty.

It seems that the EU and the British people agree on one thing only – that we don't want this to go on for much longer. The EU have European elections to focus on in May, and that's going to dramatically change the makeup of their Parliament. The populists are surging right now, and the last thing the EU needs is to be making more concessions on a Brexit deal while dealing with that.

24ᵗʰ January
EU's Latest Backstop Suggestion Leaked

The sticking point in the Brexit negotiations has long been the backstop – the provision that keeps the United Kingdom within the Customs Union of the European Union in the event of a deal on our future relationship not being agreed in the next two years. It is the issue that politicians are gravely concerned about, partly also because of the implications with the Northern Ireland/Republic of Ireland border.

Theresa May needs to get concessions on the backstop, but the European Union has time and time again refused to make any changes or offer any kind of solution – until now. The European Parliament is set to announce a possible solution to the backstop issue, according to a leaked draft of the conclusions from a Brexit steering group meeting that took place today[38].

The leaked information suggests that the EU, instead of renegotiating the Withdrawal Agreement, believes it may be possible to solve the backstop issue by making changes to the future relationship declaration between the UK and the EU. The EU could suggest that if Theresa May changes her red-lines on Brexit, then they may be able to "avoid deployment of the backstop".

Which red lines, you ask? Well, the EU is claiming that the red lines of leaving the Single Market and Customs Union, ending free movement, and stopping the jurisdiction of the European Court of Justice must be reconsidered in order for any new assurances on the backstop to be made. The EU says that these red lines mean that there cannot be frictionless trade, requiring a backstop and even a border on the island of Ireland.

Mrs May now has to make the decision – will she go back on her red lines, and switch from a position of compromise to one of out-right betrayal? May has so far shown she's willing to betray the British people in the subtlest way possible, but in order to get new assurances on the backstop and get a deal to pass through the Commons, she might have to back down on key Brexit requirements.

It might satisfy some in the DUP, but it won't satisfy Rees-Mogg and the ERG. So much for his optimism, yesterday…

20 MPs in Secret 'Club' to Block No Deal

Can our MPs stoop any lower? A new report from the Daily Telegraph suggests that 18 Members of Parliament, including Work and Pensions Secretary Amber Rudd and Chancellor Philip Hammond, are part of a secret club that's plotting to block a No Deal exit[39].

The report suggests that the MPs call themselves the 'Hair-Shirt Club' because they don't drink alcohol at their meetings, and meet every two weeks to talk about how they can stop the UK from leaving the EU without a deal on the 29th March.

Let me reiterate – these are members of the *cabinet* who are plotting to subvert the will of the people and take actions that could result in the cancellation of Brexit, the watering down of Brexit, or the delay of Brexit.

The news comes not long after Amber Rudd warned the Prime Minister that as many as 40 ministers could quit unless she gives her Tory MPs a free vote on Tuesday the 29th – the next time Parliament has a chance to vote on amendments to the Withdrawal Agreement.

The report by Steven Swinford claims that the group last gathered on Tuesday last week to discuss Yvette Cooper's amendment, which attempted to take No Deal off the table and extend Article 50.

It also suggests that other members of the club include Justice Secretary David Gauke, Business Minister Claire Perry, and Business Secretary Greg Clark.

Theresa May must be *furious* that Amber Rudd has been going behind her back and doing this despite the fact that she brought her back into government after her spectacular fall from grace during the Windrush scandal.

May helps Rudd, and this is how she repays her?

But maybe I'm being foolish – perhaps May isn't bothered by this at all. I hold out a tiny bit of hope that May will get tired of this all and just give us No Deal – but I know the reality is that May really doesn't want that to happen. She does want to use it as a negotiating tactic and threat, but when push comes to shove, I'm not convinced that the Prime Minister is all that different in her view on No Deal than Rudd and other members of the Hair-Shirt Club.

25th January
The DUP Might Have Just Saved Theresa May's Deal

The Democratic Unionist Party might just save Theresa May's Withdrawal Agreement on Tuesday, according to The Sun[40]. The DUP is reported to have indicated they are willing to help the Prime Minister as long as the deal will provide a 'short time limit' to the Irish border provisions/backstop.

While winning over the DUP's 10 votes in Parliament isn't all that significant in itself, the knock-on effect it could have could completely turn around the fortunes of the Prime Minister's deal. If May can get the DUP on board, then she can likely get a large amount of her own party on board. While her deal was shot down in Parliament by 230 votes, she only needs to win over a further 118 MPs to get the deal passed through Parliament.

If the DUP can get on board with her deal – assuming that May is able to provide some kind of assurance that there will be a time limit to the backstop – then May could potentially win over those 118 MPs and hit the 320 mark that will give her a majority in Parliament. I think that's something Jacob Rees-Mogg would go for, given the looming threat of Parliament taking over negotiations and potentially delaying Brexit. Rees-Mogg and other Brexiteers are very aware of this threat, which is why he recently suggested the Queen should shut down parliament if a No Deal Brexit is ruled out[41].

The Sun claims that private negotiations and deliberations are now taking place between the DUP and the Prime Minister. A senior DUP source told The Sun:

"If she fails on Tuesday, Parliament will take over and we lose any semblance of a decent Brexit. We have to help her now,

*so we'll vote with the Government if they
agree the right amendment. That's
looking like a short time to the backstop
at the moment".*

And while Northern Ireland is sitting down and working
with the Prime Minister to make a success of Brexit – or at
least, try and deliver some semblance of Brexit – Leo
Varadkar in the south is throwing a hissy fit. The Republic
of Ireland leader is now threatening to put Irish troops and
police officers back on the border in the event of a No Deal
Brexit[42]...despite saying just three days ago that there
would be no need for a hard border. In fact, many times
over the last few months, Varadkar has said there would be
no need for a hard border. I wonder what changed his
mind?

28th January
What is Tuesday's Brexit Vote?

If you thought the Brexit debate and vote on Tuesday
29th was another Meaningful Vote on May's Withdrawal
Agreement, think again. She first has to come up with
something agreeable in Parliament before she can take it
to the EU, get them to agree, and then take it back to
Parliament. That one even confused me – I was half
expecting Mrs May to have returned yesterday with a new
agreement that the European Union had found agreeable.
Silly me for expecting the Prime Minister to work quickly.

It turns out the actual Meaningful Vote on whatever
agreement Theresa May proposed has been delayed until
February 13th, meaning she still has a little bit of time to get
the EU to come around to new concessions on the
backstop. Interestingly, though, Brussels officials have
already said any such concessions would be 'stupid'[43].

So what's the vote? Well, it's simply an opportunity for the House of Commons to vote on amendments that have been tabled…including amendments to amendments. These would be amendments to the withdrawal legislation, but it doesn't mean that the European Union would agree to it.

The amendments include[44]:

- Backstop amendments

There are two primary amendments from the Tories – specifically from Graham Brady and Andrew Murrison – which aim to make the backstop time-sensitive. The amendments would add an expiry date to the backstop of December 2021, or simply remove it from the Withdrawal Agreement altogether.

- Indicative voting amendments

These amendments try and give MPs more opportunities to vote on matters relating to withdrawal. One high profile amendment from Labour's Hillary Benn sets out a plan for indicative votes on all Brexit options, while Dominic Grieve is putting forward a motion that says a further six days of debates should take place in February and March.

- 'No Deal' amendments

The two main amendments put forward are from Yvette Cooper and Jack Dromey. I've talked about the Yvette Cooper amendment a little previously. She aims to give the Commons the power to pass a bill that would require May to request an extension to Article 50 if she is unable to get her deal passed through Parliament. The question now is – will Speaker John Bercow allow it to be voted on? The non-binding amendment from Jack Dromey and Caroline

Spelman simply rejects no deal in principle. I don't see what impact that's going to have.

So the vote itself, on Tuesday, will really indicate Parliament's feelings on the withdrawal legislation. It could also be a stepping stone towards Theresa May gaining support from the DUP and the Tories. The DUP have already said that they are considering supporting May's agreement, and now even Brexiteer Boris Johnson is talking about it too. The former foreign secretary has said that he would support the Prime Minister if she is able to gain new concessions from the EU on a 'freedom clause' in the Withdrawal Agreement[45], which would allow the UK to leave the backstop at will.

Tomorrow's a big day, but it's still not the end.

Leaked Whitehall Plans Suggest Martial Law Could Be Implemented in a No Deal Scenario

I thought we'd hit peak Project Fear when they told us we'd run out of sandwiches after Brexit, but this really takes the biscuit. Whitehall officials have been gaming a state of emergency and the introduction of martial law in the UK, in the event of a No Deal Brexit. This is no accident. This is the next step for Project Fear, trying to scare the politicians into supporting the government's deal.

The Times reports[46] that Mandarins, the name given to Whitehall officials, are looking at how to use the powers granted under the Civil Contingencies Act 2004 to try and stop civil disobedience occurring as a result of the UK leaving the EU without a deal. As if, somehow, the UK is about to descend into total unmitigated chaos if we're no longer a part of the European project.

I'm shocked by the depths our government will sink to, to try and get this deal through the Commons. I consider it highly unlikely that these Whitehall plans were accidentally made known to the press. This information has conveniently leaked into the public domain, and now both politicians and members of the public are aware that the government might seriously consider imposing martial law on a civilised, first world country if we leave the EU without a deal.

It's funny, because I thought I'd heard Theresa May claiming that no deal is better than a bad deal...but this doesn't really ring true, does it? May and her government, or at least May and her closest allies, are doing all they can to push *any* deal through Parliament. As long as she can get the votes, she'll go for it – and that means she's willing to scaremonger about No Deal relentlessly.

It has also been reported that May has secretly told Cabinet ministers that she will not allow the UK to leave without a deal, and the only reason she refuses to rule it out is to ensure she can continue to use it as a negotiating tactic[47]. Hardly effective if your cabinet leaks that information...

So let's say we do leave without a deal, here's what it would be like:

First, it would mean public rallies and protests would be seriously limited. There could be curfews, property could be confiscated, and there could even be bans on travel.

The army could be deployed if there is any sign of civil disobedience.

Consider it the natural progression from our closely-monitored Big Brother state we already experience. You're not just monitored for the mean jokes you write online – you might be grabbed on the street and thrown in jail if you hold up a placard.

But here's the thing: if we leave without a deal, the only people protesting will be the ones who desperately want to stop Brexit and ignore the will of the people. Are the government, therefore, suggesting that the Remaniacs will finally lose their minds and start behaving like extremists and terrorists on the streets?

I'm a little confused about all this…

The only thing is clear is that the government is so desperate to get a Brexit deal through on Thursday the 29th January that they're willing to pull out all the stops to terrify us. Let's see if it works…

29th January
Theresa May Catches a Break

Theresa May finally caught a break today. Her deal was given one last chance when a majority of MPs – 317 to 301 – voted to send her back to the European Union and reopen the withdrawal negotiations. The amendment tabled by Sir Graham Brady MP, which called for alternative arrangements to replace the Irish backstop, won the support of the Commons and gives Theresa May one last shot to get the deal right.

There was talk that the Brady amendment might simply have been too vague, but the overnight emergence of a compromise deal between Remainers and Brexiteers in the Tory party just about saved it. Called the Malthouse Compromise – named after housing minister Kit Malthouse who devised it – the agreement saw Remainer Nicky Morgan and Brexiteer Jacob Rees-Mogg come together on a possible solution for Mrs May. No doubt the fear of No Deal to the Remainers and the fear of no Brexit to the Brexiteers created the sudden desire to work together.

What is the Malthouse Compromise?

This new compromise is likely to form the basis of a new Withdrawal Agreement with the EU, should they accept it. The Prime Minister warmed to the idea when she was informed that even the ERG-wing of camp Brexit in her party was willing to get on board with it, alongside Remainers like Nicky Morgan. It's being referred to as Brexit 'Plan C'[48], and it has two parts.

The first part – called Plan A – is to reopen the Withdrawal Agreement negotiations and implement an alternative backstop agreement. It would also involve an extended transition period up to December 2021. Should the EU reject this proposal, the Malthouse Compromise suggests moving to Plan B.

Plan B sees the UK negotiating an extended transition period, even without a Withdrawal Agreement in place. We will also pay the divorce bill ad offer 'no tariffs' at the end of the transition period. The idea here is to give us more time to come to an acceptable agreement.

Amazingly, extending the transition period appears to be acceptable for Jacob Rees-Mogg and even Steve Baker (fellow ERG, Tory MP). I was at Westminster today speaking to pro-Brexit protestors, and those who actually believed me Rees-Mogg would back such a thing were shocked. Most people just told me 'that doesn't sound right'. But it is. And tonight, the vote in favour of the Brady amendment means that the government is moving forward with the Malthouse Compromise.

What Happened with the Other Amendments?

The other amendment widely talked about today was Yvette Cooper's. The Labour MP has been trying to gather support for an extension of Article 50 to stop a No Deal Brexit. Labour eventually whipped its MPs to support the measure, but it failed in the Commons tonight thanks to 14 Labour MPs defying Corbyn's instructions.

Eurosceptics Kate Hoey, Dennis Skinner and Graham Stringer all voted against Cooper's amendment, along with a host of other backbenchers who unexpectedly realised the importance of leaving No Deal on the table. Corbyn of course wasn't pleased, so instead decided to focus on the success of another amendment – put forward by Tory backbencher Dame Caroline Spelman – which attempted to take No Deal of the table altogether. The motion was carried by 318 votes to 310, but that doesn't mean the government has to listen. The non-binding amendment simply told the Prime Minister that a majority of Parliament doesn't want No Deal to happen…but she knew that already.

30th January
Corbyn Finally Meets May to Talk

Corbyn's hissy fit is over. After fourteen of his own MPs rebelled against him yesterday, and Theresa May managed to win support for the Brady amendment and Malthouse Compromise, he's essentially been forced to stop talking big and finally do something. The Labour leader met the Prime Minister today to engage in talks but vowed to 'deal with' the fourteen MPs who put him in this position. He told the press that they would be dealt with 'in the next few days in the usual way'[49].

A spokesman for Corbyn said after the meeting that May had shown a "serious engagement in the detail" of Labour's suggestion for a Customs Union with the EU after Brexit[50] – but No 10 says that the Prime Minister hasn't shifted her position following the discussions. Downing Street said that while May had asked questions about his proposal, she hadn't changed her mind since telling Corbyn that the UK must be free to sign its own trade deals. That means no Customs Union.

The 45-minute meeting might be somewhat historic, but it doesn't seem to have come to much. It looks like Mrs May might be able to scrape a deal through Parliament with the support of her party (or at least most of it), the DUP, and some Labour rebels.

Will the EU Accept the Malthouse Compromise?

Still high from her victory in the Commons yesterday, the Prime Minister has vowed to renegotiate the Withdrawal Agreement with the EU, despite Barnier, Juncker and others suggestion that the Withdrawal Agreement is still the 'best and only' agreement for leaving the European Union. Donald Tusk, European Council President, almost immediately insisted that the Withdrawal Agreement was not open for renegotiation.

Given Mrs May hasn't shown much guts so far, her new ally Jacob Rees-Mogg stepped in for her and warned the EU that if they don't reopen negotiations then they could lose the £39 billion divorce settlement. Speaking to TalkRADIO, Rees-Mogg said[51]:

> *"The Withdrawal Agreement has been roundly rejected by Parliament. It lost by a majority of 230 votes. So if they think that the Withdrawal Agreement is not negotiable then we will have to leave without an agreement. That's the position that they have decided they want...But this puts it back to them. They must now decide – do they want our £39 billion? Do they want to have an agreement that has the protections for them that the current agreement has?"*

We'll see if Mrs May is willing to be as tough as Rees-Mogg. It'll be the only way she'll get the stubborn Europeans to offer something better.

Brexit Secretary Says No Deal Remains an Option, Despite Last Night's Vote

Last night MPs voted for the Spelman amendment – a non-binding amendment that suggested Parliament was in favour of ruling out a No Deal Brexit. While the government is not required to take action on the result of the amendment vote, typically this would be an indication to the government to change track. In these extreme times and circumstances, however, the government knows they must continue to pretend they're willing to leave the EU without a deal.

Today, Brexit Secretary Stephen Barclay said that a No Deal Brexit remains an option, and that the UK would leave the EU without a deal on the 29th March if an agreement cannot be made. Remainers might complain and consider it a betrayal of their Commons vote, but Barclay is only repeating what Michel Barnier has said on the matter – which is, the UK leaves on March 29th with or without a deal. The UK parliament cannot stop us leaving without a deal unless we agree to a deal.

In a BBC Radio 4 interview today[52], Barclay was asked whether the UK would still leave without a deal. He responded:

> *"Yes, for the simple reason that the way you take no deal off the table is to secure a deal, or to revoke article 50 and not have Brexit at all, which I think would be catastrophic to our democracy and go against the biggest vote in our history.*
> *Many MPs are concerned about the consequences of no deal, I share that concern as someone who oversees many*

of the plans on no deal. I'm not one of the MPs who says that no-deal can be managed in a benign way.
It is not a policy, it is reality. It is the fact that the majority of MPs voted to trigger article 50. The way you address the risk of no deal is to have a deal or to revoke article 50. That is the legal position."

Barclay also confirmed that Theresa May will today be meeting Jeremy Corbyn to discuss possible changes to the Withdrawal Agreement. The leader of the Labour Party has previously ruled out working with the Prime Minister in the hope that she wouldn't get a deal through Parliament, but following her success passing the Brady amendment yesterday, he now knows Labour's potentially in for a kicking.

With the Brady amendment passed and the Tory party unified on a new way forward for Brexit Theresa May must go back to the European Union to agree 'alternative arrangements' to the backstop. However, in the same Radio 4 interview today, Barclay failed to explain exactly what it is the UK wants. This is why Tory MPs were claiming the Brady amendment was too vague in the first place. When asked five times what the alternative arrangements might be, Barclay couldn't answer.

Mrs May now just needs to decide whether the alternative arrangements she pursues will be in line with Labour's thinking, or something her party could get behind. She just needs the votes in Parliament, and I'm sure at this point she'd choose whatever option seems most likely to pass.

31st January
Brexit Might, Realistically, be Delayed

Senior backbencher Sir Graham Brady today told the BBC that he might accept a delay to Brexit, as long as a Withdrawal Agreement has already been agreed.

The idea of extending the March 29th exit date has been thrown around before, and now it looks like it might happen so that Brexit legislation can be passed through Parliament. The European Union, however, is concerned that Theresa May might be leading the UK towards No Deal by not taking the opportunity to ask for the Brexit delay they think she needs.

According to The Guardian[53], senior figures in Brussels have been wargaming the next steps by the British government, and they think a delay to the 29th March leaving date is inevitable. However, Brussels officials fear that May's 'day to day' approach to surviving this negotiation might just mean things go wrong last minute.

The government says that their position on the date hasn't changed, but even Foreign Secretary Jeremy Hunt today said that extra time might be required to get the deal done[54]. It seems likely to me, too. The Brexit date of March 29th doesn't necessarily mean that the legislation is done and dusted, and passed through Parliament – it simply requires that the deal is in place and we're on track to leave on mutually agreeable conditions. Assuming, of course, that the EU wants to play ball.

Speaking to the BBC Radio 4 Today programme, Hunt said[55]:

> *"It is true that if we ended up approving the deal in the days before the 29th March, then we might need some extra time to pass critical legislation...but if we*

are able to make progress sooner, then that might not be necessary. We can't know at this stage exactly which of those scenarios would happen."

Since the Brady amendment passed in the Commons, May has been discussing potential new arrangements to replace the backstop with EU leaders, MPs, and Irish leader Leo Varadkar. A number of alternatives already exist that could replace the Irish backstop – from a 'trusted trader' scheme that could negate the need for border checks on the island of Ireland, to pre-destination customs checks. But the EU isn't interested. May's intention to renegotiate the Withdrawal Agreement was immediately shot down by the EU[56], and I doubt that's going to change any time soon.

So…yeah. Brexit could well be delayed.

References

[1] The Telegraph, "Theresa May uses New Year's speech to push her Brexit deal", 1st January 2019,
https://www.telegraph.co.uk/news/2019/01/01/theresa-may-uses-new-years-speech-push-brexit-deal/?fbclid=IwAR1GarUew-Nu1l-R0JeqZe14vjl4B9n9lXLZGrOmwFTiykLgJL3F1kXXww8

[2] The Guardian, "Corbyn defies calls from within Labour to back second Brexit referendum", Jessica Elgot, 2nd January 2019,
https://www.theguardian.com/politics/2019/jan/02/corbyn-tells-may-to-strike-new-brexit-deal-labour-can-back

[3] The Guardian, "Most Labour members believe Corbyn should back second Brexit vote", Peter Walker, 2nd January 2019,
https://www.theguardian.com/politics/2019/jan/02/most-labour-members-believe-corbyn-should-back-second-brexit-vote

[4] The Guardian, "Irish PM says he has escalated no-deal Brexit preparations", Jenifer Rankin, 3rd January 2019,
https://www.theguardian.com/politics/2019/jan/03/theresa-may-ring-round-eu-leaders-fails-restart-brexit-talks-irish-backstop

[5] The Telegraph, "By preparing for no deal properly, we will get the good Brexit democracy demands of us", David Davis, 2nd January 2019,
https://www.telegraph.co.uk/politics/2019/01/02/preparing-no-deal-properly-will-get-good-brexit-democracy-demands/

[6] BBC News, "Brexit: PM warns of 'uncharted territory' if MPs reject deal", 6th January 2019,
https://www.bbc.co.uk/news/uk-politics-46772601

[7] BBC News, "Brexit: Date for vote on Theresa May's deal confirmed", 7th January 2019,
https://www.bbc.co.uk/news/uk-politics-46777987

[8] Mail Online, "Commons revolt over No Deal: More than 200 MPs will tell Theresa May to rule out leaving without an agreement even if her proposals are rejected", Jason Groves, 7th January 2019,
https://www.dailymail.co.uk/news/article-6563023/More-200-MPs-tell-Theresa-rule-leaving-without-agreement.html?fbclid=IwAR0oxvAlsBlAY08sRqA0Xuu_CLh8p9MhXHcWCf7pZJi8rtusGbEpvuTsut0

[9] The Guardian, "No-deal Brexit rehearsal in Kent 'a waste of time'", Lisa O'Carroll, 7th January 2019,
https://www.theguardian.com/politics/2019/jan/07/no-deal-brexit-rehearsal-tests-traffic-congestion-in-kent

[10] Mail Online, "Use the 'nuclear option', ministers tell May: PM is urged to trigger an April 4 ELECTION to stop MPs blocking no-deal Brexit", James Tapsfield, 9th January 2019,
https://www.dailymail.co.uk/news/article-6572399/May-urged-stop-MPs-blocking-no-deal-Brexit-triggering-April-4-ELECTION.html

[11] The Guardian, "No-deal Brexit would put thousands of UK jobs at risk, CBI to warn", Lisa O'Carroll, 10th January 2019,
https://www.theguardian.com/politics/2019/jan/10/no-deal-brexit-shrink-uk-gdp-risk-jobs-cbi-business-warning

[12] Twitter, "Business Secretary @GregClarkMP reflects the voice of business. 1000's of firms in despair at prospect of no deal. Rising costs & border disruption will cost jobs for years to come.", Carolyn Fairbairn, 10th January 2019,

https://twitter.com/cbicarolyn/status/1083277399595384832

[13] *Independent, "Jacob Rees-Mogg says we should ignore the CBI on Brexit: 'They have got everything wrong in their history'", Lizzy Buchan, 11th July 2018, https://www.independent.co.uk/news/uk/politics/jacob-rees-mogg-cbi-brexit-business-uk-economy-forecast-a8443056.html*

[14] *Why Vote Leave, "Revealed: the CBI receives millions from the EU and public bodies", 3rd November 2015 http://www.voteleavetakecontrol.org/revealed_the_cbi_receives_millions_from_the_eu_and _public_bodies.html*

[15] *Gov.uk, "Exchange of letters between the UK and EU on the Northern Ireland backstop", Department for Exiting the European Union, 14th January 2019, https://www.gov.uk/government/publications/exchange-of-letters-between-the-uk-and-eu-on-the-northern-ireland-backstop?utm_source=4d883a05-f087-4365-bb56-80c7c98807b2&utm_medium=email&utm_campaign=govuk-notifications&utm_content=immediate*

[16] *Belfast Telegraph, "DUP rejects 'meaningless assurances' from EU on Brexit backstop - Dodds calls for 'real changes' to Withdrawal Agreement", Mark Edwards, 14th January 2019, https://www.belfasttelegraph.co.uk/news/brexit/dup-rejects-meaningless-assurances-from-eu-on-brexit-backstop-dodds-calls-for-real-changes-to-withdrawal-agreement-37708744.html*
[17] *Breitbart, "Theresa May Warns 'No Brexit' Is More Likely than 'No Deal'", Jack Montgomery, 14th January 2019, https://www.breitbart.com/europe/2019/01/14/theresa-may-warns-no-brexit-more-likely-no-deal/?fbclid=IwAR34I3UB_lu0f0EM6EoVSf3fkB_IxOEmv8UhBql_Gc49s8hzx5MP9LhD_LE*

[18] *BBC News, "Brexit: MPs vote on Theresa May's deal", 15th January 2019, https://www.bbc.co.uk/news/uk-politics-46868194*

[19] *BBC News, "Brexit: Theresa May's deal is voted down in historic Commons defeat", 15th January 2019, https://www.bbc.co.uk/news/uk-politics-46885828*

[20] *Itv, "Jeremy Corbyn hits out at Theresa May's 'Frankenstein' deal as MPs begin debating no confidence motion", 16th January 2019, https://www.itv.com/news/2019-01-16/government-no-confidence-theresa-may-historic-eu-deal-defeat/*

[21] *Twitter, "Early start for breakfast media. Will be meeting the Prime Minister later in Westminster.", Arlene Foster, 16th January 2019, https://twitter.com/DUPleader/status/1085533538072571904*

[22] *Sky News, "May tells Corbyn it is 'impossible' to rule out 'no-deal' Brexit", Aubrey Allegretti and Alan McGuinness, 17th January 2019, https://news.sky.com/story/jeremy-corbyn-tries-to-block-mps-from-helping-theresa-may-break-brexit-deadlock-11610101*

[23] *BBC News, "Theresa May urges Jeremy Corbyn: Let's talk Brexit", 17th January 2019, https://www.bbc.co.uk/news/uk-politics-46901217*

[24] *Express, "BREXIT BOMBSHELL: Terrified EU to be forced into MAJOR CLIMBDOWN after May defeat", Rebecca Perring, 17th January 2019, https://www.express.co.uk/news/politics/1073501/Brexit-deal-latest-news-theresa-may-brexit-uk-eu-no-deal-brexit*

[25] *The New European, "We want you to stay: high-profile Germans urge Britain to stay in EU", Matt Withers, 18th January 2019, https://www.theneweuropean.co.uk/top-stories/we-want-you-to-stay-high-profile-germans-urge-britain-to-stay-in-eu-1-5856693*

Chapter Eight: January 2019

[26] ComRess, "DAILY EXPRESS VOTING INTENTION AND BREXIT POLL JANUARY 2019",
https://www.comresglobal.com/polls/daily-express-voting-intention-and-brexit-poll-january-2019/

[27] Mail Online, "'The only option is to walk away!' BBC Question Time audience erupts in APPLAUSE and cheers at prospect of a No Deal Brexit", Alexender Robert, 18th January 2019,
https://www.dailymail.co.uk/news/article-6606705/BBC-Question-Time-audience-erupt-applause-cheers-prospect-no-deal-Brexit.html

[28] City A.M., "Boris Johnson says delaying Article 50 would erode trust in politicians", Alex Daniel, 18th January 2019,
http://www.cityam.com/271847/boris-johnson-says-delaying-article-50-would-erode-trust

[29] Independent, "Brexit news: Theresa May mocked over 'Groundhog Day' as she unveils plan B almost identical to original plan", Lizzy Buchan and Shehab Khan, 21st January 2019,
https://www.independent.co.uk/news/uk/politics/brexit-live-update-theresa-may-deal-statement-speech-parliament-corbyn-labour-conservatives-dup-a8738231.html

[30] BBC News, "Brexit: Theresa May scraps £65 fee for EU citizens to stay in UK", 21st January 2019,
https://www.bbc.co.uk/news/uk-politics-46950719

[31] Belfast Telegraph, "Downing Street rejects claim PM wants to change Good Friday Agreement", Gareth Cross, 21st January 2019,
https://www.belfasttelegraph.co.uk/news/northern-ireland/downing-street-rejects-claim-pm-wants-to-change-good-friday-agreement-37731847.html

[32] Evening Standard, "Theresa May's Brexit 'plan B' rejected by Europe", Joe Murphy, 21st January 2019,
https://www.standard.co.uk/news/politics/europe-says-no-to-theresa-mays-brexit-plan-b-a4044431.html

[33] Euro Guido, "ICM: NO DEAL MOST POPULAR BREXIT OPTION", 21st January 2019,
https://order-order.com/2019/01/21/icm-no-deal-popular-brexit-option/?fbclid=IwAR1BCyEsqiwhzqUhYqhwA3GlUHp87NFVauyE_KjhCu8k_gWelzDwxehqdVQ

[34] Sky News, "Fox: Taking no-deal off table 'not possible'", 23rd January 2019,
https://news.sky.com/video/taking-no-deal-off-the-table-not-possible-11615251

[35] BBC News, "Rees-Mogg says reformed Brexit deal could win over critics", 23rd January 2019,
https://www.bbc.co.uk/news/uk-politics-46971390

[36] The Guardian, "Michel Barnier says opposing no-deal Brexit will not stop it in March", Daniel Boffey, 23rd Janaury 2019,
https://www.theguardian.com/politics/2019/jan/23/michel-barnier-warns-against-time-limited-irish-backstop

[37] Le Monde, "Michel Barnier : "This is the only possible divorce treaty"", Cécile Ducourtieux, 23rd January 2019,
https://www.lemonde.fr/international/article/2019/01/23/michel-barnier-this-is-the-only-possible-divorce-treaty_5413347_3210.html?xtmc=barnier&xtcr=2

[38] Independent, "Brexit backstop could be avoided if Theresa May drops red lines, EU parliament to say", Jon Stone, 24th January 2019,
https://www.independent.co.uk/news/uk/politics/brexit-backstop-irish-border-theresa-may-eu-parliament-michel-barnier-negotiations-a8743851.html

Chapter Eight: January 2019

[39] The Telegraph, "'Hair-shirt club': How 19 Remain ministers have met secretly in bid to stop no-deal Brexit ", Steven Swinford, 23rd January 2019, https://www.telegraph.co.uk/politics/2019/01/23/exclusive-19-remain-ministers-dubbed-hairshirt-club-have-met/?fbclid=IwAR3V14rFYDgcIICk0O-XDMxlZb8R29i2_5tKb8ICcABaYC1I1Zw-1yCUTVM

[40] The Sun, "DUP privately agree to support Theresa May's 'Plan B' Brexit deal when she 'toughens it up' ahead of crunch Commons vote", Tom Newton Dunn, 25th January 2019, https://www.thesun.co.uk/news/brexit/8274637/dup-agree-to-support-pm-brexit-plan/

[41] Politics Home, "Queen would have to shut down Parliament if no-deal Brexit ruled out, Jacob Rees-Mogg says", Emilio Casalicchio, 23rd January 2019, https://www.politicshome.com/news/uk/foreign-affairs/brexit/news/101330/queen-would-have-shut-down-parliament-if-no-deal-brexit

[42] Independent, "No-deal Brexit: Leo Varadkar raises prospect of soldiers on Irish border if UK crashes out of EU", Ashely Cowburn, 25th January 2019, https://www.independent.co.uk/news/uk/politics/no-deal-brexit-irish-varadkar-troops-border-uk-eu-a8746871.html

[43] Evening Standard, "Brexit latest: New Meaningful Vote 'on February 13' as May clashes with Boris Johnson while urging Tory MPs to back an amendment that could save her deal", Sophie Williams and Ella Wills, 28th January 2019, https://www.standard.co.uk/news/uk/brussels-blasts-concessions-stupid-on-eve-of-crucial-series-of-votes-for-pm-a4051046.html

[44] House of Commons, Summary Agenda, 28th January 2019, https://publications.parliament.uk/pa/cm201719/cmagenda/OP190128v2.pdf

[45] Breitbart, "Boris Blinks First: Brexit Rebel Indicates He Will Support PM May's Surrender Plan", Oliver JJ Lane, 28th January 2019, https://www.breitbart.com/europe/2019/01/28/boris-blinks-first-brexit-rebel-indicates-he-will-support-pm-mays-surrender-plan/?fbclid=IwAR34bF6Kd_6ZkXzIQkDtvYj7sKBGgUULE6F79oJTO0vqOg2tPv147pKQ5kc

[46] The Sunday Times, "UK ready to declare martial law to avert no-deal Brexit chaos", Caroline Wheeler, 27th January 2019, https://www.thetimes.co.uk/edition/news/uk-ready-to-declare-martial-law-to-avert-no-deal-brexit-chaos-bfqgzzlrw

[47] The Sun, "Theresa May 'privately told Cabinet ministers she will rule out No Deal'", Matt Dathan, 27th January 2019, https://www.thesun.co.uk/news/brexit/8292363/theresa-may-rule-out-no-deal/

[48] Inews, "Malthouse Compromise explained: Here's the Brexit 'Plan C' Tory MPs are hoping to vote through", Serina Sandhu, 13th March 2019, https://inews.co.uk/news/brexit/kit-malthouse-compromise-brexit-plan-c-tory-mps-explained/

[49] Independent, "Brexit: EU negotiator and Council chief tell Theresa May deal is not open for renegotiation", Shehab Khan and Samuel Osborne, 30th January 2019, https://www.independent.co.uk/news/uk/politics/brexit-news-live-updates-theresa-may-deal-jeremy-corbyn-eu-backstop-irish-border-latest-a8753596.html

[50] The Guardian, "Labour and No 10 at odds over May-Corbyn Customs Union talk", Dan Sabbagh, 30th January 2019, https://www.theguardian.com/politics/2019/jan/30/labour-theresa-may-discussed-post-brexit-customs-union-with-jeremy-corbyn

[51] Express, "Brexit ULTIMATUM: Rees-Mogg warns EU will lose £39billion – 'it's up to Brussels'", Charlotte Davis, 30th January 2019,

Chapter Eight: January 2019

https://www.express.co.uk/news/uk/1079961/Brexit-news-UK-EU-latest-Jacob-Rees-Mogg-Theresa-May-Brexit-bill-no-deal-Ireland-backstop

[52] Twitter, "Britain's Brexit Secretary @stevebarclay says the UK is to leave the EU with no deal on March 29 unless a deal...", BBC Radio 4 Today, 30th January 2019, https://twitter.com/BBCr4today/status/1090535424530022401

[53] The Guardian, "EU fears short article 50 extension will mean no-deal Brexit in June", Daniel Boffey, 21st January 2019, https://www.theguardian.com/politics/2019/jan/31/eu-fears-short-article-50-extension-will-mean-no-deal-brexit-in-june

[54] BBC News, "Brexit: 'Extra time' may be needed, says Jeremy Hunt", 31st January 2019, https://www.bbc.co.uk/news/uk-politics-47069433

[55] The Guardian, "Jeremy Hunt admits Brexit may be delayed to avoid no deal", Matthew Weaver and Dan Sabbagh, 31st January 2019, https://www.theguardian.com/politics/2019/jan/31/jeremy-hunt-admits-brexit-may-have-to-be-delayed-to-avoid-no-deal

[56] Independent, "EU immediately shoots down May's intention to restart negotiations on the Border backstop", Gordon Rayner and Steven Swinford, 30th January 2019, https://www.independent.ie/business/brexit/eu-immediately-shoots-down-mays-intention-to-restart-negotiations-on-the-border-backstop-37764154.html

Chapter Nine
February 2019

1st February
EU Offers Visa-Free Travel to Brits, Spain Sparks Gibraltar Feud

Amidst growing speculation that No Deal is the most likely outcome of May's attempts at renegotiating the Withdrawal Agreement, the European Union has now officially offered the UK visa-free access to the EU for Brits...even if we leave without a deal[1]. The move flies in the face of suggestions by Remain activists for *years* that British citizens would face high costs and paperwork should they want to travel to EU nations.

The European Commission confirmed that as of 2021, UK visitors to EU member countries will have to pay 7 Euros for the European Travel Information and Authorisation Scheme (ETIAS) – effectively the same as the US Esta system, which grants entry to the country for most people without criminal records. The ETIAS can be purchased online ahead of travel and will last for three years, meaning Project Fear now has one less ludicrous claim to throw around.

The offer is granted upon the condition of reciprocity, meaning the EU will be expecting a similar deal for EU citizens looking to travel to the United Kingdom. This serves as a great example of the importance of cooperation between the UK and the EU. It shows the EU considers us a major trading partner and doesn't want professionals and visitors from the EU being cut off from our economy.

Today's news comes as No Deal legislation from the EU is revealed, and a simple footnote in the legislative documents have sparked a row over Gibraltar. The European Union described the Rock as "a colony of the British crown" – an addition to the documentation added at the insistence of Spain, who claims ownership of the soil.

The UK's ambassador in Brussels, Sir Tim Barrow, today expressed the anger of the British government. The official spokesman for the Prime Minister said[2] it was "completely unacceptable" to describe Gibraltar in this way, and that Gibraltar is "a full part of the UK family and has a mature and modern constitutional relationship with the UK".

Following Brexit, the relationship between the UK and Gibraltar will not change – but the potential reopening of the Withdrawal Agreement could mean that Spain tries to gain further concessions over Gibraltar's status as a part of the UK. Our government has already said they would resist any attempt to renegotiate the status of Gibraltar, and this was reiterated by the Prime Minister's spokesman today.

While it's good news on the visas, it's clear that reopening negotiations on the Withdrawal Agreement won't come without its problems.

4th February
"Alternative Arrangements" Discussions Have Begun

Discussions about a proposed alternative to the Irish backstop have begun today. The Alternative Arrangements Working Group, which is made up of both Leave and Remain MPs, have begun three days of discussion to find an alternative to the Irish backstop. Home Secretary Sajid Javid has already said that existing technology could be used as an alternative, while MPs debate whether systems like Trusted Traders schemes could be implemented to stop checks at the Irish border.

The discussions might ultimately come to nothing, however, as EU leaders continue to rule out making changes to the backstop arrangements within the Withdrawal Agreement. Irish leader Leo Varadkar told the press last night the ideas the UK were considering had 'already been rejected' and he found it frustrating that the UK would going back to considering technological replacements of the backstop.

The very fact that the government appears willing to spend three days reviewing these options means Theresa May is hoping a suitable solution might just be attractive enough for the EU to reconsider. German Chancellor Angela Merkel has said, after all, that the EU is willing to listen to the proposals outlined by the UK – but that they needed to hear, specifically, how the UK intends to solve the backstop riddle.

Tim Farron, former leader of the Liberal Democrats, has accused Theresa May of wasting time with the new working group[3], and the Irish deputy prime minister Simon Coveney was similarly negative about the ideas being considered. Writing in The Sunday Times[4], Coveney explained:

> *"This is not a new concept. The EU is committed to trying to agree alternative arrangements to replace the backstop. We want a comprehensive future relationship in place by the end of 2020 so the backstop is never used. We want to get on with the work once the Withdrawal Agreement is ratified. Yet there are no credible alternative arrangements, put forward by anyone, that achieve the shared goal of the UK and EU to avoid a hard border. The backstop is a necessary guarantee,*

based on legal certainty, not just wishful thinking".

Meanwhile, Her Majesty's Revenue & Customs (HMRC) has announced that EU imports will not get extra checks following a No Deal Brexit[5], to avoid any traffic delays if we leave without a deal t the end of March. Critics have suggested that such a measure would mean the UK wouldn't know what was being imported into the UK...while failing to recognise this is the same policy we have as members of the European Union.

HMRC said that the transitional plans would be put into place for one year, where EU goods will be waved through in the same way they are now, while other arrangements are put into place.

5th February
May Confirms She's Seeking to Change the Backstop, Not Remove It

The Prime Minister travelled to Northern Ireland today[6]. She gave a speech in Belfast, where she reconfirmed her commitment to avoiding a hard border on the island of Ireland. Theresa May used the opportunity to thank businesses who had supported her initial backstop plans, and to explain her plan to win over the EU and the Commons.

Given that the Commons has already voted in favour of the government finding 'alternative arrangements' to the backstop, you could be forgiven for assuming that Theresa May was going to Northern Ireland to discuss the potential alternatives to the backstop. But, in her speech today, the Prime Minister explained that she is instead seeking changes to the backstop, and is not planning on removing it from her Brexit deal[7].

Mrs May is no doubt giving in to the stubborn nature of the European Union after being told that the backstop is a necessity. I wonder whether her working group back in London know about that. Possibly not, given the press reported today that Downing Street had said the government is still considering alternatives.

In a bid to try and prove UK-Irish relations are as strong as ever, the Prime Minister also used her trip to Northern Ireland to float the possibility of a joint UK and Ireland bid for the 2030 World Cup. May said that the ties of 'family and friendship' between the UK and Ireland are more important than ever, and that she would work with Irish leader Leo Varadkar to get the respective football associations to approve the idea.

So all in all, a bizarre kind of day for the Prime Minister. She stood up in front of the UK press, announced that she wouldn't be seeking to remove the backstop despite what the Commons has already told her, and that she wants to improve UK-Irish relations through football.

Weird.

6th February
Labour Calls for Article 50 Extension as 2-Month Brexit Delay Seems Likely

The Labour Party has today called for a delay to Brexit, suggesting Theresa May has run out of time to pass her deal before the 29th March – the legal day of Brexit, which is just seven weeks away.

Speaking to the Commons in Corbyn's place today, Shadow Foreign Secretary Emily Thornberry said that no one could seriously think that Theresa May was going to get the concessions she needs from the EU. She also said[8]:

Chapter Nine: February 2019

"Does she not agree that the sensible, cautious thing to do at this late stage is to seek a temporary extension of Article 50 so we have time to see if the negotiations succeed or, if they do not, to pursue a different plan?".

Of course, we have to take anything that comes out of Emily Thornberry's mouth with a pinch of salt. The Labour MP is, much like the rest of her party, hell bent on stopping Theresa May getting a deal with the European Union.

Opposite Thornberry in the Commons today was de facto Deputy Prime Minister David Lidington. The Cabinet Office Minister known for being exceptionally close to the Prime Minister told Labour that delaying Brexit would "simply defer the need" for Members of Parliament on both sides of the house to "face up to difficult positions".

But, it looks like Cabinet might be on a similar page with Thornberry after all. It emerged last night that a potential eight-week delay to Brexit has already been discussed by cabinet, meaning MPs would have more time to pass necessary Brexit-related legislation through Parliament before we leave the European Union. That would mean that Brexit wouldn't happen on March 29th as planned, but on May 24th instead.

The Commons would need some time to pass immigration and trade bills, as well as hundreds of other minor pieces of legislation. We've already heard Andrea Leadsom and Jeremy Hunt talk about a potential delay of a couple of weeks, but eight weeks seems excessive. It seems to me that the politicians want to kick the can down the road a little further – with little regard for the businesses who still have absolutely no idea what they should be preparing for.

Donald Tusk Lashes Out at British Politicians

Tusk lashed out at British politicians today, in what some assumed was an angry, off-the-cuff remark. It turns out that the President of the European Council planned his words very carefully when he said[9]:

> *"The top priority for us remains the issue of the border on the island of Ireland and the guarantee to maintain the peace process in accordance with the Good Friday Agreement. There's no room for speculation here. The EU itself is first and foremost a peace project. We will not gamble with peace...By the way, I've been wondering, what the special place in hell looks like for those who promoted Brexit without even a sketch of a plan how to carry it safely".*

The Council President disguised his anger behind a dream and a desire to bring Europe together in peace, but his anger was clearly directed at those who simply want to leave the European Union. This isn't about the politicians who didn't have a plan (and they didn't, by the way) – this is about the European Union purposely making Brexit difficult, and then attacking our (admittedly useless) politicians for not having any idea how to navigate the process in a way that the EU likes.

Sorry, Tusk, but nothing we do is ever going to keep you unhappy. Unless, of course, we decide to stay in the EU.

May Meets with Northern Ireland Parties

As part of her trip to Northern Ireland, the Prime Minister today held talks with the five main political parties in Stormont[10]. Her Northern Ireland visit was primarily an attempt at reassuring the Irish that the Brexit deal she'll try and get through the Commons will not involve a hard border.

The leader of the Ulster Unionist Party, Robin Swann, called for Northern Ireland to be ruled directly from the Westminster parliament in the event of a No Deal Brexit – while the leader of the Alliance Party, Naomi Long, said that the Prime Minister had offered nothing new during the talks. It seems that the Prime Minister is just as underwhelming in her attempts to convince the Northern Irish that everything will be OK, as she is when she speaks in the Commons.

While the Prime Minister is away, Business Secretary today indicated that he and other ministers might resign from the government if Theresa May recommended a No Deal Brexit[11]. Clark said that if the Prime Minister fails to get a new agreement through parliament, then he and other ministers would regard the decision as 'unacceptable'. He also said that it's time for parliament to "grasp the nettle and agree a deal" – another indication that our politicians would rather take any deal than implement a Brexit that would return our sovereignty and offer an economic advantage for our businesses.

7th February
May Goes Back to Brussels, Corbyn Offers a Deal

Jeremy Corbyn sent a letter to the Prime Minister this morning, in which he outlined the five things his party would need to see, if they were to support her Brexit deal in Parliament. The move is a marked change to his previous position. It wasn't that long ago when Jeremy Corbyn was refusing to even talk to the Prime Minister about Brexit.

Ever since the Brady amendment was passed in Parliament, Corbyn's tune has changed and now he seems willing to set out some options that could potentially get his party on board. A combination of a looming No Deal, and pressure from his party for him to call a second referendum, are not doubt the reasons why he reached out today.

The letter, however, doesn't seem like something the Prime Minister could really get on board with. In his five demands, Corbyn suggests a Brexit that looks nothing like what Mrs May promised when she became Prime Minister. It read[12]:

> *The changes we would need to see include:*
>
> 1. *A permanent and comprehensive UK-wide Customs Union. This would include alignment with the union customs code, a common external tariff and an agreement on commercial policy that includes a UK say on future EU trade deals. We believe that a Customs Union is necessary to deliver the frictionless trade that our businesses, workers and consumers need, and is the only viable way to ensure there is no hard border on the island of Ireland. As you are aware, a Customs Union is supported by most businesses and trade unions.*
>
> 2. *Close alignment with the Single Market. This should be underpinned by shared institutions and obligations, with clear arrangements for dispute resolution.*
>
> 3. *Dynamic alignment on rights and protections so that UK standards*

keep pace with evolving standards across Europe as a minimum, allowing the UK to lead the way.

4. *Clear commitments on participation in EU agencies and funding programmes, including in areas such as the environment, education, and industrial regulation.*

5. *Unambiguous agreements on the detail of future security arrangements, including access to the European Arrest Warrant and vital shared databases.*

Mrs May has repeatedly promised that Brexit would mean leaving the Single Market and Customs Union, meaning it's likely that Corbyn's suggestion is dead in the water. However, according to Downing Street sources, the proposal was in fact seriously considered today[13]. Considerable points of differences were noted, however, and it seems that the Prime Minister's focus is staying on her discussions with EU leaders.

She has been over in Brussels today talking to EU leaders, where she gave Donald Tusk a telling of and had what looked like a pretty cold meeting with Juncker. The Prime Minister confronted Tusk today over his "special place in hell" comment, and told the press that she had taken part in "robust but constructive" talks with leaders in Brussels[14]. In a photo op with Juncker, she walked out, coldly looked at the cameras, begrudgingly shook Juncker's hand, and then left. I've never seen them both look so angry at one another – so I can only imagine how tough it's been today. Days like this almost make me feel sorry for the Prime Minister.

The EU is refusing to budge on its commitment to the current Withdrawal Agreement and backstop, saying they will not open up the document and renegotiate. However, the Prime Minister now appears to be trying to provide some certainty over the backstop through the political declaration – the document that outlines some information about the UK's future relationship with the EU.

Tusk doesn't seem all that optimistic, tweeting[15]:

> *"Still no breakthrough in sight. Talks will continue".*

The Prime Minister also told the press[16]:

> *"What I've set out is our clear position that we must secure legally binding changes to the Withdrawal Agreement to deal with the concerns that parliament has over the backstop, and that changes to the backstop, together with the other work we're doing on workers' rights and other issues, will deliver a stable majority in parliament…That's what I will continue to push for. It's not going to be easy but crucially President Juncker and I have agreed that talks will now start to find a way through this, to find a way to get this over the line and to deliver on the concerns that parliament has, so we get a majority in parliament."*

She even said that she still intends to deliver Brexit on time, going against reports yesterday that Brexit could be delayed until the end of May. We'll see.

8th February
Government Plans for Brexit "Crisis" as May's Negotiations Continue to Flop

The government has begun employing civilians to work in an emergency control centre being set up to ensure that Britain continues to function normally in the event of a No Deal Brexit. Don't get me wrong, I don't think it's bad for the government to be planning – but doesn't the media hysteria seem a little much?

Briefing notes to recruitment agencies, issued by the Department for Environment, Food and Rural Affairs (DEFRA), state that the "EU Exit Emergencies Centre" could stay open for two years. The briefing notes were seen by the Guardian, and the newspaper suggests[17] that the government is seeking to recruit "unflappable" individuals who will help brief ministers and the Cabinet on emergencies that might occur in the event of a No Deal Brexit.

No doubt the fact that an EU Exit Emergencies Centre is being set up will be used by Project Fear to reassert their claims that Brexit is a disaster, but it seems like sensible planning to me. No Deal planning was already ramped by Whitehall back in December, and I expect our government to do everything they can to make Brexit a success. If that means hiring professionals to keep the government up-to-date on unfolding matters in the event of No Deal, then so be it. Sounds responsible to me!

Meanwhile, back in Westminster, a group of Tory MPs today told the Prime Minister that the Irish backstop issue is "monumental" and that it could not be solved with a "few cursory tweaks". The warning comes as the Prime Minister suggests she is looking to change the backstop by opening up the political declaration. That option might please Brussels, given EU leaders have said the Withdrawal Agreement cannot be reopened, but it's not going to please

Members of Parliament who have already told her they want an alternative to the backstop.

The three former Cabinet ministers who put together the Malthouse Compromise – Owen Paterson, Iain Duncan Smith and Nicky Morgan – warned the Prime Minister that the Withdrawal Agreement in its current form is not going to pass in the Commons. And they're right.

They also warned that any support of Labour's plan to keep Britain inside a Customs Union with the European Union would go against the promises made in the Conservative Party manifesto. That is, of course, also true. It would even be a breach of the Labour Party manifesto, which promised an end to free movement. Labour MP Shami Chakrabarti got absolutely skewered by Andrew Neil on Politics Live over that yesterday[18]. She sat there looking absolutely terrified as Neil repeatedly reminded her that staying in the Customs Union means maintaining free movement. She just told him that it would be up for negotiation. Well, it won't – the EU will not back down on the Four Freedoms, and that means they won't give up free movement if Britain wants to remain in a Customs Union.

So Mrs May has found herself in a very tricky spot. The EU won't reopen the Withdrawal Agreement, meaning the Brady Amendment was effectively pointless. The Prime Minister is now seeking a tweaking to the backstop, but her own party won't accept it.

Should she go for the deal put before her by the Labour Party, which includes staying in the Customs Union, then she'll have to betray her own Brexit red lines.

Your move, Mrs May.

11th February
The Next Meaningful Vote Could Be Just WEEKS Before Brexit

The next Meaningful Vote on Theresa May's Withdrawal Agreement was expected to take place this week. After having met with European leaders, hopped over to Ireland to speak to NI leaders, and putting together an 'alternative arrangements' study group in Westminster, the Prime Minister thought she might have been able to come up with a workable solution by now.

EU leaders have repeatedly told the Prime Minister that the Withdrawal Agreement isn't up for negotiation, however, meaning that the Meaningful Vote is the last thing on our government's mind right now. The first step is finding the impossible impasse to this ongoing backstop disagreement. The Commons told May to find alternative arrangements, the Prime Minister has said she wants to simply amend the backstop, and the EU said "fat chance"!

So now, it looks like MPs might not get the opportunity to vote on the Withdrawal Agreement again (which should be coming with new promises and assurances from the EU) until the middle of March...just weeks away from the departure date of 29th March.

Communities Secretary James Brokenshire has said that in the event this happens, MPs would be given the opportunity to vote on their own proposals and change the course of Brexit[19]. So unless the Prime Minister finds some acceptable way forward very, very soon, then Parliament could ultimately find itself in control of Brexit and not the Cabinet. That could potentially be disastrous for Brexit voters given the majority of the Commons is looking for a way to stop Brexit from happening full stop.

In an attempt to assure MPs their voice is still being heard, the Prime Minister *has* offered further votes by the end of February – but there remains no binding commitment to a Meaningful Vote on the deal by the end of the month. The Prime Minister is simply offering MPs new opportunities to vote on amendments to her Brexit negotiating strategy on the 27th of February.

Shadow Brexit Secretary Keir Starmer isn't appeased by the Prime Minister's attempt at keeping the Commons happy, though. In a piece in the Sunday Times, Starmer said that Labour will be attempting to force the government into holding the second Meaningful Vote before February 26th[20].

Mrs May not only has the EU to worry about – she's got angry politicians at home looking for blood. As No Deal looks more likely than ever, our politicians are likely to get even more drastic in their attempts at thwarting Brexit. Either that, or they might just cave and support the Prime Minister's deal at the eleventh hour.

12th February
May Promises Meaningful Vote, Tells MPs to 'Hold Their Nerve'

Speaking to the Commons today, the Prime Minister appealed to MPs for more time to continue her negotiations with Brussels over her Withdrawal Agreement. Mrs May acknowledged that European Union negotiators had already denied reopening the Withdrawal Agreement negotiations but said the British negotiators had informed the EU that the only wait it will be passed through Parliament is if legally-binding changes can be offered.

That doesn't necessarily mean the Prime Minister is looking for changes to the Withdrawal Agreement, but signifies she still intends to find some other way of obtaining a legally-binding promise from the EU.

Chapter Nine: February 2019

Leader of the opposition Jeremy Corbyn accused May of 'running down the clock' in an attempt to blackmail MPs, to which May responded[21]:

> *"I wanted this sorted before Christmas!"*

MPs erupted when the Prime Minister seemed to suggest that those who didn't vote for the deal were the ones holding up Brexit. Shadow Brexit Secretary Keir Starmer responded:

> *"Unbelievable. Do we really have to remind the Prime Minister that she was the one who cancelled the vote before Christmas?"*

The only thing May could offer was a promise of a Meaningful Vote on the changes she will ultimately secure to the backstop clause but didn't provide a time frame. She did promise to update the House on February 26th and offer non-binding votes if she had not obtained a new deal by then[22].

Meanwhile, rumours suggest that the Prime Minister might actually be considering leaving the European Union without a deal. After years of trying to betray the vote we cast in 2016, the Prime Minister might be forced to leave the EU after failing to negotiate a deal. In a piece for the Huffington Post, Paul Waugh wrote that internal party polling, along with warnings from her Party Chairman and Chief Whip, have forced her to "think the unthinkable"[23]. In a tweet, he also suggested that the Prime Minister is now "seriously contemplating a No Deal Brexit"[24].

13th February
Hard Brexiteers Threaten New Defeat for May in the Commons

Hard Brexiteers from the European Research Group are threatening to vote down a No 10 motion in Parliament tomorrow, and inflict another Commons defeat on the Prime Minister. The motion to be voted on tomorrow outlines the "approach to leaving the EU". It asks the House to reconfirm its support to the approach set out in the Brady amendment, which was supported in the Commons on January 29th.

It was therefore considered uncontroversial, until members of the ERG noticed the wording of the motion endorsed an extra amendment made by MPs on January 29th, which tried to rule our No Deal. Remember that? It was the amendment put forward that said the House would not accept a No Deal Brexit – the same amendment that the EU scoffed at and reminded British politicians that they could not stop No Deal.

The motion being voted on tomorrow effectively endorses that amendment and asks Parliament to support ruling out No Deal. Something the ERG clearly doesn't want to do.

Speaking to the BBC, a well-known member of the ERG Mark Francois said[25]:

> *"We cannot vote for this as it is currently configured because it rules out no-deal and removes our negotiating leverage in Brussels...The Prime Minister, if she want through the lobbies for this tomorrow night, would be voting against the guarantees she has given in the Commons for months. It is madness".*

The Prime Minister denies that the motion will rule out No Deal[26] (of course) with a No 10 spokesperson saying the motion simply reflects the Prime Minister's desire to get a deal with the EU.

Mrs May has also spent today playing down reports that she could force Members of Parliament to choose between her deal with the EU or delaying withdrawal. UK Brexit negotiator Olly Robbins was reportedly heard speaking in a bar in Brussels that the European Union was likely to offer an extension to the negotiating period. The Prime Minister today said that MPs shouldn't rely on "what someone said to someone else as overheard by someone else, in a bar".

So the prospect of delaying Brexit still seems uncertain. The Prime Minister will, however, be changing a rule that requires 21 days before voting on an international treaty. That would mean she can delay the final Meaningful Vote on the Withdrawal Agreement to just days before the UK is due to leave the EU. When Corbyn says that the Prime Minister is trying to run down the clock, it's hard to disagree with him.

14th February
May Delivered Blow by Brexiteers in Parliament

MPs were set to vote on three amendments to Theresa May's Brexit negotiations today. Speaker John Bercow chose the following three amendments to be debated and voted on, which were:

1. Jeremy Corbyn (Labour) Amendment
This amendment would require the Government to hold another Meaningful Vote by the 27th of February. If the vote is not held, the amendment asks the

government to declare there is no longer a deal on the table and to present the next steps it intends to take.

2. Anna Soubry (Tory) Amendment

This amendment requests the Government publishes its most recent official No Deal briefing within a week.

3. Ian Blackford (SNP) Amendment

Requires the Government to extend Article 50 by three months at least.

MPs today also voted on the Prime Minister's motion which attempted to gain support for her current negotiating position. The Prime Minister's motion was defeated by a majority of 45 (303 votes to 258). While the vote won't have any real effect on the Brexit negotiations, it does reverse the win she had a few weeks ago when Parliament voted for the Brady amendment and agreed that the Prime Minister should seek alternative arrangements to the backstop.

Interestingly, one ERG Tory actually abstained on the vote. Sir Bernard Jenkin said that he didn't think these votes were important (given they're non-binding), and so spent the time being interviewed by Sky News instead.

None of the three amendments put forward by Tory, Labour and SNP members succeeded[27]. In fact, Anna Soubry withdrew her amendment after Brexit Minister Chris Heaton-Harris suggested that David Lidington (Cabinet Office Minister and Theresa May's number two) would meet with her and publish the information she is requesting. Soubry did suggest, however, that she would reserve the right to put forward the amendment again in February if the documents were not published.

Ian Blackford's amendment was defeated quite severely – with just 93 MPs voting in favour and 315 against. The amendment put forward by Corbyn, however, was much closer – losing to the government's majority of just 16 (306 to 322).

So while Theresa May has been dealt a blow by the Brexiteers in her own government, the other side hasn't succeeded in throwing her off course just yet. The Prime Minister will continue her attempts at getting the EU to offer some kind of concession on the backstop, while Westminster keeps playing games to try and keep us in the EU.

18th February
7 Labour MPs Defect and Form "Independent" Party in Westminster

The fracture within the Labour Party over Brexit has finally broken the party apart. This morning, seven Labour MPs defected from the party and have formed "The Independent Group".

Chuka Umunna announced the decision today at a press conference in London, where he was joined by fellow defectors Luciana Berger, Chris Leslie, Angela Smith, Mike Gapes, Ann Coffey and Gavin Shuker. Tired of Labour's shift to the anti-Semitic fringe of politics, these MPs are aiming to form a new 'centrist' grouping in Westminster.

Luciana Berger told the press:

> *"I cannot remain in a party that I have today come to the sickening conclusion is institutionally anti-Semitic".*

Chris Leslie, former Shadow Chancellor, said:

> *"We can no longer knock on doors and support a government led by Jeremy Corbyn and the team around him…This has not been an easy decision for any of us. We have all been Labour MPs for years. But the Labour Party we joined is no longer today's Labour Party".*

These MPs made anti-Semitism and left-wing extremism the reason for forming the new group, but there's more to it than that. They know that polls have shown time and time again that the British public are looking for a new centrist party to vote for, and they foolishly believe that the public consider remaining in the European Union to be part of a centrist platform.

A new anti-Brexit force is being created in Westminster, and it's only a matter of time before Tories like Anna Soubry jump on board too.

In an attempt to legitimise their work thwarting Brexit, these MPs will use the one tool that they can always rely on - the media. Their method is simple; they tell the press that they are the new centrist party the people are looking for, and the press believes them. That's all there is to it.

The people want a centrist party, these guys announce that they're centrist, the media reports it, and the voters believe them. Mark my word – in a matter of day's we'll be seeing polls that show The Independent Group (or whatever name their party ends up having) beating or competing with Labour.

We know this is all about Brexit, and Mike Gapes confirmed it when he said he was "furious that the Labour leaderships is complicit in facilitating Brexit".

Look a little closer at their policy, however, and you'll see how they're trying to casually bury the Brexit issue for now. They're not saying they want to stay in the EU, only that they want an "alternative" to the Conservatives' approach.

Their official statement reads[28]:

> *"Labour now pursues policies that would weaken our national security; accepts the narratives of states hostile to our country; has failed to take a lead in addressing the challenge of Brexit and to provide a strong and coherent alternative to the Conservatives' approach".*

This is going to be a turbulent week. So many defections from one of the two big parties is significant. It hasn't happened since the SDP. A few more defections could seriously hurt Labour in the polls (and ultimately in a general election) – and if any Tories get on board, it could put Theresa May's slim majority in jeopardy.

19th February
One More Labour MP Defects, Four Tory MPs Could Join Her

I knew it was only a matter of time. We now know that as many as four Tory MPs, including a minister, could join ex-Labour MPs in the new Independent Group. The Mail reported today[29] that Chuka Umunna is now appealing directly to Tory MPs who are "fed up with the UKIPisation" of the party, and The Telegraph reports[30] that a minister is prepared to join the new party if the Government goes ahead with a No Deal Brexit.

The minister, apparently, considers the breakaway group as "remarkably sensible people".

Anna Soubry has to be one of the Tory MPs in question, of course. It has long been speculated that Soubry would leave the Tories if given an alternative platform, with rumours ramping up after she removed her "One Nation Tory" slogan from her Twitter profile.

Oh, and as I predicted, a poll has just found that Labour voters now prefer the Independent Group. A survey by Survation asked which party "best represents the people of Britain". 23% of Labour voters surveyed said they prefer Labour, while 40% opted for The Independent Group[31].

Another Labour MP joined the defectors today, too. Enfield North MP Joan Ryan has officially joined The Independent Group, making her their eighth MP, citing Labour's failure to tackle anti-Semitism. Just like all the others, though, she's not considering a "People's By-Election". Ryan told the Today programme that she won her seat in 2017 "in spite of" Corbyn, "not because of him"[32].

Watch this space.

20th February
Soubry Defects to The Independent Group with Two Tory MPs in Tow

Anna Soubry has officially left the Conservative Party. This is wild! It's been such a long time since we've seen defections like this – and it doesn't end with Soubry. She's taking two other Tory MPs with her. Sarah Wollaston and Heidi Allen wrote a joint letter with Soubry confirming their departure from the Conservative Party. They will be joining Chuka Umunna and the seven other Labour MPs in the pro-Remain Independent Group.

The press conference was well prepared. It mirrored Chuka's press conference precisely, with specific questions from the press being expertly shared between the three MPs. Everyone knew what they had to say, and how they had to say it. The only time Soubry seemed flustered was when she was asked if she should call a byelection in her constituency. She and Heidi Allen scoffed at the idea and said the last thing the country needs right now is a general election or byelection of any kind.

Ironic, given all three of them want a second vote on Brexit. In fact, that's the entire reason they're leaving the Conservative Party today. They're joining a new anti-Brexit force in Westminster, calling for a second vote, but not daring to go to their own constituents for a second vote. Allen claimed that her political positions haven't changed since her election, meaning she wouldn't need to go back for a fresh mandate...but I remember her telling audiences that she planned to respect the decision made by the people in 2016. She flat out lied today.

Anna Soubry taking two other MPs with her is a big blow. That means the new Independent Group has a total of 11 MPs, and that's very likely to grow in coming days and weeks. It's currently only a registered business and not a party, but I suspect they're gearing up to register with the Electoral Commission very soon. There could be a general election around the corner...

Actually, let me talk about the potential of a general election – because the formation of a new party does have some interesting implications.

First of all, the Conservative Party and the DUP are at risk of losing their majority in the House of Commons. With three MPs gone, the Tories and DUP have a majority of 6 in the Commons (excluding the speaker and Sinn Fein and presuming that Labour will win the upcoming Newport West byelection). That means losing just three more Members of Parliament to the Independent Group will put their majority at 0. Four more defections, and that gives the opposition parties a collective majority of 2 – putting Theresa May in very difficult water.

Though, in saying that, it's hardly like those Tory MPs were particularly helpful to her in the party. So I suppose in the grand scheme of things, it doesn't make much difference to her.

It could in all likelihood mean another election, though. Mrs May has been presumably wanting to avoid another general election given how badly it went last time – but the defections could force her to make decisive action and could persuade her to try and take advantage of Labour's vulnerable position.

Sure, the Tories have lost some to the Independent Group, but it's the Labour Party that is suffering the most. A poll by YouGov shows that, if Independent Group candidates stand and register as a party, 14% of voters would support them. That takes Labour's position in the polls down to 26% and puts the Tories at a healthy 38%[33].

Depending on how concentrated those votes are in specific constituencies, that could either mean Theresa May wins a healthy majority...or she's stuck with another hung Parliament and no clear answer about which parties would even work together. The Lib Dems agree with The Independent Group on Brexit, but they're both small. The Tories want a deal, and Labour want a Customs Union.

Parliamentarians do think that another election could be on the cards. Labour MPs and peers are worried that the Prime Minister might be tempted to exploit Labour's split and call an election. Stewart Wood, a Labour peer as well as an academic from Oxford, said that the defections from Labour had "significantly raised the chances of a snap election being called"[34].

What's funny about these defections is that Anna Soubry, inadvertently, might have helped pave the way for Theresa May to call and win a general election.

21st February
Corbyn Meets EU Leaders to Propose Staying in Customs Union

Jeremy Corbyn was in Brussels today. I'm not sure exactly who this guy thinks he is, but no matter how useless the Prime Minister might have been throughout this negotiation process, it is absolutely not the role of the leader of the opposition to be meeting EU leaders to discuss the Withdrawal Agreement.

Corbyn met with Brexit negotiators, including the EU's very own buck-toothed mini Hitler, Guy Verhofstadt. The discussions focused on the alternative deal that Jeremy Corbyn proposed to the Prime Minister some weeks ago, which recommends that the United Kingdom remains in the Customs Union and Single Market.

Speaking to the press following the meetings, Corbyn said:

> *"We put forward a view, as you know, that No Deal must be taken off the table and we believe the Labour alternative on a Customs Union, market access and protection of rights is a credible one. It certainly has great support amongst MPs on my side of the house, and some from the other side as well. We think there could be a majority for it, we'll continue to push it, but Theresa May must end her red lines and start being serious about it. Otherwise, the danger of the No Deal exit on the 29th March becomes very real –*

and that would be very very damaging to jobs on both sides of the Channel. It would be damaging to supply chains, again on both sides of the Channel. These things have to be addressed".

Corbyn also insisted[35] that the option of holding a second referendum remains "very much part of the agenda put forward by the Labour Party" if Theresa May fails to support a close economic partnership with the EU. In short, Corbyn wants his Customs Union deal, or he wants to go back to the public in the hope that we all change our minds.

This is all the evidence you need that the Labour Party is interested only in treating Brexit like a game. They're navigating around this invented crisis as if it were a board game, making strategic moves to undermine the Prime Minister and ultimately stop the Brexit process in its tracks. Quite astounding, for a man who has campaigned against the EU his entire life.

Interestingly, Jean-Claude Juncker also said today that he is "not very optimistic' that No Deal Brexit can be avoided, following a meeting with Theresa May. He said that he clearly saw no majority in favour of the deal in Parliament.

Speaking to a session[36] of the European Economic and Social Committee, Juncker said:

"If no deal were to happen, and I cannot exclude this, this would have terrible economic and social consequences in Britain and on the continent, so my efforts are oriented in a way that the worst can be avoided. But I am not very optimistic when it comes to this issue...Because in the British parliament every time they are voting, there is a majority against

*something, there is no majority in favour
of something."*

I suppose he's not wrong, though he's hardly been cooperative throughout. The fact that he and his colleagues categorically refuse to reopen negotiations on the Withdrawal Agreement and seem reluctant to offer any assurance that the backstop will not be permanent and impossible to leave unilaterally, is a huge red flag. If they have no intention of keeping the UK stuck inside the backstop, then why are they so desperate to maintain their ability to do exactly that, within the Withdrawal Agreement text?

Or could it be that they're doing the same as the Prime Minister – running down the clock in the hope that the other side will cave at the last minute?

Despite all this, however, a Brussels reporter has claimed that the latest Brexit meeting with Barnier will trigger EU concessions and that there's "something in the air". Quite a stark difference to the doom and gloom Juncker portrayed today.

Ian Wishart, European reporter for Bloomberg, recounted to BBC Politics Live[37] that after Jeremy Corbyn and Keir Starmer met with Michel Barnier, the Attorney General Geoffrey Cox and Brexit Secretary Stephen Barclay stepped in for their own meeting. He said that the meeting with Cox and Barclay could come with a proposal and could result in concessions over the backstop.

What those concessions will be are yet to be seen, but they will unquestionably be some form of legal assurances outside of the Withdrawal Agreement that could be enough for the Attorney General to confirm that the backstop will not be something the UK will be stuck in for an indefinite period of time.

When Corbyn was asked by journalists whether he'd support the Prime Minister's deal if Cox confirmed the backstop is no longer indefinite, he simply refused to answer – once again confirming this is all a game to the Labour Party.

25th February
Corbyn Prepared to Back Second Brexit Referendum

It seems like the pressure of The Independent Group is getting to Corbyn. In an attempt to stop the outflow of Labour MPs to the new "independent" grouping, Corbyn has announced that Labour would be prepared to back a second Brexit referendum.

Jeremy Corbyn has told MPs that if Labour's proposed Brexit deal is rejected in a Commons vote on Wednesday, then the party will back a second vote. What question they will pose to the public, however, remains a mystery. Corbyn has not officially announced what he's proposing, but a briefing paper from the party to MPs has said that any second referendum would need to have a "credible" leave option, and a remain option[38].

That means Labour isn't looking to offer the public a choice between two forms of "leave"...but instead, an option to stay in the European Union, or leave under a "credible" Labour-backed exit. That means, presumably, a Customs Union.

Interestingly, a second referendum wouldn't be able to pass in the Commons at this point. It seems that this decision is a promise Corbyn can afford to make, because he knows it'll never pass and he's unlikely to have to defend it.

So what next? Well, the Prime Minister will update the Commons on her progress with the Brexit negotiations on Tuesday, and there will be a vote on Commons amendments on Wednesday. It doesn't look like there's going to be a Meaningful Vote, though. The Prime Minister has in fact ruled it out completely this week but said that she *will* hold one by 12th March.

26th February
Theresa May Offers MPs Vote on No Deal Brexit/Article 50 Extension

Theresa May today offered MPs the opportunity to vote on No Deal, and a possible extension to Article 50 and delay of Brexit day[39]. This news really shocked me for a couple of reasons.

First off, Theresa May knows she needs to keep No Deal on the table. She wants to leave without a deal, and No Deal is her best form of blackmail. There's a reason why the Remainers in Parliament are always complaining that May is running down the clock and blackmailing them…it's because she *is,* and *it's working.*

Secondly, Parliament has already had a vote on this just weeks ago. It was an advisory vote that rejected No Deal, and the Prime Minister and her Cabinet reminded the Commons that their vote doesn't change the fact that No Deal is the default position if we get to March 29th and we haven't agreed on a deal with the EU.

Offering a vote on the possibility of delaying Brexit day signifies that the Prime Minister might think she needs more time. That's interesting, given that May has said until she was blue in the face that we will be leaving the European Union on March 29th.

Speaking after meeting EU leaders in Egypt – at a conference unrelated to Brexit – the Prime Minister reiterated that she will be offering a Meaningful Vote on her Brexit deal by 12th March. If that vote doesn't happen or if it is voted down, then by the 13th March the Prime Minister would give MPs the chance to vote on a new motion.

This motion would seek Parliament's "explicit consent" for No Deal. If MPs vote against it, then on the 14th March, another motion would be put to the Commons that requires a "short, limited extension to Article 50".

May has said that, should this happen, she would expect the delay to be as short as possible...whatever that means. It leaves us with a lot of questions, though.

For instance, what happens with the May elections? If Brexit day is delayed beyond June, when the new MEPs begin their term in the EU Parliament, then will we be participating in the EU elections?

This offer by May is very, very interesting. It signifies to me that the negotiations still aren't going well, though I'm not sure what she intends to achieve with a few extra months that she hasn't already been able to achieve.

27th February
MPs Vote on New Brexit Motions, Corbyn Officially Backs Second Referendum

Jeremy Corbyn was forced to officially back a second Brexit referendum today, after the Labour Party's proposed Brexit deal was rejected in a Commons vote.

Multiple motions were voted on this evening, with one from the Prime Minister that simply outlines her commitments to hold future votes on No Deal and a potential delay to Brexit, if her deal is rejects by MPs in the next Meaningful Vote. It's an effectively meaningless vote, but it will still show how much interest there still is in the Commons to hold May's feet to the fire in the hope that her deal won't be passed.

For some time, I thought that her deal could be passed just by using the fear of No Deal, but now the Prime Minister is cutting off her only lifeline by giving the Commons a vote on that too. Why?

Labour's amendment sets out the party's five demands for a Brexit deal, which includes a Customs Union deal with the EU. The PM has said multiple times that she is not willing to make that deal.

There's also an SNP amendment that tries to rule out No Deal, regardless of the date we leave. And, there's the Caroline Spelman amendment that offers MPs the chance to vote and debate on a new legal mechanism that would instruct May to ask for an extension to Article 50.

Oh, and I can't forget Yvette Cooper's amendment. This reconfirms Theresa May's commitment to allow votes on No Deal if her agreement is shot down next month – an amendment that the government is likely to accept.

Nothing from The Independent Group, interestingly. I was expecting those snotty little brats to put forward a host of amendments to mark their territory, but nothing from them just yet.

How Did They Vote?

Speaker John Bercow selected four motions to be voted on, and here's how they panned out:

Chapter Nine: February 2019

1. Labour's Brexit Deal

This was rejected. The amendment was voted down by 323 to 240 votes, meaning that Theresa May will continue with her attempts to either renegotiate the Withdrawal Agreement or gain new assurances on the backstop.

2. SNP/Plaid Cymru Amendment – "Rule Out No Deal"

The amendment tabled by the SNP and Plaid Cymru was also defeated in the Commons today. This amendment said the UK shouldn't ever leave the European Union without a deal, even if Article 50 is extended. This motion was defeated by 324 votes to 288.

3. Alberto Costa Amendment

This amendment was put forward by Tory backbencher Alberto Costa. It gained cross-party support, as it called on the government to implement a section of the Withdrawal Agreement that ensures rights for EU citizens in the UK and British ex-pats in the EU, even if we leave without a deal.

Costa resigned his position[40] as a parliamentary private secretary in the government in order to be able to table the motion, and it was passed without a general division.

4. Yvette Cooper Amendment

Cooper's amendment, which aimed to guarantee May's promise to hold a vote on extending Article 50, was passed by 502 votes to 20. That's a huge majority of 482, choosing a clear appetite for Parliament to be given the chance to make that decision.

28th February
Labour Go Full-Steam-Ahead with Second Referendum Pledge

Labour promised to back a second referendum if they didn't get what they wanted yesterday, and that's exactly what they're doing. Shadow Chancellor John McDonnell told ITV's Robert Peston last night that Labour would support putting forward an amendment in the Commons calling for a second referendum, at the same time MPs are asked to support Theresa May's Withdrawal Agreement[41].

That means Labour could be putting forward an amendment asking for a second referendum on the 12th March – less than two weeks from now and just 17 days before the official Brexit day. That would, almost certainly require an extension to Article 50 while the vote is organised.

Speaking on Peston, McDonnell said[42]:

> *"When the Meaningful Vote comes back – and we are told maybe that might be on 12 March – there are rumours that it could be next week...That's the time when we will have to put the amendment up".*

He also stressed that the Labour Party still also wants a general election and will continue to push for its own version of Brexit. Which is interesting.

Surely the Labour Party is only saving face by continuing to call for a general election. With The Independent Group stealing MPs and posing a threat to Labour in the polls, Corbyn would be mad to want to go to a national vote. Unless, of course, he'd rather get his nightmare over and done with before the TIG becomes too big.

Tory Minister Resigns Over May's No Deal Vote Decision

George Eustice resigned as fisheries minister today[43], citing the position that May has been forced into over Brexit. Instead of resigning over May's vision of Brexit, Eustice is protesting the Prime Minister's decision to give MPs a chance to vote on whether we leave the EU without a deal.

I'm with him on this. I find it utterly bizarre that the Prime Minister would give up the only thing she had going for her. Thinking from the perspective of a Tory minister who wanted May to get her deal through, I would be furious that she has given up the only thing that could have forced dissenters to back her deal last minute. The threat of No Deal, and all the horror stories it comes with, would surely be enough to bring MPs back into line with just days to go until the 29th March.

I wonder whether the Prime Minister knows something we don't. Perhaps the threat of no Brexit at all – which she's alluding to by offering a vote on an extension to Article 50 – is the new and improved leverage. Perhaps the parliamentary arithmetic checks out, and MPs really do want to deliver *some kind* of Brexit on time.

There's definitely a lot to be scared of if the government extends Article 50. Not only are we going to have to pay for it, it hands a lot of power back to the EU. It won't be short. It could be delayed for years or even indefinitely.

I think we can give up any hope that the Prime Minister is secretly trying to achieve no deal. She really does want to pass this deal, and she'll do anything she can to get it through. It just so happens that her latest attempt could land us stuck in a Brexit limbo for many years more.

References

[1] CNN, "EU offers Britons visa-free travel for short trips, if UK reciprocates", Jack Guy, 1st February 2019,
https://edition.cnn.com/2019/02/01/europe/visa-free-travel-brexit-gbr-intl/index.html

[2] The Guardian, "Brexit: visa-free travel plans spark Gibraltar 'colony' row", Daniel Boffey, 1st February 2019,
https://www.theguardian.com/world/2019/feb/01/gibraltar-colony-row-flares-as-eu-makes-travel-visa-free-for-britons

[3] Independent, "Brexit: Theresa May accused of 'wasting valuable time' as she launches group to find Irish backstop alternatives", Ashley Cowburn, 3rd February 2019,
https://www.independent.co.uk/news/uk/politics/brexit-latest-mps-irish-border-alternative-theresa-may-a8761356.html

[4] The Times, "The backstop is about peace: Britain must stand by it", Simon Coveney, 3rd February 2019,
https://www.thetimes.co.uk/article/the-backstop-is-about-peace-britain-must-stand-by-it-hbnkc2fcq

[5] Sky News, "No-deal plans: HMRC says EU imports will not get extra checks", 4th February 2019,
https://news.sky.com/story/no-deal-plans-hmrc-says-eu-imports-will-not-get-extra-checks-11628083

[6] Belfast Telegraph, "Theresa May to travel to Northern Ireland for Brexit speech", Press Association, 4th February 2019,
https://www.belfasttelegraph.co.uk/news/northern-ireland/theresa-may-to-travel-to-northern-ireland-for-brexit-speech-37780595.html

[7] BBC News, "Brexit: PM suggests backstop will not be removed from deal", 5th February 2019,
https://www.bbc.co.uk/news/uk-northern-ireland-47123078

[8] Independent, "Labour officially calls for Brexit to be delayed with Article 50 extension", Rob Merrick, 5th January 2019,
https://www.independent.co.uk/news/uk/politics/brexit-labour-delay-article-50-extension-theresa-may-emily-thornberry-pmqs-a8765656.html

[9] BBC News, "Donald Tusk: Special place in hell for Brexiteers without a plan", 6th February 2019,
https://www.bbc.co.uk/news/uk-politics-47143135

[10] BBC News, "Brexit: Stormont parties meet Theresa May", 6th February 2019,
https://www.bbc.co.uk/news/av/uk-northern-ireland-47149298/brexit-stormont-parties-meet-theresa-may

[11] The Guardian, "Business secretary suggests ministers could quit over no-deal Brexit", Dan Sababgh, 6th February 2019,
https://www.theguardian.com/politics/2019/feb/06/business-secretary-greg-clark-part-no-deal-brexit-may-challenge

[12] Politics Home, "Jeremy Corbyn's letter to Theresa May spelling out Brexit demands", Jeremy Corbyn MP, 7th February 2019,
https://www.politicshome.com/news/uk/political-parties/labour-party/news/labour-party/101667/read-full-jeremy-corbyns-letter

[13] Twitter, "A Downing Street official says Theresa May's office is looking at Labour leader Jeremy Corbyn's Brexit proposals but there are considerable points of difference", Sky

Chapter Nine: February 2019

News, 7th February 2019,
https://twitter.com/SkyNewsBreak/status/1093578188092067840

14 Sky News, "Jeremy Corbyn's Brexit plan 'promising', Donald Tusk tells Theresa May",
Alan McGuinness, 8th February 2019,
https://news.sky.com/story/not-helpful-theresa-may-confronts-donald-tusk-over-special-
place-in-hell-attack-11630806

15 The Guardian, "Brexit deal may not be put to MPs until late March, officials say", Daniel
Boffey and Jennifer Rankin, 7th February 2019,
https://www.theguardian.com/politics/2019/feb/07/theresa-may-juncker-clash-brexit-robush-
backstop

16 The Guardian, "Brexit crisis command centre starts hiring civilians", Lisa O'Carroll, 8th
February 2019,
https://www.theguardian.com/politics/2019/feb/08/brexit-no-deal-crisis-command-centre-
starts-hiring-civilians

17 Express, "Andrew Neil SKEWERS Labour peer for free movement admission", Freddie
Jordan, 7th February 2019,
https://www.express.co.uk/news/uk/1083918/Brexit-news-bbc-news-andrew-neil-poltitics-
live-free-movement-shami-chakrabarti-labour

18 Sky News, "'Emergency zone': Brexit vote may happen just weeks before March exit
date", Aubrey Allegretti, 10th February 2019,
https://news.sky.com/story/emergency-zone-brexit-vote-may-happen-just-weeks-before-
march-exit-date-11633467

19 The Times, "Labour's no-deal Brexit ambush", Caroline Wheeler, 10th February 2019,
https://www.thetimes.co.uk/edition/news/labour-s-no-deal-brexit-ambush-3br3slght

20 Mirror, "Brexit: MPs erupt in fury as Theresa May blames THEM for crisis in 'delusional'
statement", Dan Bloom, 13th February 2019,
https://www.mirror.co.uk/news/politics/brexit-mps-erupt-fury-theresa-13988618

21 BBC News, "Brexit: Theresa May promises Meaningful Vote after more talks with EU",
12th February 2019,
https://www.bbc.co.uk/news/uk-politics-47206286

22 The Times, "Labour's no-deal Brexit ambush", Caroline Wheeler, 10th February 2019,
https://www.thetimes.co.uk/edition/news/labour-s-no-deal-brexit-ambush-3br3slght

23 Huffpost, "Why A No-Deal Brexit Is Now Theresa May's Fallback Plan To Save Her Party
– And Herself", Paul Waugh, 12th February 2019,
https://www.huffingtonpost.co.uk/entry/theresa-may-no-deal-brexit-fallback-
plan_uk_5c617348e4b0910c63f30fc8?fbm&utm_hp_ref=uk-homepage&guccounter=1

24 Twitter, "Theresa May is now seriously contemplating a no-deal Brexit.", Paul Waugh, 11th
February 2019,
https://twitter.com/paulwaugh/status/1095014218364059648

25 The Guardian, "Hardline Brexiters threaten to vote down Theresa May's motion", Rowena
Mason, 13th February 2019,
https://www.theguardian.com/politics/2019/feb/13/hardline-brexiters-threaten-to-vote-down-
theresa-mays-motion

26 Express & Star, "Government not ruling out no-deal Brexit, Number 10 insists", UK News,
13th February 2019,
https://www.expressandstar.com/news/uk-news/2019/02/13/government-not-ruling-out-no-
deal-brexit-number-10-insists/

Chapter Nine: February 2019

[27] BBC News, "Brexit amendments: How MPs tried to change Theresa May's course", 14th February 2019,
https://www.bbc.co.uk/news/uk-politics-47225819

[28] The Independent Group, "Statement of Independence",
https://www.theindependent.group/statement

[29] Mail Online, "Tory Minister FAILS to rule out joining the Independent Group saying he 'understands' why the 'gang of seven' wants to change politics as ringleader Chuka Umunna vows to make it a full-blown political party", Tim Sculthorpe, 19th February 2019,
https://www.dailymail.co.uk/news/article-6719923/Tory-rebel-Sarah-Wollaston-warns-BLUKIP-Westminster-waits.html

[30] The Telegraph, "Minister and four Tory backbenchers poised to join Labour splinter group", Camilla Tominey and Steven Swinford, 18th February 2019,
https://www.telegraph.co.uk/politics/2019/02/18/tory-minister-four-conservative-backbench-mps-poised-join-new/

[31] Twitter, "On which "best represents the people of Britain"", Britain Elects, 18th February 2019,
https://twitter.com/britainelects/status/1097640007655964672

[32] BBC News, "MP Joan Ryan quits Labour for Independent Group", 20th February 2019,
https://www.bbc.co.uk/news/uk-politics-47300832

[33] Twitter, "Westminster voting intention (if IG stand candidates)", Britain Elects, 20th February 2019,
https://twitter.com/britainelects/status/1098193444034564096

[34] The Guardian, "MPs fear May could exploit Labour split to call early election", Rowena Mason, 19th February 2019,
https://www.theguardian.com/politics/2019/feb/19/labour-mps-fear-theresa-may-could-exploit-party-split-to-call-early-election

[35] The Guardian, "Jeremy Corbyn inching closer to backing a second referendum", Heather Stewart, Daniel Boffey and Dan Sabbagh, 21st February 2019,
https://www.theguardian.com/politics/2019/feb/21/starmer-pm-is-running-down-clock-so-mps-only-get-binary-choice

[36] Independent, "Brexit: EU president Juncker 'not optimistic' about prospect of avoiding no-deal outcome", Jon Stone, 21st February 2019,
https://www.independent.co.uk/news/uk/politics/brexit-no-deal-jean-claude-juncker-theresa-may-meeting-commons-vote-mps-a8790086.html

[37] Express, "Brexit meeting with Barnier WILL trigger EU 'concessions' - 'something is in the air'", Darren Hunt, 22nd February 2019,
https://www.express.co.uk/news/uk/1090497/Brexit-news-UK-EU-Theresa-May-European-Union-Michel-Barnier-Brussels

[38] Sky News, "Sir Keir Starmer says second EU referendum should include Remain but not no-deal", Greg Heffer, 26th February 2019,
https://news.sky.com/story/labours-sir-keir-starmer-says-second-eu-referendum-should-be-leave-vs-remain-11648505

[39] The Guardian, "MPs offered vote on no-deal Brexit and possible delay", Peter Walke and Heather Stewart, 26th February 2019,
https://www.theguardian.com/politics/2019/feb/26/mps-offered-vote-on-no-deal-brexit-and-possible-delay

[40] Business Insider, "Brexit chaos as Conservative MP resigns for pushing EU citizens' plan backed by his own government", Thomas Colson and Adam Payne, 27th February 2019,
https://www.businessinsider.com/brexit-chaos-as-alberto-costa-resigns-after-pushing-eu-

Chapter Nine: February 2019

citizens-plan-backed-by-sajid-javid-2019-2?r=US&IR=T

[41] *Independent, "Labour will table bid for second Brexit referendum within a fortnight, says John McDonnell", Ashley Cowburn, 28th February 2019,*
https://www.independent.co.uk/news/uk/politics/brexit-second-referendum-labour-corbyn-mcdonnell-a8800791.html

[42] *The Guardian, "McDonnell says amendment for second Brexit referendum could happen early", Poppy Noor and Rowena Mason, 28th February 2019,*
https://www.theguardian.com/politics/2019/feb/28/john-mcdonnell-amendment-second-brexit-referendum-could-happen-next-week

[43] *BBC News, "Brexit: George Eustice resignation reflects wider Tory anger", John Pienaar, 28th February 2019,*
https://www.bbc.co.uk/news/uk-politics-47406531

Chapter Ten
March 2019

1st March
29 Days to Go: The Schedule for March

We now have just 29 days until we leave the European Union, and there are multiple votes still left to go. Here's what to expect:

On the 12th March (or before), the Prime Minister will give Parliament a Meaningful Vote on her Withdrawal Agreement. Should Parliament vote in favour of her deal, we will leave the European Union as scheduled on 29th March with her deal.

Should Parliament vote against her Withdrawal Agreement, another vote will take place on 13th March. This vote will decide whether Parliament gives consent to leaving the European Union without a deal. To the EU this is effectively meaningless, but it seems that the Prime Minister is willing to take it seriously and act if MPs vote against No Deal. If Parliament votes in favour of No Deal, we will leave as scheduled on March 29th without a deal and we'll apparently run out of sandwiches and lettuce and starve to death. If Parliament votes against No Deal, then the Prime Minister will hold a vote on an extension to Article 50, the following day on 14th March.

If MPs vote in favour of a delay, the UK will ask the EU for an extension to Article 50 that could cost as much as £7 billion for the privilege. However, should MPs vote against a Brexit delay, then we're in uncharted water. Technically, we'll be on track to leave the European Union without a deal on the 29th. EU leaders have already told us we can't stop it, but we'll have to wait and see what happens. When things get desperate, anything can happen – and with the

European elections around the corner, EU leaders might be more willing to renegotiate.

If MPs vote against a Brexit delay on 14th March, Theresa May will have found herself in an impossible situation. She will have ruled out No Deal and ruled out an extension – meaning the only way forward would be leaving with a deal. But there is no deal.

Current law says we *would* leave without a deal, but if Mrs May allows that to happen then she'll have gone back on a very significant promise. It probably wouldn't really matter at that point, though, as she would almost certainly have to resign or be forced out with a vote of no confidence.

My prediction? I suspect May will get a deal – and if she reaches the impossible situation outlined above on the 14th March, I reckon the EU will scramble for a last-minute deal that Parliament can get on board with.

EU Rejects Alberto Costa Amendment Assurance

I wrote on the 27th February that an amendment tabled by former government minister Alberto Costa was nodded through Parliament. His amendment called on the Prime Minister to enact a section of the Withdrawal Agreement that guarantees rights for EU citizens in the UK and British ex-pats abroad.

The EU, however, has rejected calls for such an agreement to be made in the event of No Deal[1]. Alberto quit his government job to put this motion forward, but the European Commission today said that they will "not negotiate mini deals", doubling down on their refusal to re-open the Withdrawal Agreement with Theresa May

That's some tough talk from a group of bureaucrats who are genuinely concerned about the effect of No Deal on the EU's economies.

This is significant for a couple of reasons. First of all, it means that the rights of British ex-pats in the EU are now uncertain. There is no way that the rights of EU citizens won't be protected in the UK, but we can't expect the EU to be reciprocal. If they like, the EU could revoke any rights of British people living in the EU purely out of spite if we leave without a deal.

It's also significant because it proves that the European Union do ultimately have some power in these negotiations. The UK Parliament seems to be under the impression that voting against No Deal means that No Deal won't happen...but it will.

5th March
Cox and Barclay Come Back from Crunch Talks...with Nothing

Everything seemed so positive today, but things didn't pan out quite as hoped. Foreign Secretary Jeremy Hunt said this morning that the UK was now prepared to be more flexible over how it aims to address the backstop concerns. He also said that European leaders were now giving "positive signals" as the Prime Minister continues to push to get concessions on the Withdrawal Agreement.

Speaking on the Today programme, he said[2]:

> *"The signals we are getting are reasonably positive. I don't want to overstate them because I still think there's a lot of work to do but I think they do understand that we are being sincere.*
>
> *They are beginning to realise that we can get a majority in parliament because they are seeing the signals coming from*

the people who voted against the deal before we are saying, crucially, that they are prepared to be reasonable about how we get to that position that we can't legally be trapped in the backstop".

Today, Brexit Secretary Stephen Barclay and Attorney General Geoffrey Cox are over in Brussels trying to secure new concessions so that Theresa May can fly over at the weekend and hopefully sign off on a new agreement. It has been reported that Cox has now dropped his attempts to get the EU to agree to either a time limit to the backstop, or a unilateral exit mechanism. So, I'm not sure exactly what Theresa May and her negotiating team have in mind that would reassure Parliament that the deal is good.

What is making Hunt believe that they can get a majority in Parliament?

Whatever they're planning, anyway, is a precursor to Theresa May's trip to Brussels this coming Sunday[3]. The Prime Minister is expected to make the last-minute trip at the weekend to finalise her amended Withdrawal Agreement, leaving just a few days until the next (and final?) Meaningful Vote.

Whatever deal she's come to will then be revealed on Monday morning, one day before the vote.

If the rumour that the Prime Minister will have to whip MPs to get it through Parliament is true, however, then it could mean the deal isn't all that great. Shocker! Eurosceptics in the Tory Party, including two Cabinet ministers, are claiming that May will be forced into an even weaker negotiation position if her deal is voted down on the 12th and MPs reject No Deal (duh). One Minister told the Telegraph that the right approach, therefore, would be to whip her MPs against voting for an extension to Article 50.

Chapter Ten: March 2019

Former Tory leader Iain Duncan Smith also told the Telegraph:

> *"It is crystal clear that the Government has to keep no deal on the table and whip against an extension. That's what she has said for two years. She has to oppose anyone trying to take it off the table and to reject an extension. That will make the EU sit up and understand that we are serious. It won't give anything until these votes are done".*

Honestly, this is what I'm expecting at this point. The EU are likely to reject everything until it gets right down to the wire, and the threat of No Deal is imminent.

That's probably why the Brexit talks down eventually broke down today. Things might have started out all positive, but Brussels sources told the press this evening that talks broke down during a crunch meeting with UK negotiators.

Apparently, Barclay and Cox were left in a deadlock on the latest Brexit deal plans after meeting with Michel Barnier with four hours. The meeting involved a meeting at the Berlaymont headquarters of the European Commission, but the press is reporting that the two came back with nothing.

Tick tock.

In Other News...

The Independent Group met officials from the Electoral Commission today to discuss the formation of a new political party[4].

Chuka Umunna claimed that the British people "want an alternative" to the "broken system". He announced that today, the TIG would discuss with the Electoral Commission the formation of a new political party, which would allow them to stand in the next general election…and potentially even the upcoming council elections in May.

The decision comes after the group recently appointed official spokesperson roles to each of its parliamentary representatives.

7th March
May Pleads with EU to Make Concessions

We've reached the point where the Prime Minister can really do nothing much other than plead with the European Union to make concessions on the backstop issues.

Mrs May today gave a speech to a green energy company in Lincolnshire, with a warehouse backdrop, where she pleaded with the Labour Party, her own MPs, and the European Union to come together behind her deal. She explained how she understands the "genuine concerns" about the backstop but doubled down on her threat that Britain may never leave the EU if the deal doesn't pass.

It's clear that the Prime Minister is now committed to this new tactic. I was shocked at first to see her pivot away from using No Deal as a threat and form of blackmail to get her deal passed but switching tactics must be her only option.

In her speech, the Prime Minister explained[5]:

> *"Back it [the deal] and the UK will leave the EU…Reject it and no-one knows what will happen. We may not leave the EU for many months. We may*

leave without the protections a deal
provides, we may never leave at all".

She went on to say that the deal needs just "one more push to address the specific concerns of Parliament" and asked the EU to not "hold back" and to "do what is necessary for MPs to back the deal". She warned the EU that if MPs reject the deal then it would be a moment of crisis. She'd be right, too – there are just 12 working days left until Brexit day. And we know both sides don't want No Deal.

The Prime Minister wants movement on the deal right now. There is talk that the EU might be waiting until a summit towards the end of the month, but the Prime Minister would naturally prefer some movement before the scheduled Meaningful Vote on Tuesday.

Chief negotiator for the EU, Michel Barnier, did offer some kind of concession today too[6]. Though it comes with a catch, and the DUP aren't happy about it. In fact, they called it degrading[7]. In a Twitter thread, Barnier suggested a unilateral exit mechanism for the backstop – but it would require a border down the Irish Sea.

Barnier explained:

"I briefed EU27 Ambassadors and
EP today on the ongoing talks with UK.
Following the EU-UK statement of 20
Feb, the EU has proposed to the UK a
legally binding interpretation of the Brexit
Withdrawal Agreement. Most
importantly:

The arbitration panel can already,
under Article 178 WA, give UK the right to
a proportionate suspension of its
obligations under the backstop, as a last

*resort, if EU breaches its best
endeavours/good faith obligations to
negotiate alternative solutions.*

*EU ready to give legal force to all
commitments from January letter of
@eucopresident and @JunckerEU
through joint interpretative statement.
This will render best endeavour/good
faith obligations even more actionable by
an arbitration panel.*

*EU commits to give UK the option to
exit the Single Customs Territory
unilaterally, while the other elements of
the backstop must be maintained to avoid
a hard border. UK will not be forced into
Customs Union against its will.*

*The EU will continue working
intensively over the coming days to
ensure that the UK leaves the EU with an
agreement".*

In short, the Single Market would have to remain in
effect in Northern Ireland if the UK decides to leave the
backstop, effectively meaning a border between NI and
Great Britain.

Both sides know this won't be acceptable, though.
Attorney General Geoffrey Cox has said that negotiations
with the EU will continue but that he expected "acceptable"
ideas to be presented by Friday so that the impasse can be
broken[8].

9th March
Labour's Second Referendum Amendment Put on Hold

Labour's demand for a second referendum is being put on hold, so Jeremy Corbyn can focus on making Theresa May's life a living hell in the last few days before the next Meaningful Vote.

The Prime Minister is yet to announce any concessions that the UK government considers 'acceptable' from the European Union but is set to announce the final deal on Monday. That means Corbyn has the weekend to plan his strategy for all potentially outcomes. Unfortunately for the ultra-Remainers in the Labour camp (and The Independent Group who would no doubt have supported Labour), that means the motion for a second referendum will be delayed.

Labour has not, however, ruled out putting forward the motion later in the week if May is unable to get a majority of MPs on her side.

Former Labour communications chief Alastair Campbell supported the decision to delay the motion, writing in The Guardian[9] that Tuesday "must belong to Mrs May being made to see her deal will not – and cannot – fly".

Referring to Labour MPs Phil Wilson and Peter Kyle who have been pushing for the amendment, Campbell said:

> "I hope they will not push their amendment to a vote on Tuesday...I think the public needs to see very clearly that even though the ticking clock may have reduced the majority against Mrs May's deal from the stratospheric level 230 of January, it continues to lack the

parliamentary support needed to go through".

I'm not convinced this is real fighting talk, though. Instead, I believe this is a measure designed to ensure that Corbyn can attack May as strongly as he likes in the event that the deal is shot down again. The motion calling for a second referendum is also bound to fail, and a Corbyn defeat on the same day as a May defeat makes it very hard for either side to attack.

10th March
Could May Resign to Save Her Deal?

Jeremy Hunt warned today that Tory MPs should back the Prime Minister's deal or risk losing Brexit[10]. This comes after the Prime Minister shifted the nature of her blackmail away from threatening No Deal, to threatening no Brexit. Hunt said there was "wind in the sails" of those trying to stop Brexit, and that voting down the deal for a second time would be "devastating".

Shadow Brexit Secretary Keir Starmer told Sky News today[11] that keeping the UK in the EU for a few more months was "probably doable", and that it would be necessary because of the position we now find ourselves in. The move could be necessary even if Parliament miraculously votes in favour of the deal on Tuesday.

With the EU still refusing to back down over the backstop, however, it looks like May's problem is the looming threat of a shameful resignation. Rather than having to deal with extending Article 50 but delivering a Brexit deal, May is more likely to find her deal being voted down in Parliament on Tuesday, and No Deal being voted down in a subsequent vote – leaving her (and the country) in Brexit limbo.

Eurosceptic MPs have said over the weekend that a defeat for the Prime Minister's deal looks certain on Tuesday. Writing for the Sunday Telegraph[12], ERG MP Steve Baker and leader of the Commons DUP Nigel Dodds, explained a defeat would be "inevitable". They even predicted a "three-figure majority" against the deal.

Rumour has it that some ministers are even suggesting that the Prime Minister could name a date for her departure as PM, in the hope it might get the deal passed – but the issue really isn't Theresa May. It's the deal.

We should be hearing from the Prime Minister tomorrow about what concessions she has (or hasn't) come back from Europe with. She might surprise us, but going by the rumours, it doesn't look like all that much has changed. The EU are waiting for a 21st March summit before anything radical happens. It could be that this next Meaningful Vote might be not end up being all that meaningful.

11th March
Theresa May's Last-Minute Dash to Strasbourg

Theresa May made a last-minute dash to Strasbourg tonight. She met with Jean-Claude Juncker to finalise her amended deal with the European Union, and it seemed like she'd made a breakthrough.

Cabinet Officer minister David Lidington told the Commons that the Prime Minister had succeeded in winning over Europe, and that she had made a breakthrough over the Irish backstop. The news sent the press into a frenzy, with rumours that the Prime Minister might have secured the assurances she needed to get Parliament on her side.

Specifically, Lidington announced that the Prime Minister had got the EU to approve a new document which made clear that trapping the United Kingdom in the backstop would be an "explicit breach of the legally binding commitments both sides have agreed". To be clear, this is not an amendment to the Withdrawal Agreement, but instead a "Joint Instrument".

What is the Joint Instrument?

After a last-minute dash to Strasbourg, Theresa May has announced that the UK and the EU have agreed to issue a "joint interpretive instrument". This statement provides additional legal assurances by both parties that the Irish backstop would only ever be a temporary measure.

But, this isn't anything new. Around the time of the first Meaningful Vote, the European Union sent a letter to Theresa May which outlined their intention for the backstop to be a temporary measure. This wasn't enough for MPs back then, and it might not be enough now. The only difference this time, is that it really could the last chance to get this deal through Parliament.

The Joint Instrument is another attempt by the EU to reassure Parliamentarians that the UK is not going to get stuck in the backstop. It is not the change to the Withdrawal Agreement that Parliament told the Prime Minister to get, and it's not an 'alternative arrangement' to the backstop, but it might just be the thing the Prime Minister needs to squeeze her deal through.

Juncker Warns: "No Third Chance"

The press conference that Theresa May and Jean-Claude Juncker gave tonight was rather eery. They sat next to each other, looking rather like a couple who had just broken up but had to sit through a family dinner pretending everything was alright.

Juncker's words made it clear that he was calling all the shots, too. In the statement to the press, which they used to announce the Joint Instrument, Juncker explained that there will be no third chance on the Withdrawal Agreement.

Specifically, he said[13]:

> The backstop is an insurance policy – nothing more, nothing less.
> The intention is not for it to be used like with every insurance policy.
> And if it were ever to be used, it will never be a trap. If either side were to act in bad faith, there is a legal way for the other party to exit.
> The Instrument which sets out these details has legal force while fully respecting the Guidelines the European Council has unanimously agreed. It complements the Withdrawal Agreement without reopening it. My team and I have been in constant contact with our Irish friends over the past days and over the last hours. The Taoiseach would be prepared to back this approach in the interests of an overall deal.
> I have just informed the President of the European Council this evening and asked him to recommend that the European Council endorses this Joint Instrument – subject to a prior positive vote in the House of Commons on the Withdrawal Agreement.
> In politics, sometimes you get a second chance. It is what we do with this second chance that counts. Because there will be no third chance. There will be no further

interpretations of the interpretations; and no further assurances of the re-assurances – if the Meaningful Vote tomorrow fails.

Let us be crystal clear about the choice: it is this deal or Brexit might not happen at all.

Hearing Juncker tell the UK that it's either this deal or no Brexit at all is rather infuriating. It's even worse when you see Theresa May sat right next to him, unflinching, and agreeing with every word that comes out of his mouth. When Juncker says it's this deal or potentially no Brexit, he means it. And he's right. If Parliament doesn't consider this offer good enough, it really could mean the end for Brexit.

I've previously outlined in this book what happens if Parliament votes down the deal for a second time, and it's not good. It lands the UK into unprecedented chaos and could mean no Brexit, or an extension to Article 50.

It could even mean Britain taking part in the upcoming European elections in May. Nigel Farage is currently making a big stink about that, threatening to stand for his new Brexit Party. I don't doubt for a moment that he'd do well if the UK is forced to take part in elections we were told we'd never have to take part in again. But I don't want to see that happen.

I'm sure a lot of politicians in Westminster don't want to see it happen, either. They know that the public would vote for any Brexiteer party they could find. If they thought 2014 was a bad showing for pro-EU parties, then European elections in 2019 would be an absolute blood bath.

Will the Deal Now Pass?

The Prime Minister needs more than 100 MPs to change their mind and support her deal. This Joint

Instrument might not be what they asked for last time, but it might just be enough. With the threat of No Deal looming for some, and the threat of No Deal looming for others, MPs might be forced to give in.

Though, it also depends on the opinion of the Attorney General Geoffrey Cox. If he gives Parliament the nod and says this Joint Instrument is legally binding, then May's deal is good to go. If he doesn't, it's doomed.

12th March
Then Cometh the End: The Day of the Second Meaningful Vote

Today is the day. This is the second Meaningful Vote, and likely the last. Parliament will this evening have the opportunity to vote for the Prime Minister's deal or vote against it and cause complete and utter chaos.

It is hard for me, and indeed for many people across the UK, to decide just how we feel about this deal. I understand this deal is bad for Britain, but I also know the threat of no Brexit at all is very real. This is the betrayal that I find most disturbing. It's not the obvious betrayal of the vote, but the way in which politicians have coordinated to get Brexiteers on the side of a Prime Minister and a deal that are clearly bad for this country. The public have become so fatigued over Brexit that voting for the deal would probably give the whole nation some comfort.

But the deal still isn't popular, and either way, we're in trouble. If the deal passes this evening, then the Brexit vote will have been betrayed. The UK will become a vassal state and the uncertainty around the Irish border and backstop will remain. There is no doubt in my mind that approving this deal will result in an extremely close post-Brexit relationship with the EU. So close, that we might as well have remained members.

It's also clear to me, however, that it's very possible we'll see no Brexit at all if this deal is rejected tonight. The fact that we have been put in such a situation is bad enough – but we're not even the ones who get to decide. It's the politicians in Westminster who have done everything so far to frustrate the process.

Geoffrey Cox Says the Legal Risk Has Not Changed

At 2pm, Attorney General Geoffrey Cox addressed the House of Commons and confirmed that the legal risk has not changed. In his speech, he explained that this was now a matter of deciding political risk instead. Cox stayed true to his word that he would provide an honest review of the Joint Instrument, and that promise means that May's deal is unlikely to pass tonight.

In his statement, Cox explained:

> *"Mr Speaker. With permission, I would lie to make a statement about my legal opinion on the Joint Instrument and Unilateral Declaration concerning the Withdrawal Agreement published last night.*
>
> *Last week I confirmed I would publish my legal opinion on any document that is produced and negotiated with the Union. This has now been laid before the House. This statement summarises the instruments and my opinion of their legal effect. Mr Speaker, last night in Strasbourg, the Prime Minister secured legally binding changes that strengthen and improve the Withdrawal Agreement and the political declaration.*

Chapter Ten: March 2019

The Government laid three new documents reflecting these changes in the House. First a joint legally binding instrument on the Withdrawal Agreement and the protocol on Northern Ireland. Second, a unilateral declaration by the United Kingdom in relation to the operation of the Northern Ireland protocol. And third, a joint statement to supplement the political declaration.

Mr Speaker the legal opinion I have provided to the House today focusses on the first two of these documents, which relate to the functioning of the backstop and the efforts of the parties which will be required to supersede it. Mr Speaker let me say frankly what in my opinion these documents do not do. They are not about a situation where despite the parties properly fulfilling the duties of good faith and best endeavours they cannot reach an agreement on a future relationship.

Such an event in my opinion, is highly unlikely to occur and it is both in the interests of the UK and the EU to agree a future relationship as quickly as possible. Were such a situation to occur however, let me make it clear, the legal risk as I set it out in my letter of the 13th of November remain unchanged. The question for the House is whether in the light of these improvements, as a political judgement the House should now enter in to those arrangements."

This sentiment was echoed in Cox's letter to the Prime Minister. He explained how the Joint Instrument and

Unilateral Declaration (which is simply a statement confirming that the UK could leave backstop if we feel like the EU acted in good faith) have "legal weight" and reduce the risk that the UK would become indefinitely detained in the backstop. He also said, however, that this doesn't mean the legal risk has disappeared.

He said[14]:

> *"If both parties deploy a sincere desire to reach agreement and the necessary diligence, flexibility and goodwill implied by the amplified duties set out in the Joint Instrument, it is highly unlikely that a satisfactory subsequent agreement to replace the Protocol will not be concluded. But as I have previously advised, that is a political judgment, which, given the mutual incentives of the parties and the available options and competing risks, I remain strongly of the view it is right to make.*
>
> *However, the legal risk remains unchanged that if through no such demonstrable failure of either party, but simply because of intractable differences, that situation does arise, the United Kingdom would have, at least while the fundamental circumstances remained the same, no internationally lawful means of exiting the Protocol's arrangements, save by agreement."*

It's no wonder that Westminster DUP leader Nigel Dodds challenged him in the Commons. He argued that the only thing the EU would need to do in order to show good faith, would be to simply consider the UK's proposals even if they ultimately reject them. This could go on forever, Dodds said, without giving rise to "bad faith".

Dodds argued that the legal risk, therefore, has remained largely unchanged and that the DUP would not vote for the deal[15]. That's a big blow to the Prime Minister. Had she gotten the DUP on board, Tory MPs would have followed suit.

The Moment of Truth

The Meaningful Vote was held today at 7pm. Speaker John Bercow chose no amendments to be voted on, meaning the Brexit deal remained the sole focus for Parliament.

The Deal was voted down by a majority of 149.

242 MPs voted in favour of the deal – a substantial increase over last time. 391 voted against it. A total of 235 Tory MPs supported the Prime Minister, with 39 switching sides since last time. May still lost 75 votes from her own party, however. That's roughly the size of the European Research Group, though we know some ERG members did switch sides. Four independents also supported the Prime Minister's deal.

Only three Labour rebels supported the deal, with 238 Labour MPs rejecting it – no doubt in the hope that the resulting chaos would result in a second referendum. Surely, while Labour is performing so badly in the polls, they wouldn't be mad enough to want a general election.

It was a crushing defeat. Theresa May has been in bad shape for the last couple of days. Since returning from Strasbourg she had completely lost her voice, struggling to talk at the despatch box. I'm honestly surprised that May has lasted this long. I don't know how she handles all of this, and amazingly I can't help but commend her for just how steadfast she has been. I don't think that anything she has done has been positive, and I do consider her to be one of the architects of this systematic betrayal of the British people. But she decided to negotiate a compromise deal, and she's done everything in her power to make it work. It's rather amazing, really.

Tonight, though, the Deal is dead. Juncker has said there will be no third chances, and Parliament has decisively rejected it once again.

What Now? Is This the End of Brexit?

As I've previously explained, voting down the deal means Britain is plunged into deep Brexit uncertainty with just 17 days to go.

Tomorrow, Parliament will be asked if they support leaving the European Union without a deal. It is extremely unlikely this will pass. That means on Thursday, Parliament will vote on whether to request an extension to Article 50. This would mean the UK's exit date would be delayed beyond March 29th – the clearest sign yet that Parliament has betrayed the people.

Should Parliament reject an extension to Article 50, there surely cannot be any future for Theresa May as Prime Minister. May will be trapped in a prison of her own making, with no way out. She will have to go.

So, what if Parliament votes to delay Brexit? This is the most likely outcome, but it doesn't solve the problem. The European Union would first have to approve the extension, which they won't do unless the UK can explain what it is we intend to achieve with the extension. Parliament would rather ask the EU for an extension so they can continue bickering amongst themselves, but Juncker, Merkel, Barnier and co want some answers.

Chapter Ten: March 2019

If Article 50 is extended, then we have a few options. May might put her deal back to Parliament with another Meaningful Vote. This would be total madness. The first time the deal was put to the Commons, she was dealt the biggest and most humiliating blow in Parliamentary history. Today, it wasn't all that much better. Unless she can remove the backstop, this deal will not pass.

An Article 50 extension could mean that Theresa May explores new options, including a permanent Customs Union with the EU. This is the deal that the Labour Party has put forward twice, and it could well command a majority in the Commons. It would of course be an even greater betrayal of the decision we made in 2016 than May's deal, but at this point, I'm not sure many people in Westminster care. They're probably hoping that most Brits are too tired of this nonsense to care either.

We may also see a general election. Labour are pretty seriously down in the polls right now. A Kantar Public poll from 7th to the 11th March puts the Tories at 41% and labour at 31%[16]. That's a substantial difference to another Kantar poll from December that put Labour and the Tories neck-and-neck at 38%. Labour would be mad to push for a general election, and May might be forced to take the same leap she made in 2017.

Failing that, we're looking at a second referendum. The Independent Group are pushing for it, the Labour Party is pushing for it, and the fact that no deal can be agreed in Parliament is fuel for the fire. Parliament is at an impasse, and there's only one way to solve it: go back to the terrified, confused, belittled, and misled British public.

Tell them Brexit doesn't work, ask them to make the right decision this time, and then cancel the whole damn thing.

References

[1] BBC News, "Brexit: EU rejects no deal citizens rights call", 1st March 2019,
https://www.bbc.co.uk/news/uk-politics-47408789

[2] The Guardian, "Brexit: 'positive signals' coming from Brussels, says Jeremy Hunt", Sarah Marsh, 5th March 2019,
https://www.theguardian.com/politics/2019/mar/05/brexit-positive-signals-coming-from-brussels-says-jeremy-hunt

[3] Express, "Brexit plan REVEALED: May set to fly to Brussels Sunday to seal FINAL DEAL with Juncker", Tom Nellist, 5th March 2019,
https://www.express.co.uk/news/politics/1095762/brexit-latest-news-theresa-may-brussels-withdrawal-agreement-meaningful-vote

[4] Express, "Independent Group starts talks to become NEW POLITICAL PARTY -'people want an alternative'", Tom Nellist, 5th March 2019,
https://www.express.co.uk/news/politics/1095943/independent-group-new-political-party-electoral-commission-chuka-umunna

[5] BBC News, "Brexit: One more push needed to get deal through, says May", 8th March 2019,
https://www.bbc.co.uk/news/uk-politics-47487320

[6] Mail Online, "Barnier's Brexit 'NON-offer': DUP immediately slaps down EU negotiator as he TWEETS out proposal that would effectively carve off Northern Ireland from the rest of the UK after May begged bloc for 'one last push'", Tim Sculthorpe, Martin Robinson, David Churchill and John Stevens, 8th March 2019,
https://www.dailymail.co.uk/news/article-6784619/May-urges-EU-leaders-help-persuade-MPs-Brexit-deal.html

[7] Breitbart, "Divide and Rule: DUP Slams 'Degrading' EU Offer to Let UK Leave Backstop Minus Northern Ireland", Jack Montgomery, 9th March 2019,
https://www.breitbart.com/europe/2019/03/09/divide-and-rule-dup-slams-degrading-eu-offer-to-let-uk-leave-backstop-minus-northern-ireland/

[8] BBC News, "Brexit: Deadline looms as ministers push for changes to deal", 7th March 2019,
https://www.bbc.co.uk/news/uk-politics-47481872

[9] The Guardian, "This is not the week to push a people's vote. May's deal has to fail first", Opinion, 9th March 2019,
https://www.theguardian.com/commentisfree/2019/mar/09/peoples-vote-theresa-may-deal-kyle-wilson-brexit

[10] BBC News, "Brexit could be lost if deal rejected, Jeremy Hunt says", 10th March 2019,
https://www.bbc.co.uk/news/uk-politics-47514248

[11] Sky News, "Theresa May told Brexit delay 'doable' but would lead to 'Trump moment'", Aubrey Allegretti, 10th March 2019,
https://news.sky.com/story/theresa-may-told-brexit-delay-doable-but-would-lead-to-trump-moment-11660842

[12] The Telegraph, "The UK must leave the EU on March 29", Steve Baker and Nigel Dodds, 9th March 2019,
https://www.telegraph.co.uk/opinion/2019/03/09/uk-must-leave-eu-march-29/

[13] European Commission, "Remarks by President Jean-Claude Juncker at today's joint press conference with UK Prime Minister Theresa May", 11th March 2019,
http://europa.eu/rapid/press-release_SPEECH-19-1635_en.htm

Chapter Ten: March 2019

[14] Attorney General Rt Hon Geoffrey Cox QC MP, Letter to Rt Hon Theresa May MP, "Legal Opinion on Joint Instrument and Unilateral Declaration concerning the Withdrawal Agreement", 12th March 2019,
https://assets.publishing.service.gov.uk/government/uploads/system/uploads/attachment_data/file/785188/190312_-
_Legal_Opinion_on_Joint_Instrument_and_Unilateral_Declaration_co..____2_.pdf

[15] The Guardian, "Democratic Unionist party will not support May's deal in vote", Lisa O'Carroll, 12th March 2019,
https://www.theguardian.com/politics/2019/mar/12/democratic-unionist-party-will-not-support-mays-deal-in-vote

[16] Twitter, "Westminster voting intention", Britain Elects, 13th March 2018,
https://twitter.com/britainelects/status/1105807724527435776

Chapter Eleven
Brexit Delayed, the People Betrayed

Deciding to end this book was difficult. The original plan was to end this diary by the time of the first Meaningful Vote, but when it became clear that the Prime Minister would take her deal to the Commons for a second time, it felt right to continue. And I'm glad I did. The weeks that followed saw Parliamentarians reaching new lows in their attempt at sabotaging Brexit.

After May lost the second Meaningful Vote, it was assumed that her deal was finished. Neither the press nor the politicians believed that the Prime Minister could possibly take her deal back to the Commons for a third vote, but Theresa May defied the odds. Just a day after May's Withdrawal Agreement was rejected in the Commons for a second time, rumours of a third Meaningful Vote began.

On the 13th of March, the government went ahead with the planned vote on an amendment that would take No Deal off the table. May had originally planned to vote in favour of taking No Deal off the table but learned that the motion had been worded more strongly than originally planned. The Prime Minister attempted to whip her own party against supporting the motion but failed. 17 Tory MPs defied her, and MPs voted to take No Deal off the table by 321 to 278.

Work and Pensions Minister Sarah Newton became the 15th minister to resign from the government over Brexit this same day, after voting to rule out No Deal.

This meant the planned vote for the following day, on whether the government should seek out an extension to Article 50, went ahead. Parliament voted overwhelmingly in favour of requesting an extension to Article 50, meaning that Brexit (with a deal) would no longer happen on March 29th. Should the European Union agree to an extension, the United Kingdom would not leave the EU before the end of March. Should the European Union refuse an extension (which would require just one of the 27 remaining EU member states exercising their veto), then the UK would leave the EU on March 29th without a deal.

The decision by Parliament to request an extension to Article 50 represented their ultimate betrayal of the British people, who trusted the politicians they elected to deliver the Brexit we were promised some three years ago.

On the 18th of March, Commons Speaker John Bercow blocked a third Meaningful Vote. He made it clear that he would block the Prime Minister from holding a third vote on her deal unless there were "significant" changes to the deal being offer. In a statement to the Commons, Bercow cited Parliamentary rules that date back to 1604, stopping votes being repeatedly held on the same legislation.

In a panic, Mrs May gave a statement on live television two days later. She effectively blamed MPs in the Commons for the mess we're in, and it didn't go down well. She soon had to backtrack and apologise, after realising she had alienated the MPs she had been trying to win around for her third Meaningful Vote.

On the 21st of March, the EU offered a Brexit delay until 22nd of May if Parliament votes to support a deal, and to April 12th if no deal is reached. The date of Brexit was moved from the 29th of March to at least the 12th of April.

Brexit had finally been betrayed.

So, on the 24th of March, May gathered MPs from across the divide in her own party to her Chequers Estate. Boris Johnson, Jacob Rees-Mogg, Michael Gove, David

Lidington, and even former Brexit Minister David Davis joined the PM to thrash out the deal and see if they could finally come to an agreement to support it in the Commons. Mogg said he'd support May's deal if the DUP got on board, but the DUP weren't so receptive.

On the 25th, MPs voted to take control of Brexit with a series of 'Indicative Votes'. These votes would attempt to show if Parliament could agree on any way forward for Brexit.

Parliament voted down every single suggestion. Not a single solution, from a 'confirmatory referendum' (second referendum) to a Customs Union could be agreed on. The results of those votes can be seen in the graph from the Institute for Government on the next page.

How MPs voted on different Brexit options in indicative votes

| | IfG |

Option	Aye	No	No vote recorded
Confirmatory referendum	268	295	74
Customs Union	264	272	101
Labour's Alternative Plan	237	307	93
Common Market 2.0	188	283	166
Revocation to avoid no deal	184	293	160
No deal	160	400	77
Standstill transition	139	422	76
EFTA and EEA	65	377	195

Source: Institute for Government analysis of Commons Divisions from Parliament Data (explore.data.parliament.uk).

(cc) BY-NC

The Prime Minister, in her desperation, also offered to resign in exchange for support for her deal. She announced to MPs that if the deal passes, she would step down and allow a new Tory Prime Minister to lead the country through the next stage of the negotiations. It was clear that this was done in a literal moment of desperation rather than calculated plotting, and it didn't pay off. The DUP didn't care. Nigel Dodds said that the DUP's problem was never with the Prime Minister, but with the deal – and when asked whether the DUP might even consider abstaining on a third Meaningful Vote, he tweeted: "The DUP doesn't abstain on matters of the Union".

29th March – Brexit Day

On the day that should have seen the United Kingdom leave the European Union, the Prime Minister would once again try and pass her deal through Parliament. It wouldn't be a third Meaningful Vote, though. Bercow made sure that couldn't happen.

This wasn't MV3, but WA1.

The Prime Minister had been forced to separate the Political Declaration from the Withdrawal Agreement – meaning a vote on the Withdrawal Agreement constituted the "significant change" Bercow demanded. It didn't pass. The deal came closer than ever to being passed, with 286 MPs (277 Con, 5 Lab, 4 Ind) voting in favour and 344 against, but it still wasn't enough. The Prime Minister had been beaten again.

The deal was dead, and Brexit betrayed. Parliament couldn't even pass a compromise.

On a day that could have seen the United Kingdom flourish once again as an independent, free and trading country, the nation was despondent, gloomy, and tired. It was on this day that the impact of this betrayal was really felt, and that we realised just how far the politicians are willing to go to reverse the decision we made. It feels rather clichéd at this point to talk about a betrayal, but it's true.

What is the use of voting if the decision we make isn't enacted? Why should I ever go out and cast a vote again?

The way that politicians have spoken about Brexit supporters over the last three years has been utterly despicable. As this diary shows, we've been called every name under the sun, we've been blamed for the chaos caused by politicians who just wanted to delay and frustrate the Brexit process, and we have been treated like children who don't understand what we did when we cast our votes.

We knew what we were doing. We knew very well what we were doing.

I know this book is not an easy read, but I believe it does something important. It documents the way Westminster set about reversing the decision made in the greatest democratic exercise in our country, and how they did it gradually over a period of three years. Small, daily betrayals became a great monster that beat the British people into submission. From the day the Chequers Deal was announced – a betrayal in itself – politicians on both sides of the aisle did everything in their power to ensure that even the rubbish compromise wasn't accepted. Nothing short of a total reversal of Brexit would be good enough.

We will always remember that the British people were disregarded, and the Brexit vote betrayed, but we may forget how they did it.

Keep this book. Remember how they did this to us.

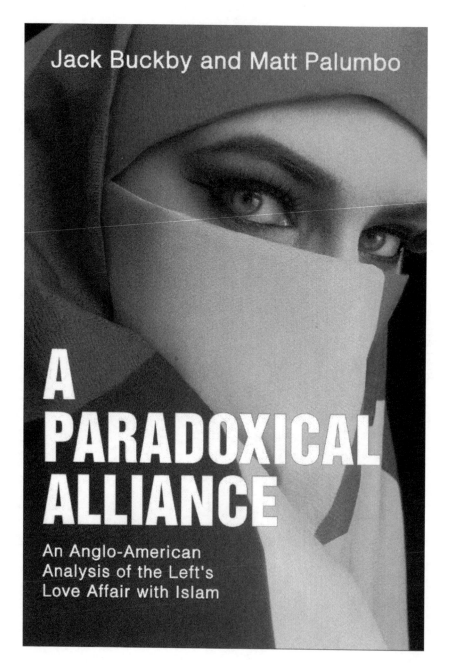

Jack Buckby and Matt Palumbo

A PARADOXICAL ALLIANCE

An Anglo-American
Analysis of the Left's
Love Affair with Islam

39893890R00217

Printed in Poland
by Amazon Fulfillment
Poland Sp. z o.o., Wrocław